CW00539256

History of

The Priory

Bishop's Waltham

History of
The Priory
Bishop's Waltham

Peter Finn

Hedera Books

Published by Hedera Books
Alderbrook
Springvale Road
Winchester
SO23 7LF
England

A CIP catalogue record for this book is available from the British Library.

Printed and bound in Great Britain.

ISBN 0 9537554 1 X

Preface

In the small attractive town of Bishop's Waltham in Hampshire, one cannot help but notice the Priory Inn, the Priory Café, Priory Motors, Priory Park, and other places displaying the Priory name, but there are few local people able to say what Priory is referred to in these names, or what kind of a place it was. Within a generation it seems that the memory of the Priory is passing rapidly into oblivion. It occurred to me that unless the Priory story was recorded, it was likely that the memory of it would be irrecoverably lost.

This book traces the history of the building from 1864, when the foundation stone was laid by Queen Victoria's youngest son, to its demolition in 1993. It relates in particular the history of the Apostolic School, which was established there in 1912.

The Priory was occupied for most of its existence by the White Fathers – a Catholic missionary society dedicated to working in Africa. They used it for educating youths who aspired one day to join their society. It was an extraordinary school, both on account of its purpose and the hardy life that was lived there. It was a direct descendant of one established in Algeria for Arab boys in the latter part of the 19th century that was forced to move to France and then to England. It was not at first intended for English-speaking boys, but circumstances dictated otherwise, and many outstanding missionaries from these islands were trained there, so that the name of Bishop's Waltham became better known in Africa than in Britain.

The age of the Apostolic School has passed and the Priory has disappeared, but history and an understanding of them require that they should not be forgotten

Peter Finn, January 2002.

Acknowledgements

I am grateful to the following White Fathers for their generous assistance: Father Richard Kinlen, Secretary of the British Province, for allowing me access to the school diaries; Father Ivan Page, Archivist at the Curia Generalizia, Rome, for providing me with copies of many of the Society's records; and Father Bill Turnbull of the Media and Information Office of the British Province for supplying many of the pictures. I am also indebted to Brother Patrick, Father Patrick Fitzgerald and Father Patrick Boyd for their reminiscences, documents, and pictures from their personal files.

My thanks also to Father Francis Isherwood, Portsmouth Diocesan archivist, who introduced me to his records and copied many cumbersome legal documents for me; to Mr and Mrs Sean McGovern for transcribing registers to computer; to Mr Paul West for lending me copies of the *White Fathers – White Sisters* magazine; and to Dr Anthony McCaffrey, Mr Michael Byrne and Mr Patrick Gritton for lending me their copies of the *The Priorian* and *The Pelican* school magazines.

Others to whom I am indebted for specific information I have mentioned in the endnotes, but I would especially like to thank Eugene MacBride for his unfailing support and encouragement, and for providing many pieces of information. I must also express particular thanks to my wife, Brenda, who made helpful comments and encouraged me to get on with it.

I am grateful to the following for the use of their pictures: Media and Information Office, Missionaries of Africa, Sutton Coldfield, 1.2, 2.3, 4.1, 5.1, 6.1, 6.3, 7.3, 8.2, 8.3, 8.4; Archivio Generale, Missionari d'Africa, Rome, 1.1, 4.5, K.1; La Société des Missionaires d'Afrique, Paris, K.2; Father Patrick Fitzgerald, M.Afr, 8.1, 9.3, 9.10, 10.1; Father Thomas Rathe, M.Afr, 6.2, 7.1, H1, H2, H4; Father Patrick Boyd, M.Afr, 5.6, 5.7; Father Kevin Wiseman, M.Afr, H.3; Brother Patrick, M.Afr, 4.2, 5.2, 9.8; Mrs Norah Rodgers, 7.4; Dr Andrew Coyle, 4.4, 9.9; Dr Anthony McCaffrey, 9.2, 9.6, 9.7; Mr Eugene MacBride, 4.6, 9.12; Mr and

Mrs Terry Butler, 3.1; Fox & Sons, Ep.1; *Illustrated London News*, 2.1, 2.2; *Magazine Mission*, Quebec, 5.4; *White Fathers – White Sisters* magazine, Sutton Coldfield, 5.3. Original photographs were not always available to me and were received via the Internet; this resulted in a loss of quality which has affected some of the printed pictures.

Much of the information in this book has been derived from the school diaries and I only reference them where I have quoted directly. Where I have used other information, I refer to the sources in the endnotes.

Contents

Chapters

Illustrations

1

The Men from Algiers

In the summer of 1912 two bearded men, dressed in clerical black, arrived at Bishop's Waltham railway station. They walked out of the station and headed westwards up the steep roadway (now Victoria Road) almost to the top of the bare green hill surmounted by a group of trees. They then turned left and walked along an open dusty lane (later named Martin Street) for about 200 paces until they came to a gateway in a long, low wall that shielded the front of a country house. Passing through the gateway and the perimeter trees, they saw at the end of the long gravel driveway what they had come to purchase – The Priory.

The two men were French Catholic priests of the Society of Missionaries of Africa, popularly known as White Fathers because of the Arab garb that they usually wore. They were Pierre Travers and Paul Voillard. Both men had led a rigorous life. They had trained in harsh conditions in Algeria and in the spartan tradition of their Society. They had lived as Arabs in North Africa, and Father Travers had also spent many years in the bush in Central Africa. These men were godly, tough, resilient, highly educated and not afraid of hard manual work. They had come to establish a school.

The Society of Missionaries of Africa had been founded in French North Africa by the Archbishop of Algiers, Charles Lavigerie, in 1868, and it was in North Africa that all White Fathers were trained. To attract young men who had not completed their general education or whose circumstances prevented them from having the prerequisite education for higher studies, the Society had established in 1877 an Apostolic School (that is, a missionary school) at St Laurent d'Olt in the south of France. It was a boarding school providing a classical education for pupils between 12 and 18 years of age who aspired to be White Fathers. At the age of 18 or so these young men could, if still willing, follow a two-year course in scholastic philosophy and then go to North Africa to continue their training for another five years before being sent into what was still known as 'Darkest Africa'.

The school at St Laurent d'Olt was originally established not for aspirants to the priesthood, but for poor Arab boys to prepare them for careers in the professions. Lavigerie had earlier set up an 'Arab Junior Seminary', that is, a residential school for teenaged boys, in Algeria. In 1874 he transferred the seminary with its 70 pupils to St Laurent d'Olt after rumours that the government was going to take the pupils and place them in its own establishments. In 1877 French boys wishing to enter the Society of Missionaries of Africa were admitted, and the number of Arab pupils steadily declined for many reasons including the austere form of life and homesickness. The perceived government threat did not materialise, and by 1882 all the Arab boys, except for a few that wished to study for the priesthood, had returned to the more congenial atmosphere of their homeland. From 1882 the school admitted only boys wishing to become missionary priests and was no longer an Arab school.[1]

Soon afterwards, the school was menaced by the renewed anti-clericalism of the Third Republic. For many years prior to 1912, religious societies in France were threatened with extinction and effectively hounded out of the country by the anti-clerical government. Many societies had been dissolved or driven into exile. Schools staffed by religious societies were the particular target at this time, for the government wished to abolish, or at least significantly reduce, the influence of the Church by laicising all schools and imposing an entirely secular curriculum. There was a fear that the 1901 Law of Associations, which declared all religious societies to be unauthorised associations that could not own property or accept gifts, would be invoked to deprive the White Fathers of their St Laurent d'Olt school and to confiscate their property. This apparent threat prompted the Society to consider moving the school abroad. Father A E Howell, a former Superior of the British Province, wrote in 1962:

> I have been on intimate terms with people who were there [at the Priory] from the beginnings of the House in 1912 and 1913, and from them I learned a few things about the foundation and early

> years of the White Fathers in Bishop's Waltham which may not have been told before.
>
> In 1912 our Society had no intention of opening a Missionary College for British students; that idea came later. In that year the anti-clerical movement in France was at its height and many members of Religious Orders were driven into exile. The Mother House of the White Fathers was in Algiers, in French territory, and there too was the Society's only Novitiate; the only Scholasticate [college of theology] was at Carthage, in Tunisia, also under French rule. There were other training houses in France itself [college of philosophy at Binson and school at St Laurent d'Olt]. This dependence on France meant, in the atmosphere of the times, that there was a real danger that the Society would be extinguished, and the Superiors decided that it would be wise to make a foundation in England to serve as a refuge and even as Headquarters if circumstances made it necessary to move from Algiers.[2]

An article in the *Hampshire Chronicle* newspaper in 1913 referred to the same danger after interviewing Father Travers, 'the respected and courteous Superior'.[3] It reported that 'The Order [White Fathers] is one of four which were not expelled from France when, a few years ago, a wholesale expulsion of religious orders from that country took place'.

1.1 Father Paul Voillard.

1.2 Father Pierre Travers.

The Society's General Chapter[4] – the governing body – met together in Algiers in April 1912, and the future of the St Laurent school was one of the many subjects discussed. It was proposed by some of those present that the school should be closed anyway as it was not providing a satisfactory level of education, but the eventual consensus was to keep the school and improve the standard. Amongst the several proposals was the recommendation that the school be divided into two parts: a junior section, which would follow a four year course of Latin and 'primary studies', and a senior section which would be established abroad.[5]

Sending only part of the school abroad would keep the options open: either to move the whole school to a prepared place if the worst happened, or to move the overseas section back if the perceived threat was not put into effect. Which country 'abroad' was not specified, though Switzerland was considered. However, another important aspect was discussed and this swayed the whole matter.

By 1912 many White Father mission stations had been established, with much suffering and loss of life, in the British possessions in East and Central Africa. It was necessary for the missionaries being sent to these regions to have a sound knowledge of English not only for establishing schools, but more especially for dealing with government officials locally and in London. The General Chapter decided that it was necessary for the young students to acquire a good knowledge of the English language and culture and it was recommended that the senior pupils should receive their education in an English-speaking country. The French government threat had presented them with an opportunity – a clear case of making a virtue out of necessity. Fathers Travers and Voillard, with the appropriate apostolic names of Peter and Paul, were appointed to find a suitable property and had now come upon exactly what they were looking for.

Father Voillard resided in Algiers as an Assistant to the Superior General and it was in this capacity that he had attended the General Chapter. Father Travers had attended as the representative of his mission territory in Nyassa, Central Africa, of which he was the Vicar General for the southern part. One of the reasons Travers would have been selected for this new assignment was that he spoke English, which very few members of the Society did at that time, including Voillard.[6] The decision by the General Chapter meant that, without notice, Travers was never to see his mission territory again; instead, he was to remain in Europe to establish a different sort of mission. It was to be hoped he had brought all his worldly goods with him for, although he did not know it at the time, the rest of his working life was to be spent in England; the door to Africa had closed behind him.

The intention appears to have been to ride out the impending political storm, even if it took decades, and then head back to France. This seems to be borne out by there being no attempt to recruit British nationals, although there were two British White Fathers (Henri Gaudibert and Arthur Prentice) in Africa at this time.[7] Whatever the intention, the move was significant for it heralded the establishment of the White Fathers Society in the British Isles, the foundation of an Apostolic College for British and Irish boys, and the setting up of a Catholic parish in Bishop's Waltham.

It was also the start of a new episode in the story of a house that had its beginning 48 years previously. It had been a distinguished beginning, graced by royalty and reported in the London newspapers.

2

The Royal Albert Infirmary

The handsome brick building that the two priests viewed stood in a fine position at the top of a hill.It overlooked the small town of Bishop's Waltham and the ruins of a medieval episcopal palace, and it had magnificent views in every direction. It had been intended as an infirmary – the Royal Albert Infirmary. However, it was never to be used as such.

In the early 1860s, at the suggestion of Mr (later Sir) Arthur Helps[8], it was decided to build a hospital 'to provide for the poor of the district those comforts in time of illness which can be secured for them by an organised establishment'.[9] As was usual at the time it was to be a charitable institution which would depend entirely on donations. A committee was formed and public subscriptions invited. Arthur Helps was the enthusiastic prime mover and major contributor. The land on which the infirmary was built was part of the Vernon Hill Estate that he owned. He donated the land[10] and contributed the profits (over £550[11]) from the sale of the published speeches and addresses of the late Prince Consort that he (Mr Helps) had edited. He raised further funds with at least two concerts in the grounds of the ruined Bishop of Winchester's Palace, one in 1864 and one in 1865. The performances were in the presence of royalty and, 'as the tickets were sold at high prices, the funds of the new infirmary must have been greatly augmented by the proceeds'.[12] He persuaded a wide circle of people to make substantial donations, including Queen Victoria's 11-year old youngest son, Prince Leopold, who subscribed a very generous £100. He also obtained the permission of the Queen for the infirmary to be named in honour of her late beloved Consort, Prince Albert.

The foundation stone was laid on the 4th August 1864 and a dedication ceremony took place a year later. Both were grand affairs at which Mr Helps was the host.

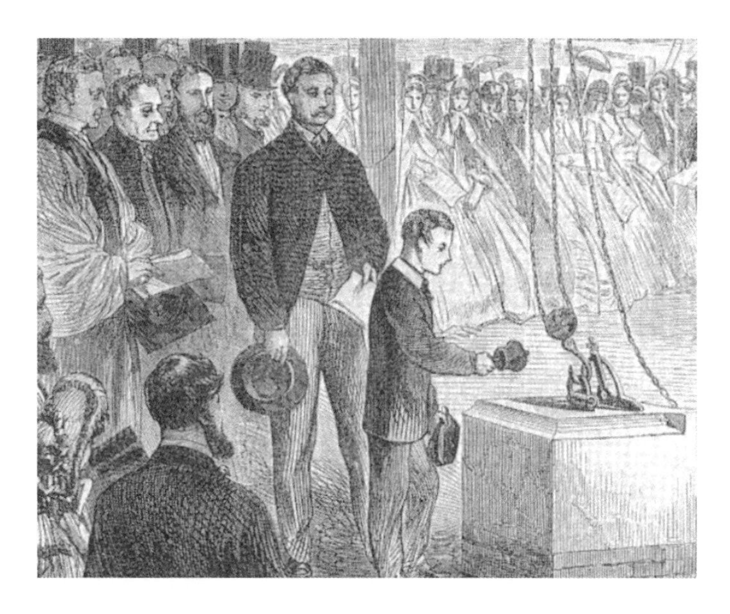

2.1 Prince Leopold laying the foundation stone of the Royal Albert Infirmary in 1864.

On the first occasion, Prince Leopold performed the ceremony and the Bishop of Winchester pronounced a blessing. The distinguished gathering included Prince Louis of Hesse (the Queen's son-in-law), Earl Granville (Lord President of the Council), General Grey, Baron Westerweller, the Anglican Bishop of Portsmouth, Mr Robert Critchlow (the architect), the local members of Parliament and the Mayors of Winchester, Portsmouth and Southampton. The 1st Hampshire Mounted Rifle Volunteers provided the escort for the royal party, the 3rd Battalion of the Hampshire Volunteers provided the Guard of Honour, and the Engineers' Band led the procession. After the foundation stone had been ceremonially laid, a very large number of guests attended a banquet in the grounds of the bishop's palace ruins. In the late afternoon the royal party returned to Osborne House on the Isle of Wight. The celebrations, however, continued with an open-air orchestral concert, singing by a choir of 200, dancing on the greensward, and 'a magnificent display of fireworks'.[13] Altogether a brilliant occasion.

The dedication, or 'opening' ceremony as it was called in the *Illustrated London News*, took place on the 7th November 1865 in the presence of Leopold's older brother and sisters: Prince Arthur and the Princesses Helena and Louisa. They had travelled by train from Windsor, and had then been escorted by a troop of the 1st Hampshire Mounted Rifle Volunteers, first to lunch at Vernon Hill House then to the ceremony at the infirmary. The highlight of the event was the unveiling of a statue of Prince Albert in a niche above the portico of the front entrance.[14] The Bishop of Winchester read a prayer composed for the occasion then, with a flourish of trumpets, a veil – the royal standard – was drawn away by Princess Helena to reveal the statue. In shallow niches either side of the statue were the armorial bearings of the Queen and of the Prince Consort. Present were again representatives of the aristocracy, senior military people, most of the gentry and clergy of the district, the Mayor and Corporation of Southampton, and 'a large assembly'.[12] The royal party inspected the inside of the building, briefly visited the newly built but unoccupied elementary school nearby[15], then went on to a concert in the palace grounds, after which they returned to Windsor.[11] Rarely can such a modest establishment have been launched with so much ceremony and national attention.

2.2. Dedication of the Royal Albert Infirmary in the presence of Prince Arthur and Princesses Helena and Louisa, 1865.

Robert B Critchlow of Southampton was the architect[16], and he designed the building to accommodate 20 patients. The construction work was started by Mr Simonds of Bishop's Waltham, and completed by Mr G S Brinton of Southampton. The cost was £2661 14s 6d. The final cost after fitting out and furnishing was estimated to be £3800. Subscriptions for £2218 15s 10d had been received at the time of the dedication ceremony, and the rest of the building and furnishing costs may well have been forthcoming, but the project seems to have foundered on the maintenance expenses for which a 'considerable sum' was required.[12] £600 a year was needed to maintain the 20 beds, but only £143 19s had been promised in annual subscriptions.[11] It was probably because the running costs, which required committed annual subscriptions, could not be guaranteed year on year that the place never functioned as an infirmary.

For a while the structure lay empty, then in 1871 we find it occupied by a butcher – Andrew Deacon and his 24-year old daughter Emma, and by a brick maker – Joseph Phillips and his wife Sarah.[17] Why this state of affairs now existed we can only conjecture. Rather than leave such a large house to suffer from dampness, general decay and possible vandalism, it would have been wise for the house to be occupied for a small rent by people seeking somewhere to live and who were prepared to act as caretakers. A couple, or couples, without young children would have been the solution.

At this time Arthur Helps must have been living in London for his country home at Bishop's Waltham, Vernon Hill House[18], was rented to James Butler Fellowes who lived there with his family.[19]

Sir Arthur died in 1875, esteemed by the royal family and by Parliament, but surely a disappointed man as far as his ambitious charitable project was concerned. The Vernon Hill Estate was broken up and sold by auction in October of the same year. Vernon Hill House was bought by Lieutenant General Frederick Elrington[20], but the infirmary was not included in the sale[21] – the subscribers still intended that it should be a hospital and it was probably still tenanted.

Within months of Sir Arthur's death, the statue of Prince Albert was removed to Southampton at the request of the donor, Sir Frederick Perkins, who doubtless realised there was no future for the building as an infirmary. This was done despite the objections of the subscribers and an encounter with the townspeople which came to be known as the Battle of Bunkers Hill.[22] In February 1876 he offered the statue as a gift to the Southampton Borough Council, who accepted it.[23] The Royal arms and those of the Prince Consort were an integral part of the brickwork and remained on the building until its final demise.

The infirmary and its grounds of 11 acres came up for auction in separate lots at the Crown Hotel, Bishop's Waltham on Saturday, 3rd November 1877.[24] The building was now vacant. The house was described as 'A desirable property consisting of a superior freehold building intended for an infirmary. Most substantially built of best red brick ... standing in its own terraced grounds, and commanding extensive views'. The description goes on:

> A capacious building ... of modern design with red brick exterior; and adequately adapted and suitably situated for an infirmary; the interior arrangements having ample accommodation, with Four Large Wards, Nurses' and Matron's Rooms, Surgery and Operating Rooms, Bath Rooms, Lavatories, and well-arranged offices; rendering it most complete as an infirmary or Convalescent Hospital ... The ground floor is completed, with the exception of a few fittings, and the first floor remains unplastered and unceiled, but the whole might be completed, fit for use, at a comparatively small cost.

One wonders which part of the building the previous tenants occupied. Presumably they lived in the very large rooms on the ground floor; the upper floor, with its bare brick walls and absent ceilings, sounds particularly inhospitable.

The property was still being offered as a potential hospital and no effort made to sell it for any other purpose. This was probably the wish of the many subscribers to the building fund and of the townspeople. It would of course have required a great deal of financing to run it as a hospital, and this was no more forthcoming than in previous years. The result was no sale, and the substantial building continued to stand empty.

In April 1881 the infirmary was still unoccupied. It is not mentioned in the census of that year, even by a different name. The census was of course concerned with people rather than buildings, so if no one were living there it would not be mentioned. It would have been one of the 33 uninhabited and unidentified buildings in Bishop's Waltham that year.

Some time between April 1881 and September 1884 the building was sold, for the next mention of it is in a local newspaper report of September 1884 where it appears with a new name – Albert House.[25] That the house was mentioned at all at this time was due to unusual circumstances – the Bishop's Waltham beer riots. The local curate had objected to the renewal of the licences of a number of public houses in the town and this provided the excuse for a mob to go around being rowdy, fighting, and carrying an effigy of the curate that they later burnt. The police were repelled in a pitched battle and a Police Constable Brown and a Mr Arnold Clark seriously injured. At one point the mob appeared at the door of Albert House demanding beer from the owner, Mr Hurley. It is not reported whether he met their demands or not, though one suspects that he must have gone some way to meeting them to prevent damage to his house.

2.3. Façade of Albert House c1885.

Richard Henry Hurley originated in London and had established himself locally as a miller and corn merchant. He was living in Albert House with his wife, six children, a governess, and domestic servants.[26] By 1898 the house was in the possession of Jacob Kalff LL.D.[27] It was he who renamed it 'The Priory'. Why he did so is open to speculation. The *Illustrated London News* had described the building as Gothic, presumably for want of a better architectural term. If it was Gothic, then it was a very restrained Victorian Gothic built entirely of brick.[28] Nevertheless, Dr Kalff must have viewed the ivy-covered building with a romantic eye and felt a frisson of attraction to what, in the right light, could be a well-preserved medieval establishment; so 'The Priory' it became.

Dr Kalff did not occupy the place for long, and when Arthur Robson and his wife bought the house in 1902 The Priory name was retained.[29]

Within six years the house (now with only three acres of grounds) was up for sale again. Mr Robson tried to sell it by private treaty and then by auction on the 30th May 1908.[30] The sale description presents a very attractive image of 'a gentleman's exceptionally well-built and substantial residence' in a fine position with local amenities that include hunting, shooting and fishing; there are ten 'lofty' bed and dressing rooms, five substantial reception rooms, domestic offices ('well shut off') including a large servants' sitting room, extensive lawns and meadow, a tennis court, coach house and 'capital stabling'. It surprisingly mentions that 'the nearest Roman Catholic Church is at Eastleigh, distant 7 miles.'However, despite the estate agent's eulogising, the property did not sell. No price is given in the sale particulars, but the property was insured for £4000. The reserve price must have been somewhere near that figure, but it was evidently too high.

Mr Robson continued to live there with his wife until his death on the 24th October 1911. After his death Mrs Robson put the house in the hands of estate agents in Winchester, so that it was fortuitously available when Voillard and Travers made enquiries.

3

The White Fathers Move In

That Voillard and Travers were enquiring in the Southampton-Winchester area was providential, for neither this area nor even Hampshire had been considered originally. Jersey in the Channel Islands was the favoured location, and the General Chapter even named the staff that were to take up residence there. They were Father Chollet as Superior, and Fathers Molin, Coutu and Falquières.[31] Jersey was a logical first choice, being close to France but English-speaking and within British jurisdiction. It was also within the jurisdiction of the Catholic diocese of Portsmouth, so permission had to be obtained from the Bishop of Portsmouth, William Timothy Cotter, to set up a religious foundation.

The two White Fathers visited Bishop Cotter in May 1912 to seek his approval. He received them warmly, but suggested that they seek a place on the mainland, particularly in the Bishop's Waltham area, where priests were needed and where their presence would be of benefit to a sparse and isolated Catholic community. This they did with exceptionally good results.

They went to visit Father Thomas Grant Hickey, the Parish Priest of Eastleigh[32], whose large parish included Bishop's Waltham. There were houses in Botley available, but Hickey pressed them to look in Bishop's Waltham. It transpired that it was he who had asked Bishop Cotter to suggest Bishop's Waltham to them for Hickey had great difficulty in getting to the Catholics there. Botley was not so much trouble for him to reach as there were frequent trains from Eastleigh.

Voillard and Travers had generously been offered accommodation in the Montfort College at Romsey by the Superior, Father Pierre Raimbault, while they looked for a suitable property.[33] When they returned there after seeing Hickey, Father Raimbault referred them to Mr John Augustus Harrington, a solicitor who, being the holder of several public offices, turned out to be a man of considerable standing and was to prove a great help to Travers in the early years. He in turn suggested they speak to Mr George Edward Gudgeon of estate agents Gudgeon and Sons of Parchment Street, Winchester. Mr Gudgeon was able to offer them three houses in Bishop's Waltham including the Priory, which proved to be the most attractive and in the best condition. It was ideal. It was in a high healthy spot, more than 300 feet above sea level and with commanding views in all directions extending even to the Isle of Wight. It was surrounded by agricultural land and close to, but apart from, a small town with good rail and road communications. The large rooms could be used as dormitories and classrooms, it had grounds of more than three acres suitable for expansion if required, and 'the price was very modest'.[34]

The Fathers were no less impressed by the warm welcome they received from Mrs Robson and decided to look no further. However, Mrs Robson wanted a reply within a week, for there was another person, 'a colonel', interested. They explained the position to Father Hickey who telephoned the Bishop asking if they could safely go ahead with the purchase, but he replied that he could not give a decision before the next meeting of the Diocesan Chapter, which would take place on the 17th September. Voillard and Travers decided to take a chance and informed the agents that they would buy. It was too good an opportunity to lose. They then embarked at Southampton for Le Havre and Paris, where they split up, Voillard going to Algiers to report the results of their trip, and Travers to the College of Philosophy at Binson.

Mrs Robson had agreed to sell for £2,300[35], which was less than it cost to build the house 48 years previously. It seems the White Fathers had got a bargain.

Voillard met with the General Council in August. They supported his decision to buy, and directed that Fathers Travers, Chollet, Coutu, Falquière, and Brother Camille would be the signatories to the contract.[36] Chollet, Bouniol, Coutu and Falquière were ordered to leave St Laurent immediately and join Travers at

Binson, where they were to apply themselves to studying English. The same order was given to Brothers Jean at Marseille, Max at Altkirch, Camille at Fribourg, and Egbert in Algiers.

At the same time Bishop Livinhac, the Superior General of the Society, wrote to Bishop Cotter seeking formal authorisation for the foundation.[37] The letter is significant for, although it makes no mention of problems actual or potential, it gives reasons for wanting an establishment in England and particularly near Southampton.

He first mentions that many of the countries in which 'our little society' is working are in the 'English sphere of influence' and that the work can be considerably advanced by having a house in England. He gives three reasons for having an English base: firstly, in case of difficulty, to be able to deal directly in London with the 'English' government; secondly, to expedite materials required by the missions in British colonies; and thirdly, for the missionaries being sent to these colonies to acquire a good knowledge of English. These ends, he maintains, would best be served by establishing an Apostolic School. He goes on:

> I have charged one of my assistants, Father Voillard, to return to England. This missionary and a confrère [Father Travers] had the honour of being received by your Grace at Portsmouth, and he has said that you received him with great kindness and encouraged him in our search ... he told us that the environs of Southampton particularly attracted his attention: connections with London are very easy, communications with France (for the students) are extremely frequent, and, for re-supplying our missions, Southampton is the port of departure for ships to South Africa ... Providence has helped him to find at Bishop's Waltham, at the place indicated by the Parish Priest of Eastleigh, a property perfectly suited to our needs.

He explains that the principal purpose is the creation of an Apostolic School 'but, to be more exact, it will be the four upper classes of the French Apostolic School'. (This was later changed to the three upper classes.[38]) The Superior of the school is to be the Society's intermediary for dealings with the British government, and also to be responsible for expediting via

Southampton materials ordered for shipment to Africa. Further burdens, financial and pastoral, to be placed on the Superior were implied:

> We have no intention of soliciting financial help either for this house or for our missions, for we cannot ignore that the English Catholics have need of all their resources to support their own works. In addition, if we can be of some help to your Grace in providing spiritual help to Catholics living in the area where we will be established, we will gladly be of assistance.

The financial and pastoral offers would have been prompted by the discovery that the Bishop's Waltham area was itself a mission territory in the Eastleigh Missionary District, where the diocesan priests were still referred to as missionaries.[39] The offer of pastoral assistance was just what Bishop Cotter was looking for as the *quid pro quo*. He needed a priest and chapel to cater for the local Catholic population and, at no cost to the diocese, it was an offer he was bound to take up.

Although Livinhac's draft letter said that Voillard would be returning to England, it was in fact Travers that returned having been appointed Superior of the school and, in effect, of the British area.

Having verbally agreed to buy, Travers was obliged at the end of August to sign a contract to that effect and confidently expected a positive reply from the Portsmouth Diocesan Chapter on the 17th or 18th September. These dates passed without any sign of the hoped-for telegram. On the 22nd the Mother House telegraphed Father Hickey for information, and he replied that they should contact the Bishop directly. A letter went off straightaway, but there was still no reply by the 27th. Travers was understandably feeling apprehensive at this stage for he had committed to sign the purchase agreement on the 30th September. He set off alone for England to discover what decision, if any, had been taken. He went to the Montfort College at Romsey arriving on the 29th, and was about to go and see the Bishop on the same day when a telegram arrived from the Mother House telling him of a favourable response. The Bishop of Portsmouth had written to the Superior General:[40]

Monsignor L Livinhac
Bishop of Pacando
Superior General of the Society of Missionaries of Africa

My Lord,
Last week, the Diocesan Chapter met for its bimonthly meeting and I submitted your Lordship's application to establish an Apostolic School for your Society in this diocese at Bishop's Waltham. I am pleased to announce to you that the proposed settlement was agreed to and I hasten to announce the news which will be as pleasing, I am sure, for you to receive it as it is for me to send it. I accept the priests you may destine for this new foundation very cordially and, as the terms of your letter, I look for much good to be effected in the locality and district where they are to establish themselves. It would be a great advantage if one or more of the Fathers could speak or understand English.
I remain, My Lord,
Yours sincerely in Xsto
W J Cotter
Bp. of Portsmouth

Travers immediately sent a telegram to Binson telling the others to leave for England, but they had already left. They had received the very welcome news directly from the Mother House earlier in the day, and Coutu and the four brothers were already on their way. Bouniol and Falquière were not there to hear the news for they had left the previous day for St Laurent where the students destined for England had arrived.

On Tuesday the 1st October, Rémi Coutu and the four brothers arrived in Southampton and Travers was there on the quayside to greet them. Coutu and Brother Jean went off immediately to buy some timber for carpentry work, and Travers and the others went directly to the Priory. Mr William, the gardener, opened the gates to them and showed them into the house. He then went off to buy some bread, cheese and beer, for the travellers now felt suddenly hungry not having eaten since the previous day because of sea-sickness. Mr William remained to tend the gardens until 1914.

3.1. The Priory as it appeared in a 1908 sales leaflet.

Mrs Robson had written from Westcliffe-on-Sea welcoming the White Fathers as the new owners, expressing her appreciation of their work and promising to leave some curtains, carpets and crockery, and a few chairs and small tables. This she had done, and she had also left some food for them. The essential items missing at this stage were beds and bedding. However, the good Fathers at Romsey, without waiting to be asked, sent 20 blankets in a motorcar, so that a minimum of comfort could be provided on the hard floor that night. Sleeping on the floor was a small consideration; the joyous fact was that they were now established in England. The first words of the house diary record that 'It was on the 1st day of October that the Reverend Father Travers, Father Coutu, and Brothers Jean, Max, Camille and Egbert took possession of the Priory'.[41]

In their typical, quick-reacting, no-frills pioneering style, the White Fathers had established themselves in another foreign land. Mass would have been offered for the first time in the house on the morning of Wednesday the 2nd October 1912, and besides thanks to Almighty God, the Mass intention must surely have been for the success of this new venture. It was the start of a noble and blessed enterprise that would provide many brave and holy missionaries for Africa.

4

The Travers Era

Monsignor Livinhac's letter to Bishop Cotter effectively set out the responsibilities of Father Travers. In addition to setting up and managing the school, he would be headmaster, government negotiator, overseas shipping manager, parish priest and, later, fund raiser – a demanding job description. Fortunately, Travers was man enough for the job. He had already demonstrated his administrative ability in Africa where, in 1906, he was appointed financial administrator of the Vicariate of Nyassa and, in 1910, a Vicar General. He would very likely have been appointed bishop if he had not been abruptly dispatched to England.[42]

4.1 Father Pierre Travers, First Superior of the Priory 1912–14, 1915–26.

The immediate task of Father Travers was to set up a school, which would follow the rule that had been approved for St Laurent.[36] There was no time to muse about it. The boys had been sent for and they had to be housed, fed, educated, exercised and religiously motivated – immediately. The logistics to support these objectives were considerable. Furniture had to be made, bedding found, regular food supplied, timetables arranged, classes taught, a chapel set up, daily religious services organised, and the divine office said daily by the ordained members of the community.

The brothers immediately started to make tables and benches and to install washing and toilet facilities. Travers and Brother Jean went to London to purchase classroom materials, bedding, cooking utensils, crockery, cutlery, an altar, and other necessary items. The Mill Hill Fathers provided them with hospitality for several days at St Joseph's College, Mill Hill, and advised them to deal with an agency to help them buy and dispatch items unavailable at the time. Their first relaxation was on the Saturday evening, after the shops and offices had closed, when they went to look at the Houses of Parliament.

On the 10th October Father Falquière and 14 boys left St Laurent for Paris where they met up with Father Bouniol who had gone ahead the day before to buy some bits and pieces for the school. The following day they were joined by 13 more boys[43] and together they left Paris on the 1pm train for Le Havre, their travel costs and those of later French students being paid by the Society.[38] It was 'a happy and lively occasion, but for the mothers it would have been a time of sadness and regret'.[44] They embarked on the *Hantonia* at 8.30pm, but it did not sail until 1am. They had been unable to book any cabins or couchettes in the time available to them, so they had to spend the whole night sitting on benches on the deck. It was 10am the following morning (Saturday) before they were allowed to disembark with their 'stomachs crying out'. They must have been relieved to be met by Father Coutu who greeted them with some cakes and took them to a nearby hotel for coffee. They then boarded a train for Bishop's Waltham and, after changes at Eastleigh and Botley, arrived at 12.15pm.Brothers Jean and Max were at the station to meet them, and while Max went off with Coutu to buy some plates in the village, Jean led the new arrivals up the hill to their new home.

The beauty of the place made an immediate impression on the newcomers. 'A low gate opened on to a beautiful long drive, broad and well cared for. There were flowers in the borders, a meadow, and a series of three lawns on the left ... We were reflecting on the charm and beauty of the lawns and flowers when we saw the magnificent house with three gables covered with ivy and with rose bushes in front of it. Father Superior opened the door, welcomed the young men, and led us all to the chapel where we said the *Magnificat* before the Blessed Sacrament.'[45] They then went to the refectory where they sat at well-made improvised tables covered by white sheets that served as tablecloths. The plates had not yet arrived, so they managed as best they could until the crockery arrived an hour later.

They had spent several uncomfortable days on the journey from St Laurent d'Olt in the far south of France and must have been feeling very tired. The first six occupants had slept on the floor, and that morning Travers must have envisaged the boys doing the same. Fortunately beds and bedding were delivered an hour before their arrival and, after eating, they set about assembling the beds in the three rooms that had been allocated as dormitories.

So on Saturday the 12th October 1912 all were assembled for the start of the first term. There were 27 pupils, four priests and four brothers. It was an entirely French community living in surroundings utterly foreign both in language, culture and religious sympathy, in crowded living conditions, and trying to run a disciplined religious and educational institution. There were relationships to be established with neighbours and local suppliers. Would they be regarded with suspicion? They were more foreign than could be expected: they were not only French, they were Catholics, priests, bearded, dressed as Arabs[46] and, except for Fathers Travers and Coutu, speaking very little English. Bishop's Waltham must have been agog.

The First Term

Sunday the 13th October 1912 was the first full day of activity with staff and pupils present. Ten local people came to the High Mass, and one of them, Captain Tighe, expressed the feelings of them all when he said how delighted they were to attend Mass locally, and Mrs Tighe added that she had prayed a long time for priests to come to Bishop's Waltham. Previously, Mass was said by the Eastleigh priest about once a month in the Mafeking Hero Inn, which was owned by the Spurr family. That evening the boy's three-day retreat began, followed by a full day of manual work. It was just as well they were thus occupied, for they could do no schoolwork as there were not yet any desks.

Classes began on Friday the 18th October. There were still no desks, so planks precariously balanced on trestles were used instead. Chairs had arrived that morning from the agent in London, but they were for eight-year old children and were sent back immediately. Benches from the refectory were presumably used as seats. The desks eventually arrived on the 24th October and the chairs on the 14th November. There were three classes: Rhetoric, Second Class (Belles Lettres), and Third Class (Syntax); Rhetoric being the highest.

Each day started with morning prayers in the chapel at 5.30am followed by Mass at 5.45am, including Sundays when there was also a sung High Mass at 8am. On weekdays, including Saturdays, classes started at 7.30am.

The interior of the tiny chapel, at the east end of the ground floor, was embellished with wood panelling by the brothers and a canopy was placed over the altar, but it was so cramped it was difficult to move. There were no pews and the thin pieces of carpet on which they knelt were hard on the knees. They got some relief after a few weeks when they produced padded kneelers for themselves. The boys had been issued with black cassocks for use in chapel. Red cassocks had been preferred but the fathers had been told (perhaps by Hickey) that only Protestants wore red cassocks.

Their first day off was All Saints Day on the 1st November. The Frenchmen were surprised to find that it was not a public holiday, but this did not prevent them getting their own holiday off to an early start with sung High Mass at 5.45am. The day was spent playing croquet on the lawn, tennis on the court at the front of the house and going for long walks. They boys wanted to play football, but there was no ball, so they each subscribed a little money to buy one on the following Monday. They were just as surprised five months later on the 4th April 1913 when they discovered that Mardi Gras was not a carnival day in England. They went ahead with their holiday, however, and enjoyed plays, songs and 'high-spirited fun'.[47]

Within a month a fully functioning boarding school had been set up from scratch – an outstanding achievement by any standard.

However, the property did not yet belong to the school. The sale agreement should have been settled on the 30th September 1912, but it had been delayed because a document requested by Mr Harrington, the solicitor, had not been delivered. In the meantime 5% per annum of the agreed price was being paid to Mrs Robson. This delay, besides increasing the cost, also prevented any modifications being made to the property until the purchase was concluded. On the 11th November 1912 a letter arrived from Mr Gudgeon to say that the vendors – the trustees of Mr Robson's estate – had signed the contract of sale. The White Fathers, however, did not have the opportunity to sign until the 22nd November. The signatories were 'the Reverend Pierre Marie Travers, the Reverend Jean Marie Chollet, the Reverend Joseph Bouniol and the Reverend Eloi Falquières all of The Priory Bishop's Waltham'.[35] The Priory name was retained although it had no relevance to the White Fathers' Society, which is not a monastic order (although it is often referred to as one) and does not have priors or priories.

As soon as the letter was received from Mr Gudgeon, the boys set about making a play area behind the house during their recreation periods. This required the felling of four poplar trees, hacking out the stumps, removing the turf, levelling the ground and putting down gravel. It took several weeks of laborious effort until the 18th December when it was declared finished. This work did not release them from their usual manual work cleaning the premises each day and washing the dishes as their successors were required to do. The brothers immediately started to dig a necessary additional cesspit and to build a covered playground for use during the winter. Brother Jean, now joined by Brother Lucien from Nyassa, continued making necessary articles of furniture using the coach house and stable as a carpenter's shop.[48]

Everybody appeared to be working very hard, but on the 16th November two boys were sent home for being idle; whether this related to their academic or manual work was not recorded, but they were the first two to be dismissed. Another boy left in the following January because he found that the regime of the school was too severe, and another shortly afterwards suffering from fatigue. In 1914 a pupil was sent home on the advice of the doctor. Physical, and maybe psychological, demands were taking their toll.

Establishing Relationships

Travers wanted to establish friendly relations with as many people as possible, but his first invitations were to those he wished to thank. On Thursday the 17th October Father Hickey and four Montfort Fathers came to supper. Others had been invited, but were unable to attend. When Travers mentioned that he intended contacting people in the neighbourhood, he was restrained by Hickey who surprisingly advised him to be 'reserved' with the Catholics until he (Hickey) officially introduced the White Fathers at Christmas, and to be reserved with the Protestants and not make the first call on the Rector whom Travers wished to meet. He must have been a little astonished at this English reserve, but abided by the advice. However, he invited Mr and Mrs Harrington to tea a few days later. Mr Harrington was a great help to Travers at this time and in the years to come.

He felt no reservations about visiting other exiled French communities in the area, including the Montfort Missionaries at Romsey, the Brothers of Christian Instruction at Bitterne, Brothers of the Christian Schools at Southsea, the Trappist monks at Martin, and the Benedictine monks at Quarr.[49] Unlike the large community at Quarr, the Trappist monastery was very small: three priests and two brothers, who came to England 'some years ago during the persecution to prepare a house in case of expulsion'.[50] The White Fathers were enthusiastically received by all, and the Trappist Superior, Father Benoît, wrote expressing his great joy and enclosing a £1 donation from his meagre resources.

On the 3rd December 1912, the Feast of the Martyrs of Uganda – a red letter day in the White Fathers' calendar, the Priory was able to welcome in return the Superior and Chaplain of the Brothers of Christian Instruction, Father Hickey (the only Englishman), and five Montfort Fathers with ten of their students. They all attended High Mass at 10.30am and then had a celebratory meal in the refectory afterwards. The Montfort contingent stayed for the afternoon to play football, and this was the start of regular, brotherly and happy reciprocal visits which, except during the war years, always included a game of football.

On the 5th November, Travers had received an unexpected letter from Father R P Elrington, a Dominican priest, living in

Bonn, Germany. He explained that he was originally from Bishop's Waltham, and he wrote of his joy at there being Catholic priests in the town of his birth. He asked to come to the Priory when he next visited his mother [Mrs Emilie Elrington] who lived nearby. He recommended his friend Dr Whittindale, the local doctor, as a helpful man, and this turned out to be very true.[51] 'He is a Protestant', said the Dominican, 'but not a fanatic like certain people in Bishop's Waltham'. The 'certain people' turned out to be his own mother, as Father Travers learnt later from Dr Whittindale. Father Elrington confirmed this when he visited the Priory in August 1913, describing his mother as one who detested the Catholic Church. Perhaps the poor woman felt she had lost her eldest son to a strange and distant religion.[52]

The doctor proved to be extremely friendly and, having spent some time in Nigeria, he found a lot in common with the outgoing Travers. He explained that the Dominican priest was the son of General Elrington of Vernon House. He and his sister had converted to the Catholic Church, but their mother remained an 'ardent Protestant'. He also told Travers that the Priory was once intended as an infirmary, and that it was Mr Robson who had had the lawns terraced (and presumably had the drive moved from the middle of the lawns to the east side). Mrs Whittindale spoke of the fine collection of roses that had been established by the Robsons and how greatly they were admired. They were no less admired by the new residents of the house, and were treasured and expertly cultivated by generations of brothers.

The following evening the local Rector, Edward Hugh Rycroft, called on Father Superior. Here was another very friendly and welcoming man, who talked easily and freely with Travers. He spoke with frankness about problems in the parish, especially with a number of difficult families who had come from Southampton, and about his fear of the White Fathers causing religious difficulties in his parish. Travers assured him that it was not his intention to violate consciences but to work only for the glory of God. Travers paid a return visit to the Rector on the following Monday and found that he lived in a magnificent property near the church. The Reverend Rycroft remarked that it was too big and too beautiful for him. He also commented that it was not good for the Priory boys to mix indiscriminately with the village boys who would be a bad influence on them. He was referring to the French boys trying to speak English with young people they met in the town. Maybe he feared that they would acquire a less than respectable vocabulary. Travers accepted this as a kindly observation and resolved to talk to Dr Whittindale about finding somebody suitable to converse with the boys, but it was several months before two young men agreed to come each Sunday to chat in English.

The only members of staff with a good knowledge of English in 1912 were Travers and Coutu – a French Canadian. Coutu was the full-time procurator (bursar), so it fell to Travers to teach English to the pupils. A 1912 instruction from the Mother House directed that 'After six months English will be obligatory during recreation periods several times a week',[36] and in 1913 it approved the practical use of English during half day holidays.[38]

In an enlightened move, borne out by his experience in Africa, Travers requested approval to replace Greek with more English lessons and with practical courses in accountancy and surveying. The response was that Greek was to be continued, but for the top two classes the lessons could be curtailed to allow more time for English; practical subjects were to be taught during the recreation and holiday periods.[53] Greek continued to be taught to the two top classes until 1948, and then intermittently almost until the school closed; it depended on whether there was somebody on the staff who could teach it and pupils able and willing to learn it. Unfortunately, the practical subjects proposed by Travers were never taught either formally or informally; they were presumably considered to be skills best acquired and used by brothers rather than priests.

Although the boys were acquiring a facility with the English language, the same could not be said about English eating habits. At Easter 1914 they were taken on a trip to London and stayed in an English college. No bread appeared on the table at lunch, but when the boys came to supper that evening, they were each carrying a loaf, having visited the local baker's on the way back from their afternoon outing. The French priests accompanying them were horrified, but their hosts found it very amusing and roared with laughter.[2]

The staff continued at their English studies in the evenings. For many months, from about December 1912, a young man named Alfred Sims came several evenings a week to coach the staff, and for this he was paid the 'usual fees'.[38] He also seems to have given a limited number of lessons, probably conversational practice, to the pupils. Mr Sims was the son of the local primary school headmaster, Ebenezer Sims, who was on friendly visiting terms with the fathers.[54]

On the 22nd November 1912, Coutu, Bouniol and Falquière ventured into the cultural world of Bishop's Waltham and attended a conference on Canada in a local public hall. Coutu was interested in what they had to say about his native country. The others went to find out if their knowledge of English stretched to understanding what was said. They all returned satisfied. There was a second meeting on the same subject in February 1913 and the three of them attended again. This time the two Frenchmen were able to declare that they had made good progress.

'Curs with Devils' Beards'

The fathers were keen to master their new language, appreciate their environment and find out as much as possible about the country in which they were now living. When they had some free time, they would cycle to different areas to learn what they could. They would go to Winchester to visit the Cathedral, the West Gate Museum, St Cross Hospital and the 'poor Catholic church'.[55] They became familiar with Southampton, Portsmouth and the surrounding countryside; and they gathered information on local history. People were, in general, welcoming and helpful. Unfortunately, there were some who regarded them with suspicion and contempt – probably a youthful element – and they did not hesitate to show it in public.

When in March 1913 Travers and Bouniol visited the Bishop of Portsmouth, their day out was marred by 'the mocking laughter of the people of Portsmouth ... We must not have the air of Englishmen' was their comment.[56] When Coutu and Falquière went to Southampton the next day to make some purchases, they were pointed at and taunted as German spies. In October 1912, shortly after their arrival, they had remarked that 'The people of the village do not seem hostile'[57], but by March 1913 they were reporting that 'Many times already in Winchester and Bishop's Waltham we have been greeted with goat bleating and insulting laughter'.[58] They bought English clerical suits with money they could ill afford, and wore them for the first time on the 4th April 1913, but their 'clergyman' outfits, as they called them, did not conceal their foreignness. In May Travers and Falquière went to Quarr Abbey on the Isle of Wight to visit Abbot Paul Delatte and again had to put up with derisive laughter and bleating at Portsmouth and on the ferryboat. The taunts continued and, later in May 1913, when walking through Bishop's Waltham in their new suits they were called 'curs with devils' beards'.[59]

Kind Neighbours

Despite the public taunts the little community was very happy in 'our little park … more beautiful each day with the coming of Spring'.[60] Other people were very kind to them. In March 1913 the Boniface children appeared at their door twice in ten days bringing a basket of eggs and jars of jam. On the second occasion the children may have intimated that they were helping people worse off than themselves for Travers visited Mrs Boniface the same day to thank her and to say he could not accept any more. Mrs Boniface was confused and embarrassed saying that Mrs Featherstone told her that they were all malnourished. Travers was able to reassure the good Mrs Boniface that they had sufficient to eat and that her kindness was very much appreciated.

Mr Carpenter, who owned the neighbouring Tangier Farm, was also ready to offer assistance. He loaned them a cow and the use of a horse in 1913.[61] This was the start of a long and friendly association with the local farming community. Many of the brothers that joined the staff were from farming backgrounds and shared a common understanding of the land and animal husbandry with their rural neighbours, and none more so than Brother Aubert who arrived in 1913 to replace Brother Jean who left for the

Unyanyembi mission in April. Aubert, and Brother Patrick in later years, became well known and respected farmers in the district.

As the first Christmas was approaching, Travers took advantage of a casual call by Dr Whittindale to enquire about the English custom of 'Christmas boxes'. The doctor's advice was not to give anything to tradesman, but to give five shillings to the postman, which was the amount he gave and which was considered generous. The same evening some children came to the door and sang carols and they were followed shortly afterwards by the Salvation Army doing likewise. Each group was given two shillings and sixpence. The pupils were also included in the Christmas giving. On Christmas Day each of them received a small 'useful present' and a small 'agreeable present'. The procurator, Father Coutu, had gone to Southampton to buy the presents where, he said, they were considerably cheaper than in Bishop's Waltham.

In their first English winter six boys, two brothers and two fathers were laid low with flu at the same time. The doctor came to visit the sick and remarked that it was a very beautiful morning when he responded to an earlier call at 4am. Father Superior told him that he too had appreciated it for he and the staff rose every day at 4.30am and the boys at 5am. The doctor was taken aback and said it was not good for them to be getting up at such an early hour. 'Give me some paper and I will give you a certificate to send to your superiors saying it is not good for your health to rise at such a time.' The wry comment was 'The devotees of a certain English culture go to bed late, rise late, and are happy to listen to the voice of science when it corresponds with their nature'.[62]

On the 2nd February 1913 a letter from the Vicar General of the Portsmouth Diocese granted the Superior and his priests permission for public Masses to be said in the chapel, to preach sermons, and to teach the catechism. However, all collections of money were to go to the parish priest at Eastleigh. Until this time only a few parishioners had attended what was a private chapel, and none at all turned up for the first Christmas Midnight Mass in 1912, although three attended the 10.30am Mass on Christmas morning. The first public Mass, the first sermon (preached by Travers) and the first collection were on Sunday the 4th February 1913 when the small makeshift chapel overflowed. Thereafter there was never sufficient room in the chapel at the parish Mass on Sundays and feast days, and the boys were compelled to stand outside on these occasions.The first catechism class with 10 children present was on Sunday the 16th March 1913.

In August 1913 Travers suggested to the Parish Priest of Eastleigh that he would like one collection to help furnish the new chapel, which was being built as part of the school extension and which would serve the parishioners. Hickey referred the request to the Bishop who replied that they had 'come with a promise not to make collections, the chapel is not a chapel-of-ease, and all collections must go to the Parish Priest'.[63] The fathers were not only serving the parishioners in an area of 100 square miles around Bishop's Waltham, but from the beginning of 1913 they were helping out at parishes around the diocese every weekend. From 1918 onwards some of the parish priests expressed their gratitude with special collections for the White Fathers or contributed from their own pockets sums varying from £5 to £10. Father Doran, who replaced Hickey at Eastleigh and who many times depended on the fathers to run the Eastleigh church and parish when he was away, was especially generous.

Canon Gunning was also kind in a practical way by inviting the fathers to visit him whenever they were in Winchester. On Easter Monday, 24 March 1913 – six months after their arrival – he gave the boys and three of the fathers a conducted tour of the cathedral and the West Gate museum, and then took them all back to his house at 9 St Peter Street for a meal. They were delighted to find themselves ushered into a comfortable, brightly lit room with a twinkling fire and a table laid with food, bread and beer. Bread, beer and cheese figured prominently on the menu during the first few years.

A New School Building

Travers had wanted to extend the house since he first agreed to buy it. On the day he moved in, Mr Harrington and Mr Jenvy (a builder) had come to survey the kitchen wing, which protruded from the back of the house, with the intention of building a storey above it to provide a dormitory for the brothers, but nothing could be done before the contract of sale was signed. The delay gave time for a reassessment of building requirements. In early 1913, 18 more boys arrived[64] and more were expected. This prompted Travers to propose the addition of a substantial new building. He engaged Jurd and Sanders, a firm of architects in Southampton[65], and after meetings with Father Travers and Brother Egbert, Mr Henry Sanders[66] drew up a set of plans, which were sent to the Mother House on the 19th March 1913 for approval. The plans were accepted but with some changes that increased the cost by 20,000 francs (about £650).

The initial price quotations submitted by nine building contractors were considered very high, even by the architect. Travers asked for modifications to reduce the costs and insisted on a single total price that included all the materials. On the 13th June the architect personally presented the final quotations of three contractors: Messrs Nichol of Southampton, Draper of Fareham, and Hale of Bishop's Waltham. The staff council would like to have given the business to the local builder, Mr Hale, but the total price quoted by Mr Draper was lower at £5735 and so the business went to him.[67]

At the end of June work began on a fine three-storey building that would be behind and parallel to the house and connected to it by a two-storey structure, all in terracotta brick in keeping with the original building. Mr Sanders, the architect, took a reassuring interest in the project. He visited the site every two days and he himself pulled down some of the roof tiles because they were substandard. When he was paid the first part of his fee, he returned £15 as a gift to the school. The end of August was scheduled for demolition of the kitchen wing to make way for the block that would connect the house to the new building. Above the kitchen was an attic that served as an inadequate dormitory for the brothers who now had to be evacuated. No doubt Max, Camille and Egbert were happy to go off to France at this time for their annual retreat leaving their quarters to the demolition men. Jean, Lucien, Aubert and Nicaise must have been allocated even more restricted accommodation, possibly in the coach house.

On the 12th November of the same year the first occupants moved into the new school. It seems extraordinary that in little more than four months such a large building was started, completed and occupied. The brothers had completely furnished the classrooms and study hall with desks and chairs, and the chapel with a high altar, two side chapel altars and pews. (The pews are still in use in the parish church.) The refectory tables were completed in April 1913 and were recorded as 'firm, massive and strong. The labour and skill of our two good brothers [Jean and Lucien] will serve many future generations'.[68] How right was the remark. The tables were still being used when the school closed. As the pioneering work came to a close three of the brothers went off to new assignments before the end of 1913: Max left for Tunisia, Camille for Algeria, and Jean for Unyanyembi.

The new building was solemnly blessed by Bishop Cotter of Portsmouth on Monday the 1st December 1913. Travers and Coutu had met the Bishop at the railway station and together they had walked up the hill and entered the grounds through a floral archway to cries of '*Vive Monseigneur!*' The Bishop must have admired the large statue of Our Lady with the Child Jesus in her arms that now occupied the niche above the front entrance. It had been installed two months previously on the 6th October, and was the most obvious feature of the building as one approached along the main drive. Lunch in the large new refectory was followed by a few short speeches and the official ceremony took place at 3pm in the chapel. The Bishop left immediately afterwards for the station, passing through the archway again with further cries of '*Vive Monseigneur!*' This was the first event since the arrival of the White Fathers to be reported in a local newspaper.[3] The report referred to the excellence of the work and the speed at which it was finished which, it said, reflected great credit on the architect, Mr Sanders, and on the builder Mr Thos. Draper. It also mentioned that the new building was 'some 146 feet long, about 30 feet in width, and 50 feet high'.

Within a week, two hovering revenue inspectors appeared. They had come to value the building for taxation in accordance with the recent Finance Act. Travers seems to have claimed that as a school it should be exempt from rates, but this was rejected and it remained rateable. The duties based on this valuation became a heavy burden and were disputed by Travers for many years afterwards.

4.2. The Priory in the 1930s.

The school complex was now in the form of a capital letter H. One upright side of the H was the original two-storey house that became the Fathers' House, that is, the staff quarters with bedrooms, bathrooms, offices, library, staff recreation room and oratory. The other upright side was the three-storey building that had on the ground floor a chapel, sacristy, study hall for 60 boys, toilets and store rooms. Below ground level and to one side of the chapel was the boiler room. The first floor had a shower area with six cubicles at the west end, four classrooms occupying the main area, and, at the east end, the Prefect of Discipline's room, an infirmary, and a room that served over the years as a storeroom, classroom, small dormitory and oratory. The top floor had a dormitory that occupied almost the full length of the building. At one end of the dormitory were a boot room and a spacious toilet area with two rows of washbasins supplied with cold water only.

The crossbar of the H had on the ground floor a recreation area, known as the 'covered quadrangle', which was glazed along one side and had wide half-glazed doors that provided access to the quadrangle. The covered quadrangle ran the length of the building and served as the main thoroughfare between the Fathers' House and the Boys' House. Also on the ground floor and running parallel with the covered quadrangle, but isolated from it by a wall, was the kitchen with doors and windows that opened on to the kitchen garden. The whole of the upper floor was occupied by the refectory, except for a large scullery at one end where boys did the washing up and slicing of bread. Also here was a dumb waiter that communicated with the kitchen below.

Surmounting the junction of the two new buildings was a belfry whose thin-sounding bell was only rung for the Angelus at mid-day and in the evening. The school bell was, and remained, a very large hand bell. The bell-ringer was an older boy – with a reliable watch – appointed each term.

In the same year (1913) the grounds were enlarged with the purchase of two adjacent meadows, for which approval was given by the Mother House 'as long as the price is reasonable'.[38] Presumably it was, for they were acquired and later used as playing fields.

4.3. The quadrangle (looking north) in the 1930s. The 'covered quadrangle' is on the right with the refectory above it.

4.4. The quadrangle (looking south) in the 1950s. The 'covered quadrangle' is on the left. The door leads to the Superior's office.

Hens, Huts and Harmoniums

In 1913 Bouniol discovered auctions. He was appointed procurator in 1913, and at once he and Falquière started to attend house sales and auctions around the county. They furnished the Fathers' House, school and farm from these sales; beds, bookcases, museum display cases, textbooks, crockery, huts, harmoniums; they even came back with livestock – hens, pigs and cows. They also bought bicycles: 16 of them, which were used in common by staff and pupils for many years. In December 1919 a particularly good second-hand Alexandre harmonium ('still in new condition') was purchased for 48 guineas, and delivered in early January. Father Doran of Eastleigh sent a contribution of £5. The harmonium lasted until February 1935 when a new organ was installed.

Throughout 1913 there were many comings and goings – a pattern that was never to change throughout the history of the school. Brothers Camille, Jean and Max departed, and Brothers Aubert and Lucien arrived. In July Fathers Hephan and Brassac stayed for a little while on their way from London to the missions. They had been in London on an English language course and were the first of a continual stream of foreign White Fathers who, for more than 50 years, came to improve their English. They were closely followed by Father Emile Lefebvre who had also been studying English in London, but he had come to join the staff – his first posting. He only stayed a year before going on to teach at Binson, France, in September 1914. Father Louis Montaud , who arrived in September 1913, stayed for an even shorter time. He was posted to the St Maurice Apostolic School in Switzerland after just one term. Father Albert Folliot, who replaced him in January 1914, came for much longer and made an impressive entry by turning up from France on a motorcycle. It was not the first motorcycle at the Priory, for one had been delivered a few days before and was soon enhanced with a sidecar. It had been bought to enable the priests to travel around the country on promotional work, to assist at distant parishes and to attend conferences. Father Breslin, the parish priest of Tichborne, had given Coutu driving lessons before the bike arrived and Coutu was now the instructor for the other staff, all of whom made great use of it. In 1914 the fathers were helping out at many parishes at the weekends, including Fareham, Gosport, Tichborne, Borden Camp, Netley, Bursledon, Romsey, and Winchester. Usually they travelled by train, but sometimes walked. If the motorbike was available they used that, but Travers was the one who used it the most and consequently it was he who suffered the most breakdowns, for it was far from reliable.

War intervenes

The third year had brought a further small increase in the number of students, so that in early 1914 they numbered 50. This rapid and happy development was brought to a sudden halt in 1914 by the outbreak of war. The morning papers of the 2nd August reported general mobilisation in France, and Frenchmen abroad were instructed to report to the nearest consular office. Falquière went to the French Consulate in Southampton that day and returned with mobilisation papers for himself, Travers, Bouniol and Chollet – conscripted not as chaplains, but as soldiers. (The French government had abolished military chaplains and introduced the compulsory conscription of clergy in 1886.) Travers was in France recruiting pupils – the Priory was still considered to be a French school in exile – and he went into the army without an opportunity of returning to England. Falquière had also brought mobilisation papers for Fathers Godineau and Tessier – two visitors who were about to return to Africa after their studies in London. The boys greeted the news with passionate cries of '*Vive La France!*' and this fervour was maintained until the following day when the fathers left on the 7.20pm train from Bishop's Waltham with all the boys standing on the station platform singing *La Marseillaise*. The people of the town must have found out very quickly what was happening for many of them came along to cheer the Frenchmen and to sing *God Save the King*. After this outpouring of patriotic spirit and mutual expressions of support, the boys returned to the school where a cloud of melancholy descended upon them. The fathers left behind were Rémi Coutu, Albert Folliot, and Albert Ducourant who was a visitor who had been studying in London and was now stuck in England until he was able to leave for Banguelo, Northern Rhodesia, in April 1919.

Coutu and Ducourant were Canadian citizens, and Folliot was unfit for military service.

The war affected not only the staff but the students too: six of the older ones were conscripted almost immediately. One of the young men conscripted was Joseph Boudon who had been amongst the earliest arrivals in 1912. He was later to become the Provincial Superior of France 1940–1951.[69] When the others reached the prescribed age they too were called into the army, so that by mid-July 1917 all the French students had disappeared.

A declaration of war by King George V took effect at 11pm on the 4th August 1914 and Parliament gave formal approval on the 6th August. A few days later a couple of ladies from the Red Cross appeared asking if the school would accommodate wounded soldiers. They were offered the Fathers' House and the staff moved themselves and their belongings into the Boys' House, but a week later the ladies returned to say that the premises were not suitable for a hospital because the kitchen was inadequate. The fathers still wished to be of some assistance and, as the number of students dwindled, the unused beds and mattresses were lent to a nearby hospital. In February 1915 soldiers were billeted on the ground floor of the Fathers' House and in all the external buildings. Presumably, the soldiers were fed and did their training elsewhere for there is no mention of these activities, or of any contact with the staff and pupils.

The Mother House, aware of the anxiety of the parents, had, in mid-August, directed that boys were to be returned to their homes immediately if their families requested it. Getting them home however was another matter for the cross-channel ferry schedules had been abandoned. When the family of pupil Raymond Gueret asked for him to come home, he was taken to Southampton, but there were no ferries sailing to France, whereupon he embarked on a merchant ship as the ship's boy. He disembarked near Cherbourg and from there made his way home to Rennes. A week later François Gornouvel was luckier and was able to return to his family by the ferry.

The first news of those who had been conscripted arrived on the 18th August. Bouniol had been sent to the front in Alsace,

Falquière to Perpignon, and Travers was working as a medical orderly at a military hospital in Rennes. In November Bouniol was incarcerated as a prisoner of war in Westphalia, Germany. They were all to survive the war, but many White Fathers, students and relatives did not. The first of many reported deaths was on the 28th October when Father Folliot learnt of his brother's death from wounds at Pécigneux.

At the end of August Father John Forbes[70], a Canadian passing through England on his way to Uganda, was appointed Superior in place of the conscripted Father Travers. Forbes was the first Canadian White Father and an outstanding linguist. Besides French and English, he was fluent in Latin, Greek, Hebrew, Arabic, Kabyle, Kiswahili and, later, Luganda. He had previously been professor of French and Greek at the Melkite seminary in Jerusalem[71], and assistant director and professor of Arabic at the novitiate in Algiers. At Bishop's Waltham he quickly made up for what seemed his only deficiency: he learnt how to ride a bicycle.[72]

4.5. Father John Forbes, Superior 1914–15.

The new school year started on the 21st September 1914 with just four teaching staff: Folliot took the class of Rhetoric, Forbes the Second Class, Ducourant the Third Class, and Coutu was assigned to teach English, History and Geography throughout the school. The four teachers were soon reduced to three when, within a few weeks, Coutu was diagnosed with tuberculosis and was ordered into hospital. Father Piet Op den Kamp came to replace him and, not knowing it was a short (but steep) walk to the Priory, he took a taxi from Bishop's Waltham station. It cost him a shilling.

An unexpected visitor appeared in October and stayed for five days. This was Father Jolicoeur, Chaplain-in-Chief to the Canadian Expeditionary Force stationed on Salisbury Plain. He made a big impression: he arrived in an army staff car, was very energetic and lively, and sported an 'English officer's khaki uniform and superb pair of moustaches ... He does not look like a priest'.[73] He was to become a regular visitor throughout the war for he always spent some time at the Priory when on leave from France.

In November, Father Balthazar Drost (a Dutchman), Father Alban Delaey (a Belgian) and Brother Modeste (also Dutch) arrived to replace the departed French nationals. They joined two other Dutchmen, Brother Aubert, who had arrived the previous year and Brother Nicaise who came in June 1914. Forbes and Drost were old friends for, in 1901, Drost and a Frenchman, Father Saule, had assisted Forbes insetting up the first Canadian community in Quebec City.[72] Delaey, unfortunately, was a sick missionary with a serious chest condition and was unable to continue with his classes. On the advice of the doctor he left within three weeks for the sanatorium in Algiers. Father Pierre Kappel (a Belgian) was sent from St Laurent to replace him. He stayed until the end of January 1915 when he moved on to Boxtel, Holland, which was where he was going when he was diverted to the Priory. Drost and Op den Kamp also left in January 1915 for Uganda and were immediately replaced by three highly regarded professors from Jerusalem: Fathers Brutel, Lassoumery and Madeleine, experts in Middle Eastern languages, but it was French, Latin and Greek that they were required to teach. Joseph Robert, a French priest too ill for the missions and unfit for military service, joined them in September 1915. Robert and Folliot were kept on the military hook and had to report regularly for medical tests, on one occasion being sent for two days in April 1917 for checks at the French Military Commission in London. They were again exempted.

Coutu returned from hospital in Ramsgate in December 1914, but was still very sick and unable to take classes. When the new staff arrived, he was designated to teach Lassoumery English and to help the newcomers buy the kind of 'suits that are necessary for them in England'.[74]

Travers Returns

Travers also returned in December 1914 having been invalided out of the army. Because he was unwell, Forbes continued as Superior and Travers taught English to two of the classes. In February 1915, and on a number of occasions after that, he had to go to the French Consulate in Southampton for a medical check, and each time was declared unfit. He may have been considered unfit for the army, but not for the White Fathers and on the 15th February 1915 he resumed the office of Superior – a position he was to hold until taken seriously ill in 1926. Forbes stepped down to take Travers' classes and those of Father Madeleine who had injured his head in a bicycle accident. In April 1915 Forbes at last gratefully continued his interrupted journey to Uganda, where he was later appointed Bishop. But just before he departed he cycled 67 miles to London to bid farewell to friends, and cycled back the next day.

By July 1915 all the top class had gone, either conscripted or returned to their families. Brutel left for a teaching assignment at St Maurice in Switzerland, and Brother Nicaise left for Boxtel, Holland. Coutu returned to Canada in October to convalesce and later moved to Denver in the United States where he died in June 1918.

Staff and pupils appeared so regularly at the French Consulate for medical checks and soldiering duties that the Consul himself, Monsieur Barthèlemy, became very familiar with this source of military manpower. He knew the staff well and on at least three occasions in 1915 he came to spend a relaxing day with his countrymen. In 1916 he was posted to Chicago. His successor at Southampton also came to the Priory from time to time with his wife for afternoon tea.

The White Fathers may have been keeping the military section of the French Consulate occupied, but they were keeping the British police even busier.

Undesirables, Spies and Zeppelins

From the start of the war the police had been checking the school and its residents at frequent intervals. Spies seemed to be what they hoped to find.

Three days after the declaration of war by Britain, the police turned up at the school to check each person's nationality and to ensure there were no 'undesirables' on the premises. The boys may not have been designated as undesirables, but they were many times suspected of being so. The first time was on the 11th August 1914. It was a warm and sunny day during their summer holidays and a group of them had set off on bicycles for a day out, but at Portsmouth they were arrested as spies. They were not detained for long. They returned at 4pm accompanied by a policeman who said they were not to venture beyond Bishop's Waltham. There was no apparent authority for imposing such a restriction. The policeman was either being officious or simply suggesting that they should stay in the neighbourhood where they were known. His advice, officious or well meaning, should have been heeded for henceforth they were often stopped when they went out of the neighbourhood. A week later Father Coutu took a group on bicycles for a short holiday at a Salesian College in London. Two of the boys fell behind on the way and were again arrested as suspected spies by the police. They were searched, manhandled, and eventually released. This did not deter them from other outings. At the beginning of September they spent two days at the Trappist monastery at Martin, about 40 miles from Bishop's Waltham, again going by bicycle. No boys arrested this time, the only comment after this outing being *'Ah! le bon cidre de Père Gérard!'*[75] But Father Gérard was not around to make the next season's cider for he was called up into the army. That left only two priests in the monastery, and in October 1916 they returned to Normandy, the threat of expulsion from France having receded.

On the 3rd January 1916, the police came to tell Travers to black out all the windows. This meant buying curtains which they could not afford, so Father Folliot was dispatched the next day to buy wrapping paper which the fathers then set about sticking to all the windows. Maybe it was just as well for that evening a couple of Zeppelins passed overhead. These were not the first aircraft to pass close by. In March 1914 a very loud noise in the sky above the school brought everybody out to see an aeroplane skimming the rooftop and landing in a nearby meadow. It took off again shortly afterwards, presumably having fixed a fault or having refuelled from a can.

Father Corneille van Uden arrived in January 1916 from Europe and immediately the police came to search his belongings, but they found nothing incriminating. He was Flemish-speaking and had come to take over from Travers who had been acting as chaplain to Allington Manor, which was being used as a hospital for Belgian soldiers most of whom spoke only Flemish. Van Uden returned to France in September the same year, but before leaving he had to sign a commitment not to return to England.

On the 15th February 1916 all those in the school over the age of 18 had to report as foreign subjects to the police station at Fareham where they felt that they were treated as criminal suspects. The circumstances appeared threatening and for a while they thought they were to be imprisoned. They had their fingerprints taken and had to sign a form, despite their objections, in the place marked 'Prisoner's signature'. In March they returned to Fareham to collect their 'identity books', which all aliens above the age of 18 were required to have, and they were told that the boys were not to be allowed out of the school unless accompanied by a teacher (presumably with his identity papers).

A few weeks later the police came to the school to check that boys who had reached the age of 18 had obtained an identity book, but they found that all those aged 18 had left to join the army and those approaching that age were about to do so. They came again after a couple of weeks to check on the pupils, but found that no 18-year olds had suddenly popped up. After this all those aged 18 or above had to report each month to Fareham with their identity papers.

In April 1916 the police called again. This time it was to tell Travers not to ring the bell from one hour after sunset until one hour before sunrise otherwise it could be interpreted as a signal to Zeppelins. The fathers considered the whole business absurd, but one could not be certain as to what might be reported to the authorities. On the night of the 26th–27th September, those that were asleep were awakened by shouts of 'Zeppelins!' Thinking they were overhead, everybody ran to see where they were. In the converging beams of the searchlights they could see one Zeppelin some way off like a great vulture with little power in its wings. It then disappeared without dropping any bombs. A couple of days later the police arrived accusing them of making signals to the Zeppelin. Someone had reported seeing a signal light at one of the windows, but the charge was dropped when the witness admitted he was not sure that he had seen a light.

The fathers felt that they were being persecuted. In one month alone – August 1916 – the school was visited by the local constable, a sergeant from Droxford, a detective from Fareham, and by Mr Carman, the police superintendent. The purpose of this surveillance was ostensibly to check the Dutch nationals. On the 21st August, the honour fell to Brother Lucien, who had his correspondence searched by the Superintendent, his letters having already been checked by the Post Office. One of his recent letters, which he had received with considerable joy, was his appointment to Nyassa where he had previously spent 12 years. However, he was unable to leave the country until July 1919, so there was no relief from the continuing attention of the police. Travers took the opportunity of the latest superintendent's visit to complain about harassment, having previously complained to him about having to report to the Town Hall in Portsmouth whenever he went to St John's College at Southsea or to see the Bishop. Mr Carman had arranged for the Town Hall reporting to be cancelled and Travers was able, on this occasion to thank him. The police were always charming and amiable, and one suspects that it was a duty they rather enjoyed, for they were always treated to tea or coffee and a few hours in very pleasant surroundings.

Holidays – But Not At Home

The principal holidays until 1917 were a week between Christmas Day and New Year, eight days at Easter and 15 days at the end of the school year – all spent at the school. The top class on leaving school for the College of Philosophy took their 15-day annual vacation at home.

During the year the pupils were allowed 15 half-day holidays starting at midday, and 15 three-quarter-day holidays starting at 10am. Until midday or 10am the normal classes and studies were pursued; the rest of the day was spent in practical lessons for English, plainchant singing, and natural sciences, which the teachers were instructed to make interesting and not impose as schoolwork.[38] The part-day holidays were also spent playing sports, including football on the downs. When not otherwise engaged on their half days, the boys were expected to take long walks, often to Winchester or Romsey. These were an 18 to 22 mile round trip, which might seem physically demanding to a modern schoolboy.

They often cycled to distant places including Bournemouth, Chichester, Bognor Regis, Alton, Aldershot, and London. The seaside was a favourite destination where they would swim and from which they would occasionally return with fish and mussels that they had caught. They picnicked in the Meon and Itchen valleys, and went camping at Quarr Abbey and at the Trappist monastery. They all considered it a privilege to be in England, to be able to visit the splendid cathedrals of Winchester, Salisbury and Chichester, the abbeys and ruined abbeys of Romsey, Netley and Beaulieu, the archaeological sites to which Father Ducourant was fond of taking them, and to spend time in the many attractive and remarkable villages. They even gained admittance to some grand houses such as 'the beautiful Hursley Park' in August 1916 and, in the previous year, to an unnamed 'Lord's house' where his Lordship plied the boys with beer and sandwiches. Perhaps it was an indication of solidarity with the French. This was certainly the case in January 1917 when Father Mahoney, the Parish Priest of St Edmund's in Southampton invited them to the cinema. When the manager discovered who the visitors were, he introduced them to the audience and then played *La Marseillaise*. The occasion even earned a report in the local Southampton newspaper.

... And Then There Were None

The number of pupils was diminishing steadily and the 1916 Christmas term started with only 16 pupils (four of them British) divided into two classes. Because there were so few boys in the school, they had not played any competitive games with other teams for some time, but in January 1917 a young man from Wickham challenged them to a football match that was drawn 1-1. They had no pitch of their own and the next game against an Eastleigh team in February was in Mr Dougal's meadow. It was again a draw: 4-4. Three days later they played in Droxford. No score was recorded, but 'the Droxford team played like foul-mouthed brutes'.[76] After this game they could no longer put together a team for they were disappearing rapidly into the army. Even the two remaining British boys, Hughes and MacKenzie, were conscripted.

In July 1917 the seven remaining pupils – all French, who had not been home since they arrived several years before, departed to a war-ravaged Europe. None returned to England. They had reached military service age, so it is likely that most of them, if not all, went into the army. Travers was left with a big building, few staff, and no students. What now? A decision had to be made quickly for it was likely that the Society would be left with a large empty school on its hands.

An Apostolic School for British Pupils

In 1914 the General Council had advised that if any young Englishmen asked to be admitted they were not to be sent to the lower classes at the schools in France or Switzerland[77], but were to be provided with appropriate lessons at Bishop's Waltham.[78] With this advice in mind, four British applicants had been admitted: three in September 1916 and one the following month. They were Francis Edmunds, Joseph Hughes, John MacKenzie, and Ronald Walker who was a local boy from Bishop's Waltham. Edmunds and Walker left after one term, and Hughes and MacKenzie were conscripted in March 1917. John MacKenzie entered an officer cadet unit in Lancashire and Joseph Hughes was called into the Home Service, which meant he could continue his studies after basic training, but would be called for active service when needed.

When the final group of pupils left for France in mid-July 1917, Father Travers, by now very much an Anglophile (his Christian names henceforth always appear as Peter Mary rather than as Pierre Marie), decided to seek English-speaking students until French students returned. With this in mind he had invited all the local parish priests to lunch in April 1917 and 15 of them turned up. It proved a good public relations exercise with the local clergy, but no new students resulted from this effort. In August he set off for Portsmouth to do some recruiting, but he met with little success, only Henry Godbold came from St John's College, Southsea. The school year thus opened in September 1917 with just one pupil – 'the first piece of the edifice which we shall build'.[79] Joseph Hughes from Lancaster, who had completed his Priory studies and his Home Service basic training, returned later in September to start a lone philosophy course for he was unable to travel to France for higher studies.

The Priory was far from empty, however, for on the 13th September 1917 the school was made available to six professors and 27 novices and scholastics of the de la Salle Brothers of the Christian Schools. Having previously been forced out of Nantes by the anti-clerical circumstances before the war, they had now been evacuated from Dover because of frequent bombing raids and because the Red Cross wished to take over their house. They stayed at the Priory until the 1st April 1919 when their house was returned to them. Two weeks after their return to Dover, an Assistant of the Superior General of the de la Salle Brothers, accompanied by Brother Simon, Superior of the community at Southsea, came to thank Father Travers for the hospitality given to their confrères, and handed him a cheque for 40 guineas to buy a monstrance for the chapel. Five days later, on Easter Sunday 20th April the 'magnificent monstrance' was displayed after Mass and *O Salutaris* sung in three voices.

The three British students, MacKenzie, Hughes and Godbold, on whom Travers had placed many of his hopes, unfortunately did not complete the course. MacKenzie was gravely wounded during the war and was invalided out of the army. He tried to carry on and, in September 1918, went to Carthage to study philosophy. When the war finished he was sent to France to continue his studies, but on his way there he was taken ill at Marseille when his wound opened up. The wound refused to heal and he then contracted tuberculosis, forcing him to return to his home. Because of continuing ill health he was obliged to give up hope of becoming a White Father. He went to the Westminster diocesan seminary to study for the priesthood and was ordained in 1923. During his student and teaching days at St Edmund's College, Ware, Hertfordshire, and later as a parish priest he was a regular visitor to the Priory for part of his Christmas and summer holidays. Hughes completed his philosophy studies in 1919, and then went to the Novitiate in Maison Carrée, Algeria, having taken the London University matriculation examinations just before he left – the first time a Priory student took a British university examination. There must have been high expectations that he would be the first British pupil to become a White Father but, alas, he left the Novitiate in December 1919. He continued his studies in England and, like MacKenzie, was ordained as a diocesan priest. Godbold left the Priory in 1920 and pursued a career as a layman. Others, however, quickly replaced these three.

At the start of the school year in September 1918 Travers had enrolled nine pupils. The new boys included Arthur Hughes, destined for high ecclesiastical office, and two Belgians: George van Hoorn of Louvain and Cecil de Kerkhove of Vervius. As it was virtually impossible to get in or out of Belgium where the bloodiest and most destructive battles of the war were raging, it is very probable that the Belgian pupils lived locally. By the middle of October 1914 there were several Belgian refugee families in Bishop's Waltham who were regularly visited by the White Fathers, and it was likely that it was from these families that the two boys came. In February 1919 van Hoorn's father, who did not approve of his son's vocation, 'came for his son who has been living in England since the beginning of the war'[80] to take him back to Belgium. George must have been cheered to some extent when the other pupils insisted on accompanying him to the station to see him off.

Philip Corio also arrived in 1918, and on the 5th April 1919 he and Henry Godbold were invited to play football for their former school, St John's College, Southsea. They did so, but on the way back a policeman in Fareham stopped them for not having lights on their bicycles. This resulted in their receiving a summons to appear in court on the 12th April 1919 where they were each fined a shilling. Godbold presumably had other outings, but the only other one mentioned was when he and Joseph Hughes (the only students at that time) went with one of the fathers to the town on the 5th March 1918 to listen to a talk on the Battle of Jutland. They had gone expecting to applaud the British Navy, but they returned disappointed. The speaker, who was a retired admiral, turned out to be an old fogey who knew little other than what he had read, was hazy about the geography of the battle and was unable to answer any of the questions put to him.

Another of the pupils who arrived in April 1918 was Samuel Rogerson. He had come not to study for the priesthood, but to be a missionary brother. Unfortunately he was taken ill with tuberculosis in 1919 and had to return home for good.

By now the pupils were being taught in English, but outside the classroom and the recreation periods the language was still French. French was the language of all written instructions, staff correspondence and school records. The boys' concerts were in French, their prayers were in French and their hymns, when not in Latin, were also in French. It was on the Feast of All Saints, 1st November 1918, that some English hymns were sung for the first time. The morning and night prayers in chapel were translated into English in 1920. About this time the timetable was slightly amended so that the pupils were awakened at the later time of 6.15am (the staff rose at 5.30am). After morning prayers and meditation in the chapel there was a period of study followed by Mass at 7.45am and breakfast at 8.30am. It was the same on Sundays with, additionally, a sung High Mass at 10.30am.

Return from the Trenches

When the end of the war was announced on the 11th November 1918, the Priory bell rang out for all it was worth. There was a great sense of joy, and in the evening nearly everybody, boys and staff, joined the local people in a hall in Bishop's Waltham for an evening's entertainment. Mr Lang, who was chairing the occasion, invited Father Travers to join the prominent townspeople on the stage and then presented him with unexpected compliments especially on the triumph of France. Father Travers replied with an impromptu speech in his charming and friendly manner and briefly recounted the efforts of the White Fathers during the war. For this he received a long and enthusiastic ovation. The following day he received a letter from Mr Austin, a wealthy local estate agent, who would occasionally send a sack of apples for the boys and invite Travers round for tea.[81]

> *Dear Father Travers,*
> *We rejoice with you in the salvation of your country and the overthrow of the guilty Kaiser. It is indeed a victory of justice over wicked oppression for which we humbly return thanks to the Almighty. Vive la France!*
> *Yours sincerely,*
> *W P Austin.*

There were more celebrations locally and throughout the country on the 19th July 1919 when the peace treaty formalising the end of the war was signed. Mr Robson of Bishop's Waltham gave over his house and grounds for the local celebrations, which included music and sports. The Priory boys were invited and did well by winning several prizes.

Father Travers' spirits must have been buoyed up in April 1919 when two of his staff returned: Joseph Bouniol and Eloi Falquière. Bouniol had spent most of the war as a prisoner in Germany. Falquière had spent most of it in the trenches. In February 1916 he came to spend his leave at the Priory, but had to return to his unit within seven days. Throughout the war many conscripted White Fathers and students came from the front line for a few days' respite. Falquière returned for a fortnight's leave in March 1917 and came for his third leave to what must have seemed an oasis of peace in October 1917. When he arrived he was dirty, spattered with blood and worn out, not unlike British soldiers who were well known for returning home from the front unwashed and covered in lice. He returned to the front on the 17th October. This was his last leave for he was taken prisoner in July 1918. When he was released in 1919, Travers received a copy of a citation. It was from General S Spire, commanding the French 22nd Division, who commended Corporal Falquière for his service at the battles of Malmaison (1917), the Somme (1918), Vermeuil – Chemin des Dames (1918) and as a prisoner of war. Falquière arrived home at his beloved Priory three weeks after the citation and soon afterwards he left for Carthage for his 30-day retreat. Bouniol, who had gone from his army prison to his family home in Paris, joined his confrère in Carthage.

Writing in 1919, Father Bouniol commented on how pleased he and Father Falquière were to be back in England. 'It [England] must know we will be going to Africa. There is all the sunshine we could wish for, and a complete absence of rain.'[82] Unfortunately neither of them was to return to Africa as a missionary. Bouniol was appointed procurator in place of Father Drost who had departed for the missions. Falquière, who had been badly gassed, continued to be very ill and was unable to teach regularly for some time. In 1921 he was appointed to teach at St Laurent d'Olt, but continued to be ill. He then went to the Society's sanatorium at Pau in southwest France where he died in 1924.[83] Father Joseph Déry, another member of staff, also died in 1924. He left the Priory to visit his family in Canada before going to the missions, but he was never to reach Africa. He left England in good health, but contracted typhoid and then meningitis from which he died while in Quebec.

The School Fills Up

The war had changed the anti-clerical stance of the French government, which now promoted national unity and the setting aside of religious and secular conflicts. There was no longer any likelihood of the St Laurent school being closed down and the senior boys could continue their studies in France.

However, there was some concern as to whether the Priory could continue without French students, and Travers was asked to comment on having a mixed Anglo-French school at Bishop's Waltham. A letter from Father Bouniol to the Superior General in 1919 opened by saying that Father Travers had asked him to write giving his views.[82] Speaking from his own experience, he suggests that the only advantage would be in learning each other's language. Some subjects, such as geography, he considers could be taught in either language, but with others there would be considerable drawbacks. He comments that many students do not take to science subjects even in their mother tongue, and in an imperfectly understood foreign language the antipathy for these subjects would increase. Learning Latin and Greek would be even more difficult, for they would be using a language they did not know very well to learn another language they did not know; 'the obscurities of one adding to obscurities of the other'. He then comments on the 'formation' of the pupils, saying that with youngsters of different nationalities and between 14 and 18 years old, it is more likely they will imitate each other's faults rather than each other's qualities. He adds that the discipline and organisation adopted for the convenience of both groups would not be acknowledged by either of them. He is optimistic that the house can be filled by British students, but cannot back up this optimism because 'it is Father Travers that occupies himself with recruitment'. He suggests that the French students should stay in France and that the position should be reviewed in a year or so.

Travers' comments have not survived, but no doubt they were similar to those of Bouniol, and must have been convincing, for at a meeting on the 9th June 1919 the General Council 'having considered very carefully the reasons given by Father Travers, decided that this apostolic school will be reserved exclusively for English [-speaking] recruitment'.[84]

The setting up and maintenance costs of the first several years had been met entirely by the Mother House, but now that it was a British foundation Travers had to go about the country seeking donations to support this new enterprise. There was an income from fees paid by the parents, but these were reduced and sometimes waived altogether if parents could not afford them. Another small source of income was the fees or casual offerings to the priests for their services; this money went into a common account.[38]

In 1919 Travers asked for permission to have fee-paying day pupils to help offset the monthly salaries of two lay teachers he was employing. He was granted permission to do this as long as it was approved by the local bishop, especially if non-Catholics were admitted[85], for there were insufficient grammar school places for Catholics. In the event, day boys were not admitted. His recruitment drive was proving successful and the school was starting to fill up and was likely to reach its capacity of 60 in the following year. The two lay teachers he was employing were Mr Couche[86], who was living at the Priory and probably teaching English, and Mr Gilbert[87] who lived in Winchester Road and came in to give music lessons on Mondays, Tuesdays and Thursdays.

Mr Couche must have left in the summer of 1919 for Travers was seeking another layman to teach English at that time. In August two convert former Anglican clergymen come to discuss taking up the post. One of them, Mr McGillervery, wished to study for the priesthood in Rome as soon as the opportunity arose and was not sure how long he could stay. The other applicant, Mr Anderson, was therefore offered the position, and he took up his post on the 6th September 1919, moving into the room formerly occupied by Brother Lucien. Mr Anderson translated into English at least one of the White Fathers' prayers (an Act of Consecration to the Blessed Virgin Mary), and it was very likely that he translated the morning and night prayers, which were said in English from this time forward. When he left in 1921, Father Arthur Prentice took over the teaching of English. Mr Anderson remained a good friend of the school and came for Easter or summer holiday sojourns nearly every year from 1922 until 1936.

Although he had a very small staff and few pupils in 1919, Father Travers was a busy man. Besides teaching and managing the school with its 33 de la Salle guests, he went about the country giving talks and lantern-slide lectures, seeking recruits and the means to keep the work going and, as requested by the General Council[88], publishing articles to promote knowledge of the Society, its missions in British Africa, and the school. It was a wearisome task and by no means easy. However, the school year of 1919 started with a total of 31 pupils including a Bishop's Waltham boy, John Oliver Miller, who was to spend 30 years in Uganda as a White Father. From 1919 onwards many applications were received for places in the school, and sometimes Travers had as many as 20 on his desk at a time, but the majority were turned down. In 1922 an entry of 61 boys, which filled the school to capacity, and 31 applications, which could not be accepted for want of space, showed that his promotional work had not been in vain.

His travelling and that of the other fathers was hindered considerably during the general railway strike of 1919, and their motorcycle was far from dependable. It was forever breaking down and permission was sought from the Mother House to buy a replacement. The new bike was a Rover from '*chez Rooks*' – price £152. From the day of its arrival it was in constant use both locally and criss-crossing the country with Travers in the saddle. Within a few weeks of its arrival he set off on it to preach, run conferences, and recruit in London, Birmingham, Manchester, Stonyhurst, Reading, Oxford and several other places. It was also used for ferrying visitors to and from Southampton and around the country. Father Voillard, Assistant-General, was no exception. He experienced its questionable comfort as a passenger in the sidecar when he made an official visitation from the 8th to the 14th December 1920. It proved particularly useful again during the long railway strike from March to June in 1921.

As the number of pupils increased so did the need for furniture and recreational facilities. Father Bouniol, Father Robert and Brother Aubert attended many of the auction sales in the district in search of much needed articles of furniture, and many were the bargains they picked up – bookcases, showcases for the museum (later the library), bales of wool to be teased and used to replace the straw of the mattresses, beds, desks, chairs, school books for Latin, English and Mathematics, and a considerable amount of crockery.

Something in addition to the 'covered quad' was necessary for wet recreation periods, so Bouniol, in July 1922, acquired a long wooden building at auction from the Royal Victoria Military Hospital at Netley. It was the buyer's responsibility to dismantle and transport it and so a group of privileged boys were deputed under the supervision of Aubert to attend to it. 'The Hut' was erected, complete with glass-covered veranda, and given a coat of paint in August by the fathers and brothers while the boys were on holiday. When the boys returned it had a billiard table installed, boxing gloves and a punch bag. It was to serve its purpose well for more than forty years as a recreation room, overflow dormitory, classroom and study hall. Here all manner of indoor games, sports and entertainments took place for generations – billiards, cards, chess, darts, boxing, table tennis and concerts. When the gymnasium was erected eight years later, concerts, table tennis and boxing tournaments took place there.

4.6. The recreation hut in the 1930s. A stovepipe is in the middle of the room.

Former student James Smith described the campus as it appeared in 1922. Except for the appearance of the recreation hut and the bicycle shed, not much had changed since December 1913.

> The Priory compound was not so extensive as it was to become later, and the buildings were fewer. The college building towered in forbidding isolation on the hill, with the staff quarters in its shadow, and there was one small bicycle shed standing on the ground that was later occupied by the gym. This shed sheltered motorcycles with names little known today, like 'Douglas' and 'Osborne'; and as for bicycles, who now ever hears of the 'Kynoch'? These were the bicycles which served generations of Priorians and which Father Marchant strove to preserve for posterity by some embalming process which he had learned from Mr Bob Symes.[89] [They were probably the same bicycles that were bought at auction by Father Bouniol in 1913.]

Gaslight provided the illumination for many years. By 1925 it was defective and possibly dangerous, but despite much chivvying from a very sick Father Travers, the gas company refused to do anything about it and did not even reply to his later letters. In 1926 therefore he decided to install electric lighting. Mr Pink, the local contractor quoted £180 for the work, but the job went to a London firm who quoted £1.5s per lamp. Installation started in March and was completed, except for the boys' dormitory, a month later, and what a difference it made. They all felt it was money well spent. During the summer holidays in 1926 Fathers Roy and Lefils completed the work by installing electric lights in the dormitory. This saved a quoted price of £9. A representative of the company that installed the first phase came to inspect the priests' work, found that it had been well done and approved the installation. In August 1934 Mr Symes, who was now the local electrical contractor, and an assistant worked on a 'new electric installation' – probably installing a more up-to-date 110-volt DC generator.

Short-term Students

In Britain at this time there was little opportunity for Catholic boys to obtain a classical education, there being very few places available to them at grammar schools. It was therefore necessary to provide a complete secondary education to university entrance level, so that they could pursue higher academic courses. Some of those recruited after the First World War did have a grammar school or public school background and after a year or two at the Priory they moved on to higher studies. The first stage of the higher studies was a two-year course in scholastic philosophy at a college in France where the textbooks were in Latin and the teaching in French. This was followed by five years of further studies and training in North Africa where the same languages prevailed. It would be impossible to pursue the course without a good grounding in Latin and French, and this is what the Priory provided for those who came with an otherwise completed secondary school education.

One of those that came for a short period was 26-year old Alfred Ernest Howell, a future Provincial Superior, who arrived on the 29th March for the start of the Easter term in 1919 after completing his army service. He stayed for only five months in order to improve his Latin and French. Five others who arrived with him stayed longer, though one of them, a former soldier, left in 1920 because 'the discipline was too difficult'.[90] Two fellow pupils were Charles Woodward and Leo Gill who were probationer brothers. They went to the Brothers' Novitiate at St Laurent d'Olt, Woodward in August 1919 and Gill in January 1920. Woodward became the first professed brother from Britain and adopted the name Leo. He joined the Priory staff in 1922, but sadly left the Society in January 1923. Gill was the second professed British brother and was known as Brother Patrice.

Howell described his time at the Priory in a 1962 issue of the school magazine.[2] There was a staff of three teachers: Father Travers and two others. 'One was Father Folliot, whose Latin tuition was enchanting. We honestly loved Latin. He was both a master and a lover of the classics, and possessed considerable personal charm. His health was very poor, and many a time I and my companion sat at his bedside while he tried to teach us Latin. Another delightful teacher was young Father Robert[91] destined to die of tuberculosis in a few years.' He recalled how the fathers worked very hard at their English, but with one of them the boys were unable to distinguish his pronunciation of 'can' and 'can't', which led to some confusion. Another took pride in his colloquial English but with comic results for schoolboys when he used expressions such as 'five bobs' for five shillings.

James Holmes-Siedle, a future Bishop of Kigoma in Tanganyika, was another of the boys who, having completed his grammar school studies, came for an intense course of Latin study. He was there for only one academic year in 1926–27, but remembered his stay with great delight. Like others, he reminisced about many aspects of school life, but not scholarly achievements. Amongst the things he recalled were the prefects' caps with tassels on them, 'famous men' on the staff (Bouniol, Côté, Richard, Howell and Hughes), food parcels from home, long walks and cross-country runs. However, his brightest and most enthusiastic memories were of 'the best [Priory football] team of all time' and the cricket team made up mostly of Londoners and staff members. He reckoned he learnt a little Latin and a lot of football.[92]

Philosophy Students at the Priory

Alfred Howell and another young man, Bernard Gill, an ex-RAF officer, went in August 1919 to Colombier, France to study philosophy. They would have gone to Binson, but it had been destroyed in the last year of the war, and a temporary college had been set up at Colombier. Two of their fellow-students were former French Priorians who had served in the army. The Englishmen were there for only 12 months, for it was decided to establish a British school of philosophy at the Priory. So in 1920 they found themselves back where they started, joined by three other Priory students who simply continued their higher studies in another part of the school. Their sleeping and classroom quarters were in the Fathers' House. A large upstairs room at the east end of the building was their dormitory (previously and later an oratory) and a large upstairs library at the west end was their classroom. They ate in the community refectory and used the community chapel. Their professor was Father Arthur Prentice, who had been brought back from Katigondo, Uganda, for their benefit.

They must have appeared a sober little group. Father Travers told the five that they were far too serious and wanted to see a bit of fun in them. He soon regretted this advice, because practical jokes became the order of the day. On one occasion Alfred Howell dressed up as an old White Father with long beard and blue-tinted glasses. He waited for the last train to arrive at Bishop's Waltham then, allowing time for a walk up the hill, he appeared at the front door and rang the bell. He introduced himself to the receiving brother as Father So-and-So just back from Uganda. He was invited to the parlour, but before he could reach it, Father Travers and the other fathers came to greet him and embraced him with Gallic enthusiasm. Eventually his French and his nerve failed him, and he was recognised. He tells of more tricks being played all of which were taken in good part until the Superior made it quite clear that they had proved their point to his satisfaction and beyond!

Of those five philosophers, two became illustrious White Fathers. Alfred Howell, the first Priorian to become a White Father, was ordained in 1926 and became Superior of the British Province in 1947. Arthur Hughes, ordained in 1927, became an Archbishop and the first Papal Internuncio (ambassador) to Egypt, having previously served as a representative of the Holy See at the court of the Emperor of Abyssinia.

The school of philosophy experiment lasted only a year, and Howell and Gill, who had completed their two-year course, went off to the Novitiate in Algiers. The remaining philosophers went to Hennebont[93] in France to continue their studies, but were not accompanied by Father Prentice; he remained at the Priory on the teaching staff until 1924 with special responsibility for English, music, discipline and teaching the parish children their catechism. Prentice was an accomplished pianist and choirmaster who so elevated the singing in chapel that it was described as 'of great assurance and sublime beauty'.[94] He introduced Masses by Palestrina and other classical composers, motets in five voices, and more stylish musical concerts with pupils performing at the piano and with the violin. In September 1924 he took up a new appointment as a professor at the new St Mary's College of Philosophy at Autreppe in Belgium. The Autreppe building belonged to the Belgian Province, but in the previous July Travers had acquired it for English-speaking students and as an extra-territorial asset of the British region.

Father Murphy of Gosport Comes to Teach

Father Armand Roy arrived from Canada to take Prentice's place, but the number of pupils had increased and it was difficult to find other White Fathers who could be released from their duties in order to teach. Father John Patrick Murphy[95], a curate in the parish of Gosport, generously offered his services to teach English to the two top classes all day on Thursdays. He took his first class on the 18th September 1924, and thereafter every Thursday in term time until 1939. Even when he was appointed parish priest at Gosport in January 1928 he continued to teach at the Priory. At the request of Travers, he also wrote an article about Cardinal Lavigerie, which was published in *The Month* in September 1925. The boys thought highly of his teaching and particularly admired his ability, year after year, to identify the questions that would be asked in the London University matriculation examination. He was admired even more for being an enthusiastic and able performer at billiards, for he always stayed to supper and spent the evening recreation period that followed with the fathers in what was variously described as the salon, fumoir, drawing room, or fathers' recreation room.

From September 1923 until some time in 1924 a Mr Stewart was resident, but in what capacity he was employed can only be guessed – probably teaching.

Father Travers – A Nationally Respected Figure

Travers was not one who waited for things to happen. Besides managing the school and teaching, he was often visiting parishioners and neighbours in his far-flung curacy and inviting them to visit him. He was also continually establishing and maintaining relationships with his neighbours and with all the religious orders and societies he could reach: priests, nuns, brothers, and monks, as well as every parish priest in the diocese. And they were not just social calls; he and his priests were supporting as many as they could as chaplains, confessors, retreat preachers, and locums for parish clergy every weekend and often for longer periods when clergy were on holiday or sick. The White Fathers were called on continually for assistance and it was never refused.

The Cardinal Archbishop of Westminster and the Director of the Association for the Propagation of the Faith (APF) recognised Travers as a respected figure who could be called on to represent the foreign missions in an effective way at national level. In the middle of December 1917 while he was busy trying to get the school back on its feet and at the same time travelling about the country promoting the African missions and the Society, Cardinal Bourne, the Archbishop of Westminster suddenly called him to a meeting in London. The Government had declared that all foreign missionaries in the British Empire had each to be personally licensed to work, the implication being that they could be interned or deported if they did not meet the as yet unspecified criteria.

The Cardinal had immediately called a meeting of representatives of the missionary congregations in England and Wales to formulate a petition to the Government. On the second day he appointed Travers and five others to deal urgently and energetically with the problem, but before they left the meeting, a Jesuit priest made a formal declaration in favour of licensing. This was contrary to the wishes of the Cardinal and to the position agreed the day before, but it suited the Government to take it as the Church's view and it went ahead. The ramifications in terms of administration, education, health, agriculture, and social work as well as evangelisation for every pink spot on the world map could hardly have been appreciated. Presumably the colonial administrators exercised discretion and the Dominions ignored it for little was heard of it afterwards. On the 26th March 1925, Travers was invited, through Monsignor Canon Ross, Director of the APF, to a dinner in London given by the Labour Party. In the previous year a group of Labour Members of Parliament while visiting British Africa were struck by the accomplishments of Catholic missionaries there and wished to indicate their appreciation. On the 11th May 1925 he was invited to say the first Mass at the opening ceremony of the Missions Chapel at the great Wembley Exhibition.

The Priory was always available to the clergy and laity of the diocese for retreats, holiday breaks and conferences. On the 13th June 1919, for example, the Bishop of Portsmouth chaired a conference of diocesan priests at the school, and the visitors took advantage of a sunny afternoon to play lawn tennis before departing. The priests of the cathedral still recalled their first memory of Travers when, having travelled from France to Southampton and having gone straight on to Portsmouth to meet Bishop Cotter at 11am, his main concern was to say Mass. He did so immediately after his interview with the bishop. He was still fasting, not having eaten since the day before. It was also noticed that throughout his life he never lost the practice of poverty. He possessed little, he ate little, and his sermons, study notes, and memoranda were all written in his small clear hand on the inside of used envelopes neatly cut open and folded over.[96] His zeal for the African missions was obvious to all who met him and he was in constant demand as a preacher and speaker at local, diocesan and national events. To the bishop and others the Priory must have seemed a real powerhouse and Travers a dynamo. The esteem and affection in which he was held was given some concrete expression on the 25th anniversary of his ordination.

His silver jubilee was celebrated on the 16th April 1925, and the occasion was reported at some length in the press.[97] By this date, except for his army service, 13 of his 25 years as a priest had been spent at the Priory. In that time he had made his mark not only on the school, which was now filled to capacity, but also on the Portsmouth diocese where the bishop and diocesan clergy had great affection and respect for him, and throughout the country where the White Fathers were now well known. Bishop Cotter of Portsmouth and about 45 of his priests came to the Priory to take part in the celebration. Also present were Bishop Biermans, Superior General of St Joseph's Society, Mill Hill; Bishop du Boisrouvray, Abbot-Coadjutor of Farnborough; Monsignor Canon Ross, Director of the APF; Father Onstenk, Superior of Autreppe, Belgium; Father Lagrée, Superior of the Montfort College, Romsey; and the Brother Superiors of Beulah Hill, Southsea and Bitterne. The High Mass was an impressive and moving occasion with Father Travers as the celebrant assisted by Fathers Bouniol and Roy, and the school choir, conducted by Father Robert, beautifully rendered the Mass of *L'Hora Passa* (Viadana). Luncheon was followed by several speeches expressing admiration and affection, and Father Travers was presented with a generous gift of £100. In the convention of the time the list of contributors was noted and it is interesting to see, in addition to those that attended, subscriptions from convents and from Miss Elrington, Professor Philimore, Mr Harrington of Romsey and other local friends.

The previous such event was on the 29th December 1919 to mark the 50th anniversary of the Society. Being so soon after Christmas the refectory still had its decorations of holly and ivy and, additionally, the flags of Britain and France were prominently displayed. Most of the same people who would attend in 1925 were present. On this occasion, and perhaps for the 1925 celebration, Mrs Spurr, an hotelier and owner of the Mafeking

Hero Inn, was in charge of the dining arrangements with many ladies helping her; and Mrs Cooper, the resident cook, was valiantly engaged in the kitchen.

Death of Father Travers

At his jubilee celebrations Travers appeared as vigorous as ever, and was the life and soul of the occasion. Soon afterwards, however, he was having disquieting dizzy spells, and by Christmas 1925, he was very ill. It was not until the 8th February 1926 that he was referred to the Royal Hampshire Hospital where he was diagnosed with an incurable tumour at the left side of his head, but after later tests the doctors were not so sure of the cause of his illness. On the 3rd May 1926 he left for Paris to consult specialists there. By now he had gone deaf in his right ear and the right side of his face was paralysed, but this did not prevent him from addressing the assembled pupils and staff at 7.15am and receiving an affectionate address of farewell from the school captain. He got away just before the General Strike took effect on the same day. The doctors in Paris were unable to help him and he was taken, gravely ill, to the Society's sanatorium at Pau.

He found the inactivity of the sanatorium very trying and begged to be sent back to England. He thought he might still be of some use taking small classes, hearing confessions and so on. Father Bolduc brought him back to the Priory on the 17th September 1926, to the place he preferred to be and where he wished to die. An armchair and a wheelchair were bought for him, and he was granted a special dispensation to say Mass sitting, but after three weeks he was incapable of doing even that; he became a complete invalid confined to his bed. Realising that death was close, he was visited in October by his brother and sister, by Bishop Cotter, and by his old friend Father Voillard now Superior General. The end seemed not far off, but he was physically and mentally a strong man and survived well into the new year. On the 16th April 1927, the doctor visited him, and although he gave him only hours to live, he declared that he had 'a wonderful heart. Here is a man built to live to 80'.[98] The following day, Easter Sunday, 17th April 1927, Peter Mary Travers died at 3.40pm. The bell was tolled, and Miss Bostock came to console Mlle Travers who was present at the death.

Father Bouniol, having acquired all the necessary authorisations for a cemetery in the school grounds, had himself prepared a 'little square' during the Christmas vacation. The burial took place on Easter Wednesday after a Solemn Requiem Mass. In addition to the White Fathers present, there were 39 clergy and six nuns, representing parishes and religious congregations. Bishop Cotter, who was detained in Plymouth was represented by Canon King of Winchester.

Later in the year Bouniol worked with some of the boys to enlarge the little square into a cemetery. A headstone was placed on the single grave and a large crucifix mounted at one end of the burial ground. Bouniol perhaps envisaged himself being buried next to Travers, but that was not to be.

From almost nothing and with very little in the way of funds and materials, Father Travers established a flourishing school, made the Society of Missionaries of Africa known throughout Britain, put in place the base for a British province of the Society, and won the affection and respect of all he met. His determination, vigour, winning manner, organisational ability, kindness, cheerfulness and life of prayer made him the ideal man for the task he so capably undertook.

5

The Bouniol Years

Travers had set the pace, finding a successor to keep it up could have been a problem. Fortunately, the man for the job was right there on the staff – Joseph Bouniol, the procurator and former teacher at St Laurent. Innovation, development and expansion were needed and Bouniol was the man to provide them. He was appointed Superior on the 11th August 1926, while Travers was in Pau. A letter from Father Marchal, the Regional Superior, informed him of the General Council's decision.

5.1. Father Joseph Bouniol, Superior 1926–38.

Father Bouniol (known as 'Bunny' to the British boys) had been there from the beginning for it was he who had brought the first students from France in October 1912, and he was one of the signatories to the purchase agreement for the Priory. Jack Maguire, who was one of his pupils, remembered him vividly.

> We all stood a little in awe of him, for despite his kindly heart and ready sympathy he was a strict disciplinarian, capable of reducing

> a boy to complete submission with a few well-chosen though often mispronounced sentences. He was a man of deep humility, and when one of his outbursts had pulverised a lad he would often take him aside and apologise for being so hard on him. When therefore he decreed that a football pitch was to be cut out of the sloping field adjoining the house, everyone turned out in force and maintained their efforts over a period of long and weary months; our flagging energies would be restored and our enthusiasm renewed by his words of encouragement and by his own generous example with spade and pickaxe.[99]

An anonymous contributor to *The Pelican*, who as a student knew Father Bouniol, described him thus:

> The impressions as a youth were of a great man not only confirmed but strengthened in later life. As a new arrival at the Priory, I soon learnt that Father Bouniol was a man of authority. Some are fortunately blessed by Providence with certain physical aids to help them in inspiring obedience – piercing eyes, beetling eyebrows or a resounding voice. He had none of these. When needed, he showed his displeasure and that was enough. He did not delay his withering remarks and on those occasions when corporal punishment was considered necessary, it was administered there and then. Father Bouniol inspired reverential fear. After a few months I was surprised to discover that he also inspired confidence and affection. Anybody could go and talk to him. I went along to his room one evening and was obliged to queue up. Before his appointment as Superior his confessional was always crowded on Saturday evenings. All this is a long time ago but I remember how patient, kind and sympathetic he was every time I went to see him ... His untiring energy and devotion to the task committed to his care was based on one thing alone – prayer. We did not need lengthy conferences on the value of prayer. We had before our eyes a living example of solid piety. Father Bouniol instilled in all of us the ambition to work on the missions in Africa.[100]

'There was never so radiant a Fr Bouniol as when one of his past students came to the Priory as a priest.'[96] He must have been overjoyed when the first of them returned. That was Alfred Howell whose first appointment after ordination in 1926 was to the Priory teaching staff. It must also have been a great consolation and joy to Father Travers, by then a dying man, to see Howell – the first fruit of his many years of labour. Howell was the first former Priory student, but not quite the first native English speaker to join the staff for Father Prentice had preceded him.

Howell shared the teaching of English with the visiting diocesan priest, Father J P Murphy, and was also given the much more burdensome task of promoting the Society in Britain and Ireland. He was given further responsibility in June 1928 when the Mother House appointed him Director of the School. He was also appointed to the new post of games master and seems to have been the only one so called. By the mid-1930s all sports and games were being arranged and managed by the prefects, and that was how it continued. Until 1927 sport had been an *ad hoc* business considered by the French staff as a robust form of recreation, but not organised. Howell wanted it put on a proper footing and, as the proposer, he was put in charge. The French house diarist was moved to write that 'Games are an important element in English schools and we want to conform to the English spirit for the good of the boys and of the school. That is why this year the games will be properly organised ... We are making a new pitch, the rules for the indoor and outdoor games have been acquired, and the boys must conform or [here breaking into English] "the trespassers will be prosecuted".'[101] The first football game played after this remark was won 15-1 against 'Eastleigh Youth'.

The new pitch was the lower part of the school meadow, which had less of an incline than the upper part, but after many months of trying to make the best of it, the pupils complained that they could not invite other teams to play on such a slope and they preferred to play on the downs as they had done previously.

Making the Playing Fields

At a staff council meeting on the 11th May 1928 the need for a playing field was discussed and it was decided to level the upper (and steeper) part of the meadow. It was also agreed that the teaching staff would work with the boys during recreation periods and holidays to do it. That same evening at 9pm Bouniol with a group of boys started digging. As one pupil put it: 'He soon afterwards appeared with measuring tape and level and after some measurements and calculations announced"We begin here" and promptly filled the first wheelbarrow with earth; the work of levelling the field had begun. His enthusiasm was catching, and fathers and students were to be seen day after day digging furiously'.[100] It was a massive undertaking with pick and shovel, but the new level playing field was finished a year later on the 3rd May 1929.

5.2. Making the playing fields in 1929. Fathers Bouniol and Bolduc can be seen shovelling.

At the beginning of October 1934, everybody was taken by surprise when the new owner of Stephen's Castle Down forbade anybody to use the land, as he wanted to train horses on it. The school had used this downland for sport since 1912, and still used it for the annual Sports Days when a cooked lunch would be taken out to them by horse and cart.[102] Others had also used it for sporting activities, horse riding, walking and picnics. It became a subject of heated local debate and of impassioned letters to the local newspaper. The understanding was that it was common land and Bishop's Waltham Parish Council wished to retain the public right of way.[103] The new owner insisted by writing blistering letters to the council and the press, rather than by legal argument, that there had never been any right of way over the down; it had simply been overlooked. It was as well that the school sports field was completed for this was the end of using the downs for recreation. It forced the decision to construct a second sports field by levelling and terracing the lower part of the meadow adjacent to the first playing field. This was constructed more quickly and efficiently by laying a narrow gauge railway with a hand-pushed truck for moving the earth. The project was completed in the summer of 1936 and the first football game was played on it on the 29th November 1936. The labourers must have thought they were working like miners for the project was known as 'The Mine' and the pitch was known by that name ever after.

Heston

In August 1927 Father Paul Lefils, who had been on the staff since 1925, was assigned with three newly arrived priests (Fathers van Riel, Guerrier and Duthoit) to studies at London University to enable them to teach at places of higher education in British Africa. Bouniol was spending a great deal of time dealing with university student problems, as well as administering the comings and goings of missionaries passing through England, managing the procurement work, and continuing the promotions programme. He was also publishing and distributing *The Bulletin* magazine and writing two books. This was in addition to running the school and teaching mathematics to the two top classes. He got some relief in November 1927 when Father Henri Hoynck van Papendrecht arrived to take charge of the London students. Van Papendrecht, who had come from being the brothers' Novice Master in Algiers, resided with the students at the La Sagesse Convent in Golders Green, but he was only available to Bouniol for nine months before departing for Nyanza.

As the number of students in London increased so did the need for suitable permanent accommodation. There was also a pressing requirement for a Procure (a procurement and logistics centre) in the capital because of the many dealings with shipping agents and government departments. Bouniol visited Cardinal Bourne in October 1927 to get his approval in principle to establishing a house in the archdiocese. The Cardinal, already very familiar with the Society's work, did not hesitate in giving permission. The practical implementation was more of a problem.

Monsignor Bidwell, Coadjutor Bishop of Westminster, with whom Bouniol had to deal, wanted the priest-students to board at Strawberry Hill College and the Society to take charge of a parish in return for establishing a Procure. This was not acceptable to Bouniol. In September 1928 he sent Howell to continue the negotiations and on the 19th September he agreed, with Bouniol's approval, to take charge of a parish where a Procure and residence for students could be established in the same place. The matter was referred to the Mother House, and on the 8th October 1928 they were surprised to receive a letter authorising them to go ahead. The Society was, in general, not in favour of running parishes as it absorbed manpower that should be dedicated to the work of the Society, but sometimes it was the only way they could get a bishop's permission to establish themselves in a diocese. The parish agreed upon was at Heston, Middlesex, which was conveniently located for access to central London. Father Joseph Laane, on his return from Entebbe, Uganda, was nominated the first Superior of the new foundation and took up his appointment in January 1929. Van Papendrecht had left for Nyanza in the previous September.

It must have been exhausting for Bouniol and Howell, and the teaching routine of the boys must have been affected by their frequent absences on other business. The teaching timetable would have been even more disrupted by departures in mid-term of other teachers while Bouniol or Howell were away. Father Armand Roy, for example, left in November 1927 to help in establishing a new foundation in the United States.[104] In July and August 1927 Howell toured England on promotional work. From the 30th October to the 17th December 1927 he toured Ireland and also visited Glasgow, Liverpool, Bradford and Birmingham. He returned with little to show from his exhausting travels: £50 in donations and some subscriptions for *The Bulletin*. In October of the same year Bouniol was away in London and Preston. Both men, however, tried to arrange their long tours for the school holidays. In July and August 1928 Howell toured Scotland. He made a second long visit to Scotland in November of the same year and returned with £45 in donations, but more importantly he was able to report that the White Fathers were now well known in Scotland, and parish priests in Glasgow had asked him to return. While in Scotland he had raised the possibility of opening a house there, but 'the bishop' had poured cold water on this suggestion for he was currently concerned with establishing an inter-diocesan seminary at Blairs near Aberdeen.

The opening of the Heston house was compensation enough for the time being. The first sermon preached in the parish was by Howell on the 26th January 1929. It should have been Bouniol, but he was confined to his room with flu, as were three of his staff and six of the pupils.

Flu Epidemics

A flu epidemic was sweeping through the country, and when Howell returned to the Priory on the 4th February 1929 he also was infected. On the day he arrived back he was appointed 'Vicar in London' and returned the following day, ill as he was, to Heston. This must have thrown the teaching arrangements into further disarray. He returned at Easter to continue teaching, but was still going off on promotional tours and to settle business in London. Although a strong, youngish man of 36, the amount of work and travelling while still afflicted by flu was stressful and physically exhausting. Understandably, he fell seriously ill. The school physician, Dr Mitchell, diagnosed pleurisy in June 1929, and he was moved from his own room, which was next to a classroom, to a quieter place in the Fathers' House. His condition worsened and he was taken by ambulance to the Enniskerry Nursing Home. On the 15th June he underwent an operation to remove fluid from his lungs, at which time symptoms of tuberculosis were discovered. He underwent another operation 10 days later and in November was sent to the sanatorium at Pau.

Major infectious diseases have thankfully become rare in this country, but in the first half of the 20th century it was a different matter. Infectious diseases such as tuberculosis, scarlet fever and diphtheria were common and antibiotic treatment was for all practical purposes still in the future. Pulmonary ailments were the greatest health hazards in the school until the 1940s. There were flu epidemics in the first two months of 1913, 1919, 1925, 1929, 1933 and 1940. Sometimes classes had to be abandoned because so many of the pupils and staff were confined to their beds.

In March 1929 two of the pupils who were down with flu became dangerously ill with pneumonia. James Patrick Walsh spent three months in hospital and was then sent home. He eventually recovered his health and returned to the school. Peter Murphy, however, was not so fortunate. After a short while in hospital at Winchester he died on the 6th April 1929, and was buried on the 9th April opposite Father Travers in the new school cemetery. He was 15 years old, 'a hard worker in class, a good sportsman, and chapel organist'.[105] Another pupil, Peter Joseph Flanagan, died on the 24th October 1932. He had been taken to the Winchester hospital a few days before with appendicitis. He was also 15 years old, 'a hard worker, always amiable, and good at sports and singing'.[106] He was buried on the 27th October in the plot next to Peter Murphy.

In October 1932 the first occurrences of diphtheria occurred and five pupils were taken by ambulance to the Alton Isolation Hospital. In January 1935 there was another outbreak of diphtheria and four boys were taken to the isolation hospital. Scarlet fever made an appearance in February 1937; one pupil was taken to Alton, and three others and Father Keane were isolated in the recreation hut. Also in 1937 one boy (Patrick Hopkins) in his fifth and final year was taken home suffering with 'pains in his lungs' and sadly died 10 weeks later. The final major outbreak of flu was in January 1940 when more than 40 boys were ill with it and four had German measles. The last case of serious illness was in 1954, when one boy who contracted tuberculosis had to leave. There were few cases of tuberculosis at the school but many students contracted the disease when they went abroad and some of them died as a result, including two brothers, Gerard Monaghan at Pau in 1936 and Patrick Monaghan at Carthage in 1943.[107] Patrick Monaghan's twin brother, Hugh, also contracted tuberculosis in North Africa, but survived to be ordained and to work at the Priory and in Burundi. After the Second World War there were no further epidemics at the Priory and this probably reflected the better health of the nation.

The students sometimes had to contend with illness, difficult circumstances or tragedy at home. This could put great pressure on them to abandon their calling and return home to support their families by living with them and attending school nearby or by finding employment to support them financially. Father Pat Donnelly came to the school for the first time a few weeks after his mother died. Some returned to the Priory after an interval. Father Tom Moran was one who returned as a fourteen-year old after the death of his mother. The last recorded family tragedies were in September and October 1956 when the mothers of two pupils and the father of a third all died.

Full-time Promotional Work

In August 1927 Arthur Hughes – another of Bouniol's pupils – had joined the teaching staff. In September 1929 he was appointed to promotional work in Howell's place. This was a full time job with no teaching work. His first tour was one of three months in Scotland from September to December 1929. He visited parishes, schools, colleges, universities and families. He addressed a meeting of 2000 people in Glasgow, attended 14 conferences, established 300 new 'circles' of helpers, wrote a large part of the next edition of *The Bulletin*, and visited the Archbishops of Glasgow and Liverpool. He returned with £80 for the APF and £53 for the White Fathers. He stayed one night at the Priory and then went off to Sheffield to preach an eight-day retreat.

A year later another member of the staff, Father Bolduc, was appointed to promotional work, but this time in Canada, where his powers of persuading the hardest hearts to give generously to the missions became legendary. He was better remembered at the Priory, however, as an earnest football player who constantly called 'Pass the ball, my boy, pass the ball, I say'.[99] He was a very popular teacher, and was accompanied by many of the pupils to his ship at Southampton where they bade him an emotional farewell.

Howell seems to have been remembered by his pupils more for his prowess on the football field than for his teaching. It was rumoured that he had played for Woolwich during his army career, and his services on the pitch were always in demand from the house teams. Father Hughes seldom appeared on the sports field, his gifts being more academic. He was a disciplinarian in the classroom. Father Jack Maguire, a pupil at the time, records how one youngster, destined to be an army colonel in the Second World War, tried to put Father Hughes to the test, but was reduced to tears by the quiet but determined little priest.[99]

Howell returned from Pau in June 1930 and was assigned to work with Monsignor Ross of the APF, probably to hone his promotional skills. In January 1931 he replaced Father Laane as Superior at Heston, and the newly ordained Owen McCoy – destined for the episcopacy – joined him in June 1933 as his curate. Arthur Hughes left for Uganda in 1933 and was consecrated bishop in Cairo on the 20th May 1945. Alfred Howell followed him to Uganda in 1934 and remained there until 1938. Former pupil Bernard Brown, who had recently returned from Rome with his doctorate, but with no field experience, was appointed Superior at Heston in Howell's place.

5.3. Archbishop Arthur Hughes.

Following Their Stars

Father Henri Côté, who came in 1925, had succeeded Father Roy as procurator in 1927. His many journeys in this capacity were made on the motorcycle combination, which was a familiar sight in the neighbourhood. Jack Maguire remembers him on one occasion in 1929 pulling up outside the Superior's office at daybreak and producing a youngster from his sidecar. 'This youth had decided that his stars were calling him elsewhere, and instead of arranging matters with the authorities had set off on his own, only to be caught near Andover [about 25 miles away] and brought back in disgrace by the procurator ... he eventually left in a more regular way.'[99] The miscreant settled in the Middle East after the Second World War as an oil company executive. This was not the only time pupils went off for no apparent reason. In September 1946, 'two of the smaller students' went missing. There was a widespread search without any positive result, then a night phone call discovered them at home in Grantham. They explained that they had set off on an adventure to London and had just kept on going. They had no intention of running away and were happy to return in the company of Father Superior who went to fetch them.

5.4. Father Henri Côté.

As well as teaching and having the duties of procurator, Côté was following a teachers' training course at Southampton, which entailed inspections of his teaching in the classroom. Whenever an inspector was due, he made it clear to his pupils that they were to co-operate fully and were not to open their mouths if a French language inspection was taking place. Young Maguire and his classmates took this as a slur on their ability in that language![99] Côté left in 1934, after nine years, for Heston, then for the missions. He became the Provincial Superior of Canada and, in 1947, Assistant to the Superior General.

Celebrations and New Statue for the Portico Niche

In January 1930, a huge timber gymnasium that was surplus to military requirements was acquired at auction by Bouniol. Fathers and pupils were sent to Netley to dismantle it, and on the 5th February they began erecting it, under the expert direction of Mr Moon, adjacent to the roadway leading from the quadrangle to the farm. It came fully fitted with a large stage, dressing rooms, parallel bars, vaulting horse, climbing ropes and beams. An opening concert was performed in it on St Joseph's day, the 19th March, Bouniol's patronal feast day, and Mr Moon attended as an honoured guest. The building, although used as a gymnasium, became primarily a recreation area and concert hall. Two table-tennis tables occupied the large floor area, and these occasionally gave way to a boxing ring for inter-house boxing competitions.

Another event that honoured Father Bouniol was on the 28th June 1934 to celebrate his 25 years as a priest. After a Solemn High Mass there was a festive lunch served by the pupils. The guests included fellow White Fathers from around the country, the Superior of Autreppe, the Abbot of Farnborough, superiors of local religious orders, many of the diocesan clergy and several of his former pupils now diocesan priests.

There were more celebrations a year later on Sunday the 5th May 1935 – the silver jubilee of King George V's coronation. Again there was a Solemn High Mass, a celebratory lunch with speeches followed by toasts honouring the King, the Royal Family, and the Pope. A strong sense of patriotism had prevailed since the first days of the school. When the French boys were present *La Marseillaise* was often sung. From 1918 until the 1950s *God Save the King* brought all concerts to a close, reflecting the common patriotic sentiment of the time; the feasts of St George, St Andrew, St Patrick and St David were marked with a special Mass and a half-day holiday; and Empire Day on the 24th May was celebrated with an additional hour of recreation. The day following the King's silver jubilee was a national holiday. The weather was warm and sunny – ideal for the festivities that took place throughout the country. The boys spent part of the day in Bishop's Waltham admiring the decorations and attending musical events. In the evening the King lit a bonfire in Hyde Park, London, and this was the signal for lighting bonfires in towns and villages around the country. The school had its own bonfire with fireworks, and the local people had theirs on a piece of common ground on School Hill just outside the school gates. The noise, including loud dance music, of the local revellers went on through the night, making it difficult for early risers to get any sleep.

Two years later on the 12th May 1937 the coronation of King George VI was also celebrated with a public holiday, bonfires and fireworks. This time, however, apart from the religious services in the chapel and lunchtime celebration, the boys joined in the local festivities and gathered at the bonfire and fireworks display on School Hill.

5.5. Statue of Our Lady above the front entrance.

Earlier in 1937 the statue in the niche above the front entrance had been replaced. Unfortunately the original statue had deteriorated because of exposure to the weather, and on the 23rd January 1937 a new, weather-resistant, white statue of the

Blessed Virgin holding the Child Jesus in her arms arrived as a replacement. It was installed and then blessed by the Father Superior on the 2nd February after sung High Mass for the feast of the Purification. The new statue was removed when the school was sold and it now stands at the entrance to the parish church of Our Lady Queen of Apostles, Bishop's Waltham.

A Bishop's Waltham Parish

In May 1931 Father Voillard, the Superior General, had, during his visitation, called on Bishop Cotter of Portsmouth and at that meeting had agreed to Bishop's Waltham becoming a Catholic parish in the care of the White Fathers with the Father Superior as parish priest. Subsequent to the concurrence of the Portsmouth Chapter, the erection of the new parish was announced in a letter from Cotter to Bouniol, which he received on the 17th October 1931. Bouniol, as the new parish priest, informed the parishioners at Mass on Sunday the 25th October.

Until this time the chapel had been considered by the bishop as a private place of worship in which public Masses could be said for the benefit of Eastleigh parishioners. About once a month Father Hickey (until 1916) and then Father Doran (until 1931) cycled, or came by train, from Eastleigh to say a public Mass. They would arrive on Friday evenings to hear parishioners' confessions and stay overnight to say the Parish Mass at 8am on Saturday morning. This was considered convenient both for the priests, who had to attend to services at the parish church in Eastleigh on Saturday evening and Sunday, and for the Bishop's Waltham parishioners because there was no satisfactory public transport on a Sunday.

Now that the chapel was a parish church it was dedicated to Our Lady Queen of Apostles, which was the same name that had been adopted for the Heston Parish Church in 1929.

Bishop's Waltham was a scattered rural parish of about 100 square miles with few Catholics. In 1913 the Catholic population was about 30.[102] The number of parishioners grew very slowly, but from this small number in the 1930s came a White Father (John Miller), a White Sister (Myra Spurr, who took the name Sister Mildred), and a Jesuit priest. In addition to services in the school chapel, Mass was said on Sundays in parishioners' homes in outlying areas, mostly by Father Kingseller who from 1943 dashed from one place to another in a tiny Austin Seven car. Regular venues from 1942 were: Beachcroft at Curdridge from 1942–1960; the hall and Station Hotel at Droxford from 1957 to 1960; and the racing stables and village hall at Owslebury from 1956 to 1960. Maybe Masses in the outlying areas ceased in 1960 because parishioners had their own cars and could get into Bishop's Waltham on a Sunday.

In 1955 the first full time parish priest, Father Gerard Burton, was appointed, and the White Fathers continued to provide full time pastors until a diocesan priest was appointed in 1970.

St Columba's College

In 1930 a new member of staff arrived from Algiers. This was Father Francis Walsh, later to be Bishop of Aberdeen. It was while he was at the Priory that he began writing his book *Mosaic of Man*, which was completed a few years later. He returned to Algiers after a year, and Father Bouniol reported that 'He is an outstanding person; throughout the year he has given me complete satisfaction, and he has exercised a deep salutary influence on both fathers and students. He is certainly the best educator on the staff here'.[108] The Mother House must have considered him a better administrator and organiser than educator, for he was sent back to Britain at the end of 1931 to promote the Society in Scotland and to explore the possibility of a foundation there.

5.6.Father Francis Walsh.

Fathers Howell and Hughes, having visited Scotland on their promotional tours, saw there an opportunity for recruiting future missionaries. Once Francis Walsh was working there permanently, a regular high level of applications ensued. He was joined in December 1932 by Father Balthazar Drost, who had returned from Uganda, and by Brother Modeste from the Priory. They lived for a while in a rented semi-detached house in Melrose until Walsh persuaded Mr and Mrs Douglas to sell him their 60-acre Hawkslea Farm at Newtown St Boswell's, Roxburghshire. Mr Downey, an artist and friend of Father Walsh's, provided the purchase money and the farm was renamed St Helen's in memory of Mr Downey's late wife, Helen. Father Walsh's intention in buying such a large piece of land was to build an Apostolic School with a home farm. Like Father Travers in England, he went about soliciting donations saying that it was with the pennies of the poor he would build it, and so it was. The foundation stone for the school was laid in June 1935, and in September 1936 the new College of St Columba was ready to receive its first students. Brother Modeste then returned to the Priory, leaving St Helen's Farm in the hands of Canadian Brother Phillippe de Neri. Father Drost remained at St Columba's where he died and was buried in 1959.

5.7. St Columba's College, Newtown St Boswell's, Roxburghshire.

By 1933 the number of applicants for places at the Priory had risen so much that they exceeded the places available. Another former military hut was purchased for £45 to serve as an additional dormitory for seven boys and as an overflow study hall. Some space was released in September 1934 when one of the boys, while passing through London on his way back to school, decided on the spur of the moment to join the army. Perhaps a recruiting poster offered him more adventure as a soldier than as a missionary. '*Un coup de tête*. Typical of today's young people' was the comment.[109] By September 1936 there were 80 students living in crowded conditions. This was in addition to ten boys at St Columba's. There were neither sufficient staff nor a high enough number of Scottish boys at this time to justify a school of five forms in Scotland, so the decision was taken to move the Priory's two lower classes to St Columba's in 1937, and for all the higher classes to be at the Priory. There would be a single curriculum for both places geared to the London University matriculation examinations.

Significant Developments

By 1936 the British area had developed significantly with foundations at Bishop's Waltham, Heston, Newtown St Boswell's, and Autreppe (Belgium). In 1936, the General Chapter of the Society formed the four houses into a British regional group with Father Bernard Brown as the Regional Superior and making him, in effect, Bouniol's superior. Father Bouniol was left with responsibility for the Priory and the parish of Bishop's Waltham.

Having overseen a flourishing Priory, new foundations in London, Scotland and Belgium, fruitful promotional activities, and Britain designated as an autonomous region, Father Bouniol was suddenly transferred to France as Treasurer to the French Province. He was informed of his posting in December 1937 and left in the first week of January 1938 after a farewell luncheon attended by many of his friends. At the luncheon Bouniol recalled a brief meeting many years previously. By coincidence, when changing trains on his first day in England in 1912, he chatted with a young English priest who was travelling from Portsmouth to an appointment at Winchester. The young priest's name was John Henry King, who had now come to bid him farewell and who would soon be the next Bishop of Portsmouth.

As teacher, procurator, rector, parish priest and superior in Britain, Bouniol's accomplishments were many. He had inherited responsibility not only for the Priory and the Bishop's Waltham parish, but also for the Society in Britain and Ireland, and he had developed all of them significantly. He had also set about his wider duties energetically. In February 1927 he arranged a system of collecting-boxes throughout the country for donations from benefactors, and established a network of collaborators to help in promotional activities. In July of the same year he published the first edition of *The Bulletin*, a magazine that was later renamed *White Fathers*, a publication which continues to this day, though now titled *White Fathers – White Sisters*. He wrote *The Martyrs of Uganda*, which was translated from his French by Miss Messervy of Southsea and published in November 1928. In 1929 he published *The White Fathers and their Missions*, a wide-ranging and detailed view of the Society's work at that time; he was the editor of the book and its major contributor, and was again assisted by Miss Messervy.

He was still at the height of his powers when he was recalled to France. It must have been a dreadful wrench to be torn from such successful ventures and from the connections he had built up during his long years in Britain. Despite the burdens of his several offices, Bouniol had continued as a physically and intellectually energetic man always ready to be personally involved and to lead from the front. But it was now time to put the Society in Britain into the hands of its own native people. This was the result of his success. In a spirit of loyalty and obedience he did not demur, but it could not have been easy for him to leave. It must have been an additional personal sorrow that he never went to the African missions to which he was dedicated and for which he worked all his life. His apostolate had been to train others for that work, his thwarted ambition being realised through his students. He remained in France until his death in December 1950, returning to his beloved Priory six times for brief visits.

The upward curve of the Priory's progress under Bouniol was suddenly to dip. Uncontrollable forces were to have an unforeseen effect that would disrupt the quiet and steady advance. A period of instability lay ahead.

6

A Time of Turmoil

In January 1938, Father James Smith, who had returned from Uganda the previous year, was the Superior who greeted the boys on their return from their Christmas holidays. James Smith's inherited responsibilities, unlike those of his predecessors, were related entirely to the Priory. Now that there was a regional superior for Britain and Ireland, he could give his entire attention to being superior of the community, rector of the school, teacher of Greek, and parish priest.

Father Smith had taken over at an unfortunate time. War and rumours of war filled the newspapers, and the government and local authorities were advising people to prepare for the worst.

6.1. Father James Smith, Superior 1938–44.

Gas Masks and Trenches

The 64 pupils that arrived on the 6th September 1938 were overwhelmed three weeks later by the arrival of 100 pupils and their teachers from Finchley Grammar School (now Finchley

Catholic High School for Boys), who had been evacuated from London. This had been arranged by Father Parsons, formerly Deputy Director of the APF and now headmaster at the Finchley school. Where they were all accommodated is not mentioned, but it must have been in the gymnasium and recreation hut. Parsons and several of his students were used to this for they had been coming to the Priory over several years for camping holidays. On the day they arrived, the Priory boys and staff were issued with gas masks in the expectation of a declaration of war. Presumably the Finchley contingent had brought their gas masks with them. The following day all the pupils and visitors set about digging air-raid trenches in the meadow. The population had been advised in 1938 to dig trenches as temporary shelter from air attack. These trenches were intended as short-term measures and were advocated in areas without standard shelter accommodation. They were even recommended as in some ways being better than air-raid shelters.[110] They had been digging for two days when Prime Minister Chamberlain returned from Munich with his declaration of 'peace for our time'. With that reassurance, the visitors returned to London on the 2nd October 1938.

Ten months later, in August 1939, another party of unwitting trench diggers arrived. They were a group of 11 Canadian pilgrims (two priests, six young men and three young women) on their way to Rome. They were unable to continue from England to France because of the unsettled political situation caused by the renewed threat of war. They were considered very devout and earned their keep by working in the kitchen, in the refectory and digging an air-raid trench. Surprisingly, they got clearance to proceed through France and set out on the 29th September after war had broken out and after exactly one month at the Priory. One can only wonder just how far they got and even if they survived their perilous journey.

War is Declared

War was declared on the 3rd September 1939 just before the start of the new term. Some worried parents refused to let their sons return. Those that did so arrived in small groups over a period of a week because of the difficulties of travelling at that confused and disordered time. Classes eventually started on the 18th September.

On the 6th November the pupils again found themselves being crowded, this time by the arrival of 22 philosophy students who were transferring from their requisitioned college in Yorkshire to France. The fateful move of these students to France, and to many years of internment, was in two separate groups on the 8th and 26th December.

It must have been a bustling Christmas period for as the second group of philosophers left the house on Boxing Day a group of unexpected guests arrived at the door. They were five French White Fathers conscripted into the army while abroad. Their ship had arrived at Southampton on Christmas Day 1939 and on the following day they had walked the thirteen miles to the Priory. They only stayed one night for they had to leave on the 27th December to board another vessel for France. Travelling across the Channel still seemed to be considered safe for Father Tom Moran left on the 5th March 1940 for a teaching post in France where he also was interned.

Father William Burridge, who had been on the staff since 1936, went to Heston in October 1939 to replace Father Bernard Gaffney who had joined the army as a military chaplain. Father Bernhard Hartmann, aged 29 and studying in London, took Burridge's place. Unfortunately, Hartmann, a German national, was arrested and interned in May 1940, and two months later he was deported to an internment camp in Canada for the duration of the war. In what turned out to be a relaxed confinement in Canada, he was allowed to have contact with the White Fathers there, and from 1942 to 1947 he was even permitted to teach at the St Martin Novitiate. He stayed in North America after the war, teaching at the Belleville Seminary from 1947 to 1952, then at the Franklin and Alexandria Bay Novitiates in the USA from 1952 to 1969.[111]

Air Raids and Evacuation

It was on the 1st June 1940 that the first air raid warning sounded, but the Lufwaffe attacks on the Channel ports began in earnest on the 5th June with raids over the Portsmouth and Southampton areas. The boys witnessed the first raid on Southampton from their dormitory. Air raids, or warnings of air raids, became a nightly occurrence and staff and boys repaired regularly to an air-raid shelter for a few hours almost every night. They had built the underground shelter themselves by digging into the embankment at the side of the upper football pitch, adjacent to the stretch of drive that ran from the farm to the quadrangle. It was formed of curved corrugated iron sheets with the excavated earth piled on top.[107] The uncomfortable dormitory beds 'took on a mystic aura of peace and comfort when contemplated from the dank depths of the air-raid shelter'[112] where the boys and staff sat on long wooden forms until the raids were over. Father Patrick Boyd who was a boy at the time records that 'The students sat on a long line of benches which ran almost the width of the football field. They wrapped themselves in blankets and waited. They could hear the regular drone of the planes and the occasional explosion of a bomb in the distance'.[113] The sleepless nights and sojourns in the damp shelter were not conducive to study, so they were sent home for their summer vacation ten days early on the 2nd July 1940.

On the 16th July, Hitler issued Fuehrer Directive 16 for the invasion of England and the Luftwaffe intensified the bombing. On the 13th August 1940 four bombs fell on the local brickyard about 400 metres distant. It was a daylight raid. Brother Patrick vividly recalled that afternoon. He was working in the fields when the air raid warning sounded. He watched as the bomber dropped its lethal load and clearly saw the occupants of the cockpit before the plane could regain height. He also recalled seeing dog fights high up in the sky during the Battle of Britain and night attacks when the anti-aircraft guns poured missiles towards the head of the searchlight beams.[102]

The Priory suffered only three broken windowpanes as a consequence of the brickyard bombing, but it was possible that another raid might result in a direct hit. The proximity of the explosions and the frequency of the air attacks caused concern about the safety of the boys. Father Brown met with the staff in mid-August and decided it was too dangerous for the pupils to return for the school year 1940–41. Arrangements were hurriedly made for the English and Scottish pupils to go to St Columba's and for the Irish boys to pursue their studies in the Jesuit College at Mungret in County Limerick, Ireland. These decisions were taken during the school holidays, so it was necessary to send hurriedly a circular letter on the 21st August to all the parents telling them that their sons were to report to their different schools on the 10th September 1940. The fathers then spent the rest of the vacation packing and dispatching books and other school materials to Scotland. Fathers Rijkers, Ryan and Murphy left for St Columba's in the first week of September 1940. Fathers Smith and Kingseller with Brothers Aubert, Modeste and Patrick remained behind to run the parish and to maintain the farm and the property. The Bishop of Portsmouth was informed of what was happening and he asked that the chapel be reserved for religious services if the buildings were requisitioned by the military.

The Priory Barracks

There was no question that such a large building would be allowed to stand empty. The army immediately requisitioned the vacant students' house, the refectory, the kitchen and all associated rooms, except for the chapel and three rooms above it where the school furniture was stored. They also took over the gymnasium, the recreation hut and other outbuildings. The Fathers' House continued to be occupied by those of the staff that were left behind, but they were compelled to convert a small room on the ground floor into a kitchen.

The first army unit arrived on the 20th September. It was a detachment of the Royal Electrical and Mechanical Engineers that had been evacuated from Dunkirk. It was they who made what became known as the Burma Road. It had been known as the Boys' Drive and had been made by the pupils in 1922. It was on the western side of the property parallel with the main drive and between the lawns and the meadows. It stretched from Martin Street to the quadrangle and led eventually to the farm. It had a gravel surface and in October 1922 pine trees was planted along it to form a very pleasant avenue. The army laid railway sleepers side by side to form a new surface on which vehicles could be parked and remain concealed from the air by the trees that lined the roadway. The REME was followed by an infantry unit that did its training on the football fields.

The intrusion was irksome, but it was never resented. Relations with the army were always cordial and even produced mutual benefits. From the start of the occupation, the farm supplied the army with six to eight gallons of milk a day for which they paid 2s 1d a gallon. Eggs were also provided as they became available but the Luftwaffe occasionally broke them before they could be delivered. The army also paid for the water and electricity they used.

Unfortunately bureaucracy soon descended on this mutually happy arrangement in the form of the Milk Marketing Board who said it was illegal to sell milk without their permission. The permission was forthcoming after the nuisance and expense of exchanging contracts all round. When this had been settled, representatives of the Cow-Keeper Board, a department of the Ministry of Agriculture, appeared saying the milk must conform to the Ministry's directive of 1926 and that milk should not be sold directly to the army but only to an approved dairy. Selling to an approved dairy turned out not to be a legal requirement, so Kingseller (the procurator) continued supplying the army, and Brother Patrick went out and bought a new milk-cooling machine for £7 on the strength of assured future orders. Within a few days Mr James Hann, the proprietor of a large dairy, put in an appearance. Perhaps prompted by the Ministry, he tried to persuade the procurator to sell the milk to him. When he refused to do so, Mr Hann conceded that there was an economic benefit in selling directly to a customer, but warned that the Sanitary and Health Department could give them trouble. Not unexpectedly, the men from the Sanitary and Health Department turned up within a week. They were satisfied with all they saw and licensed the farm to sell milk retail. By November the farm was producing enough milk to supply the military tenants and Mr Hann's dairy.

The farm received from the army food scraps, which were not to be despised, for they were used to feed the pigs. This pigswill had by law to be boiled and so a boiler had to be purchased. It used solid fuel, but as there was little available and what could be had was expensive, the ever-inventive Brother Patrick developed a system that would burn spent engine oil of which there was plenty available from the army. Probably the biggest advantage of the army's presence was the installation of mains electricity, which remained permanently connected when the army departed in 1944. The small 110-volt DC generator installed in an outhouse had been overloaded for years causing the lights to flicker annoyingly[102] and was quite incapable of meeting the demands now placed on it. Other compensations resulting from the military presence were a payment of £200, a reduction in the rates, and a contribution by the army to the property insurance premiums.

The soldiers organised dances in the gymnasium at the weekends despite the frequency of air raid alarms. In fact, the gymnasium became a social centre for the area, used not only by the soldiers, but by the local people as well. In October 1940, for example, an event was organised there for the benefit of the Red Cross. The Priory must have been one of the better postings for soldiers. They were in an oasis of reasonable calm, were well housed and fed, were provided with regular weekend entertainment, and had co-operative and friendly people around them. On the 20th November 1940, General Ackland visited the Priory Barracks with its 150 soldiers and was impressed by all he saw, declaring it the best-regulated barracks he had visited.

In September 1940 Father Leo van den Hoeven, a Dutchman, arrived from Heston to help in the parish and in other parishes of the diocese, especially Bursledon. As an alien, he had to report to the police regularly and was prevented from using a car, motorcycle or even a pedal cycle. This severely restricted his movements, so Father Smith had to drive him to wherever he was required to go, unless an army vehicle was going in his direction and would give him a lift. There was relief all round when in mid-October 1940 the police gave permission for him to drive himself to Bursledon.

The three Fathers repainted the chapel for Christmas 1940 and built a crib, but because of the continuing night raids, the Midnight Mass liturgy was celebrated at 3pm on Christmas Eve. The Christmas 'Midnight Mass' was celebrated at the same time in 1941 and 1942, and on each occasion the chapel was completely full.

From November 1940 onwards the bombing raids became more intense, the 17th November being the date Southampton was most heavily bombed. The only damage to the Priory was plaster falling off the ceilings. On the night of the 1st December 1940 incendiary bombs and flares fell near the quadrangle, but St Mary's College in Bitterne was badly damaged and every window broken. Seven of the brothers, one of them injured by shrapnel, and their chaplain came to spend the following day and night at the Priory. On the night of the 9th–10th January 1941 there was a ferocious air attack on Portsmouth. This was the Portsmouth blitz. The Bishop's house was completely destroyed and four domestics killed. Bishop Cotter had died in the previous October and had been succeeded by Monsignor John Henry King, who had continued to live in Winchester where he had been parish priest and so avoided the devastation and probably death.

Civil Defence

The public had been told early in the war to take all precautions to frustrate an airborne landing. The brothers, two Dutchmen and an Irishman, therefore placed in the Long Field, behind the farm buildings, at various angles, upright lengths of the railway track that had been used for the construction of the football pitches. They also produced blackout curtains for all the large and numerous windows.

The school was required to have three fire watchers on duty during an air raid, so members of staff were compelled to act in this capacity. They were issued with stirrup pumps to control fires caused by incendiary bombs, and they attended fire watchers' meetings where they were shown different types of bombs and gas used by the Germans and where they sometimes had NFS (National Fire Service) drill. The meetings were either in the gymnasium or in a hall in the town. At one such meeting in early 1944, there were furious complaints about insufficient protection from air raids. There were few fire watchers in the town and the Bishop's Waltham schools were not allowed air raid shelters. Apparently the town was not considered a dangerous area, but many of those present considered it very dangerous and demanded improvements, but the heated exchanges do not appear to have achieved any progress or any change in policy.

Internment of the Class of 1938–39

Since 1924, those completing their studies at the Priory went on to study philosophy at St Mary's College at Autreppe in Belgium. The diplomatic crises of 1938 and 1939 prompted the British Embassy in Brussels to warn the Autreppe staff and students that war was likely and that British nationals should return home.[114] In June 1939 they did so and the Autreppe building was returned to the Belgian Province. Those who had completed the two-year philosophy course set off for North Africa in August to continue their training there; the rest, now joined by first year students from the Priory, were instructed to proceed to Rossington Hall, Yorkshire, which had been purchased to accommodate the British and Irish philosophy students.

Some of the students arrived at Rossington Hall in July and August to help prepare the place for its intended purpose. However, before the main body of students arrived in September 1939, the building had been requisitioned by the military. The 22 students and two professors (Father Jan Deltijk and Father Jack Maguire) were told to report to the Priory while alternative premises were found. It was impossible to accommodate them satisfactorily, but some study was attempted while they waited there.

6.2. Father Jack Maguire.

An expedient solution was to send them to the Kerlois College of Philosophy at Hennebont in Brittany. They could be easily accommodated for it was practically empty, most of the French students having been conscripted into the forces. The obvious disadvantage – and a grave one at that – was the imminent invasion of France. However, Father Bernard Brown, the British Regional Superior, and his advisers incredibly considered it a safe destination. They had been assured by their French contacts that Brittany would not be invaded as it was so far from the war zone. The invading German army had a different view and occupied the area in July 1940. All the members of the British group were immediately arrested and interned in a camp at St Denis, near Paris, for the duration of the war.

They lived for several years in squalid and confined conditions, but their deprivations did not prevent them from continuing their religious life or continuing with their studies under the direction of their able Superior, Jack Maguire, a man not much older than his charges. Jan Deltijk, a Dutchman, was released because of his nationality. One of the students, Kevin Wiseman, was sentenced to death. He suffered severely in solitary confinement until reprieved after interventions by the Swiss authorities, the Archbishop of Paris and probably the German military governor of Paris. Another of the students, Billy O'Shea, died in the camp; and another, George Fry, died shortly after liberation in August 1944.[115]

The School Reopens 1942

St Columba's College in September 1940 was crammed full for it housed its own pupils and those who had been evacuated from the Priory. The first year philosophy students had also to be found a home for they could no longer travel to Europe where the philosophers of the preceding year were prisoners of war, nor could they use Rossington Hall, which was occupied by the army. The only place that could be found to accommodate them was St Helen's farmhouse near St Columba's. It was far from satisfactory as the building could not be adapted to a house of studies. Patrick Boyd, one of the students, tells us that 'There ensued a year of

Spartan frugality, freezing in cramped dormitories and forced to study in damp classrooms'.[113] With an additional intake of philosophy students in September 1941, the previous year's students moved into huts near the college.

In January 1941 an unusual arrangement was made when Father Smith was assigned to St Columba's to help with the teaching though still continuing as Superior of the Priory. He went to fill a gap caused by Father Stanley being taken ill. Stanley's illness continued and, later in the year, he came to the Priory to convalesce. In the September Father Howell was posted as Superior to St Columba's from Heston where he had been since 1938 after returning from Uganda. Unusually, and perhaps uniquely, because it was wartime, one of the boys, Bernard Duffy (a future Priory Superior and Provincial Superior) sat the London University matriculation examinations in Glasgow.[107]

Stanley's convalescence was alarmingly disturbed several times in 1941 by bombing raids in the vicinity. On the 23rd July another four bombs fell on the brickworks, which had been demolished in an earlier raid, leaving the school unharmed but covered in brick dust. The raids continued throughout 1942, and on the night of the 20th–21st June 1942 a great number of incendiary bombs fell in the school grounds and all were busy after the raid putting out fires especially Brother Patrick who was wielding fire extinguishers for several hours. There was no serious damage to the school, but a neighbouring farmer lost several of his cows.

There was more damage done by the soldiers than by the bombs. A company of Royal Engineers that had replaced the infantrymen moved out in February 1942 leaving eight damaged radiators, a broken central heating system and many windows open in the extremely cold weather. It must be said that the infantrymen had left the place in good order and had been very willing to lend a hand on the farm. When, for example, there were no pupils or fathers to help with the haymaking in June 1941, the soldiers offered their services freely.

To relieve the cramped conditions at St Columba's, the two senior classes, Rhetoric and Poetry, returned to the Priory in September 1942 with Father Smith, the chances of being bombed apparently having diminished. Two classes were all that could be accommodated in the Fathers' House as the army still occupied the main school buildings.

John O'Donohue was one of those that arrived at that time. He was to spend a year at the school before going on to higher studies. He had been told that he would be going to St Columba's, but ten days before leaving home he received a letter telling him to go to Bishop's Waltham; like many other new students he had no idea where that was. He eventually made it on a packed wartime train to St Pancras Station, London. There he was met by Father Smith, who expressed surprise that he was not wearing a school cap, and then insisted on carrying his suitcase on the journey to Waterloo Station. They met up with half a dozen other boys, some of whom, to O'Donohue's amazement, were wearing kilts. These were boys from St Columba's. They took the train to Winchester and a bus to Bishop's Waltham, where all the boys assembled in the temporary refectory. O'Donohue was expecting to see about 100 boys, but was astonished to find that there were only eleven of them. He went to bed rather bewildered that night in a makeshift dormitory on the first floor of the Fathers' House and with blackout blinds on the windows.[116] This had been the dormitory in 1912 and 1913, and an oratory since then.

The teachers were Fathers Smith, Stanley, and Kingseller, whom O'Donohue considered 'excellent teachers' which may account for all the boys passing the university matriculation examinations in crowded and difficult circumstances. Other members of the staff were Father Ryan, who was convalescing, and the three brothers, so that there were almost as many men in white habits as there were boys.

The increased numbers required a larger kitchen so one was set up in the Father Superior's office on the ground floor, which was next to the refectory (the former staff recreation room) and had access from the quadrangle. The visitors' room became the Superior's bedroom and office, and two staff bedrooms – one downstairs and the other upstairs – were the classrooms. Mr Pink's men fitted out the new kitchen and installed two additional toilets. Brother Cuthbert came from Scotland for a few months as a stopgap to look after the kitchen, and he was followed by another stopgap, Brother Terence from Algiers. The arrival of Mrs Rodgers as cook in July 1943 brought a semblance of normality at least to the tiny kitchen with its two small gas ovens.

The boys spent time nearly every day working on the farm. The Ministry of Labour had exempted the older pupils from military service if they were pursuing full time studies before the 3rd September 1939 and if they worked on the land 'to help sustain the supply of food to the nation'.[117] In general students were conscripted into the services if they interrupted their studies to go elsewhere. This may have been the case with Frank Mallon who in June 1943, without explanation, was called up into the Royal Navy. Afterwards he was ordained a priest for the Archdiocese of Glasgow. Several years later, in February 1947, Hugh Beattie was similarly conscripted.

The school buildings and grounds were filled with soldiers and their equipment, but the boys had no acquaintance with the troops except for football matches. Father O'Donohue recalled that the great benefit of these games was not so much the competition as the tea provided afterwards. '... it was very pleasant to share now and again in the abundance which His Majesty's Forces seemed to enjoy'.[116] The boys' own fare was austere: 'We lived for the most part on bread and potatoes, but we kept healthy enough. Sunday morning's breakfast consisted of a slice of spam and dry bread'. Enough bicycles had been left behind for all the boys to go on long cycle rides, though they often became lost because all the road signs had been removed for fear of invasion. Despite the restrictions, Father O'Donohue was able to write of his 'very happy year at the Priory', which he described as 'a happy house with a real family spirit', and 'though we boys stood rather in awe of Father Smith, we did not feel unduly pressed and there was a relaxed atmosphere about the house which made it a real home.'

On the 22nd July 1943 another large troop of soldiers arrived – this time Americans. They were more extrovert than the previous contingents and readily expressed their appreciation and enchantment, remarking that they had never seen such a beautiful spectacle as the school grounds. The weather was warm and sunny, the roses and other flowers were in full bloom, the lawns were in excellent condition and the English countryside was probably at its best. The fathers in return admired them for they worked so well and so hard, and they could not help but notice that all the officers were white and all the NCOs and other ranks were black. It was remarked that everything they had looked new. This comment must have been suggested by a comparison with the military equipment that had gone before. After only eight days they reluctantly departed and a British REME contingent moved in.

In September 1943 there were 12 boys at the Priory. Peter Barry was one of those who arrived in that month and he recalls how the 12 were packed into the same dormitory as the boys of the previous year. There were three rows of beds each with a locker, and Father Kingseller had to pass between the beds to reach his own small room. The grand silence was forgotten whenever an air raid siren sounded and all 12 rushed to the window and pulled back the blackout curtains to watch planes being caught in the searchlights' beams. On at least one occasion the bedding of one of them was hidden while watching the aerial combat, causing a cry of pain or surprise when the unfortunate student made a high-speed landing on the wire bedstead at the approach of Father Kingseller. He also recalled a soldier arriving in 1943 and, seeing Father James Smith in his white habit, parroted a line from a recent film (*The Road to Morocco*) saying to his mate 'Look, Charlie, a gen-yu-ine Bed-yu-ine Ay-rab!'[118]

In January and early February 1944, the grounds filled up with army vehicles. On the 9th February they started to move out. The rest left the following morning at 7.30am with a great deal of noise, and again leaving the central heating system out of order. With vehicles from the surrounding area they formed a mile long convoy and the troops could be heard singing until their voices were lost in the distance. In Bishop's Waltham, Mr Pink was about to be awarded a government contract to make coffins for the Second Front – the expected invasion of the continent.

The Bombing Continues

A day later another REME unit moved in. There were no vehicles, so it was a time of brief and relative quiet. The soldiers must have had electric room heaters for, considering they were engineers, they made no effort to repair the damaged central heating, and the chapel remained at freezing point. It was also very cold elsewhere. The only warmth available seemed to be from a fireplace in the temporary refectory (the fathers' former recreation room), where Father Kingseller had enlarged the fireplace so that it would burn coke, which may have been the only fuel they could get. However, in April 1944, the army redecorated the part of the school that they occupied, and a soldier artist painted large brightly coloured rural scenes on the walls inside the gymnasium, which was used by the army as a dance hall as well as a fitness centre.

Nearly every night during February 1944 there were air raid warnings and the sound of heavy gunfire. This continued with less frequency during March when the massing of troops for D-Day began in earnest. On the 6th March a detachment of US troops arrived but, because British soldiers occupied the school buildings, they laid large concrete rafts on the lawns and erected tents on them. On the 27th March a group of British Military Police arrived and they were followed by another detachment of soldiers so that in May there were 250 men in the school buildings in addition to those in tents.

The drains were unable to cope and consequently fractured, but they were quickly repaired. While this was being done another party of soldiers arrived to swell the numbers even further. Then airmen arrived. All the external wooden buildings, including the gymnasium and the soldiers 'drying hut', which had been erected in the orchard the year before, were turned into barrack rooms with bunk beds. Despite the occupation of the gymnasium as sleeping quarters it was still used for dances on Friday nights. On the evening of the 26th May 1942 a greater throng than ever tried to get in. 'The overcrowding of the Priory has not stopped this noisy entertainment as we had hoped' and 'Many young ladies were tempted by the first blooms of Modeste's roses'.[119] This last remark prompted the only recorded complaint against the army:

that those attending the dances should be told to respect the property of the house. The pupils never recalled the noise that so often disturbed the fathers. What they vividly remembered were the air raids, the multitude of soldiers and the army vehicles.

Those billeted at the Priory were not the only soldiers to appear just before D-Day. The brother-in-law of one of the pupils turned up for a visit with some of his paratrooper friends and ate the month's jam ration at one meal. As compensation they persuaded the Superior to give the boys a day off.[120]

In March the dreadful carpet-bombing of Germany was intensified. On Wednesday the 15th March 1944 at 8.15am a long procession of bombers flew over the house heading east, and on the 18th April about 200 four-engined planes passed over going in the same direction. On the roads what seemed like endless convoys of lorries and tanks passed by. Many of the roads had been widened to allow the convoys to pass, and signposts, which had been absent for several years, reappeared almost overnight. The boys witnessed it all for they were still going for long cycle rides to the coast, to Brighton, Chichester and Portsmouth, and to other towns beyond the New Forest.

The air traffic was not all one way by any means. The Southampton area was heavily bombed from the 14th to the 16th May. The searchlights could not penetrate the low cloud, and the raiders came in very low. Two planes were shot down at 2am on the 15th May, and 15 were shot down on the night of the 15th–16th May. The windows rattled and shook but were not broken, a lot of heavy shrapnel fell in the grounds and some steps were shattered. Between midnight and dawn on the 23rd May 1944 the school witnessed the heaviest barrage since the blitz of 1940. Shrapnel rained down, white flares lit up the sky over Portsmouth, and six enemy planes were reported destroyed. A particularly spectacular crash was seen on the 29th May when a plane hit a fuel dump and lit up the sky with a huge blaze in the direction of the Isle of Wight.

The Second Front opened on the 6th June 1944: D-Day. Most of the soldiers and their vehicles were suddenly gone, and the spectators' interest turned to watching aircraft towing gliders in the direction of France. The gliders, carrying troops and towed by DC3 aircraft, filled the sky as they headed for the landing grounds. That evening hundreds of heavy bombers swept overhead and the air was filled with the deafening roar of aircraft engines. At 10pm, the bombers started to return singly and in small groups.[102]

The occupants of the school had witnessed air battles, bombings and aeroplane crashes nearly every night for the previous three months, then at the beginning of June the appearance of enemy aircraft became less frequent until it seemed that the raids had ceased. But it was only an interval. In mid-June 1944 pilotless V-1 flying bombs put in an appearance. From the 18th June until the end of the month, nearly every night there were warnings of their approach. 'It is a jet-propelled machine, flying about 300 mph. There is a red light at the tail, caused by the heating of the metal. It makes a noise similar to that of a locomotive. When the light disappears, the plane dives and explodes on hitting the ground ... Already a church, a convent, a hospital and residential areas have been hit.'[121] A week after their first appearance the V-1 bombs were being referred to as 'doodlebugs'. Peter Barry vividly remembered seeing a procession of 21 'doodlebugs like glowing cigarette ends following each other'.[118] When a V-1 passed overhead, an explosion would be heard shortly afterwards. At 12.30am on the 7th July 1944, the engine of one doodlebug ominously cut its engine directly above the Priory, but no explosion was heard. Later in the day the soldiers told them that it had landed at Fair Oak.

Several of the bombs fell close by, and there were night alerts so often that staff and pupils could only manage a couple of hours sleep, much of the time being spent in their homemade shelter. There were usually only a few moments between the warning and the planes arriving overhead, giving hardly any time to get to the protection of the shelter. Everybody was invariably in the house when they arrived.On the 11th July 1944 it was only a few seconds between the warning and the V-1 above them cutting its engine. It fell nearby and the explosion shook the whole house. The boys were hurried to the shelter, but the fathers on fire watch duty were in the front porch when they saw another doodlebug coming straight towards them. Searchlights and streams of tracer bullets threw bright lights on to it, but it was not brought down. It continued coming towards them, its engine stopped, and then mercifully it glided past and exploded nearby. The fire watchers made for the football field and sat there all night, and watched more than 20 doodlebugs going about their deadly business. The following night at 12.45am, the air raid alert sounded as the bomb passed over them. It exploded in the direction of Winchester. The wry comment was 'Experience shows that "alert" means a plane is within reach ... [The] second came soon afterwards flying parallel to the house. Caught in the searchlight, it resembled a speck of silver speeding along. Tracer bullets made a pattern of red in the sky, and big shells were sent up to form a barrage across its path. The A-A [anti-aircraft] man could not hit it and it burst a few seconds later'.[122] It came down on an army camp at Mill House on the Waltham Chase road and forty men were seriously injured. The spectators continued watching as more bombs descended on Portsmouth.

From 1am until 5.40am on the 13th July 1944 there was continual bombing. The air raid warning had not sounded until several of the planes had already passed over, one of them exploding in a field near Durley church. It made a crater 16 feet in diameter and eight feet deep; fortunately there were no casualties. Father Superior sheltered under the piano in the recreation room, Father Kingseller in a corner behind a sofa in the same room, and Brothers Aubert and Modeste sought doubtful refuge in a shed. But life had to go on, and the end of year exams began that morning.

The following night a doodlebug dived on to Cross Lanes Farm and shook the whole house. Fortunately there were no casualties. The next day, a Saturday morning, at 7.30am another landed nearby as the boys were about to leave for their summer vacation. There was no let up and the bombing continued throughout the summer.

The Blackout is Relaxed

In July Father Smith departed for Uganda, and Father Stanley Lea, who had been on the staff in the mid-1930s, returned in August as Superior after an absence of eight years. He had most recently been professor of Dogmatic Theology at Rossington Hall, but despite this apparent handicap he proved he could still play football in the first game of the season when the staff played the pupils. Cornelius Kingseller left, after 14 years on the staff, for the novitiate at Sutton Coldfield, his departure marked by 'a wartime feast of adieu'.

6.3. Father Stanley Lea, Superior 1944–47, 1966–67.

During the summer holidays of 1944 the garrison engineers repaired and resurfaced the quadrangle and main drive, which had been damaged by the army traffic. They also dug up the concrete tent bases on the lawns. The broken concrete proved useful as a base for the foundations of a new hard tennis court. Mr Matthews came in the same week to say that the fire watch was dissolved, and that the civil defence equipment – 'souvenirs of some exciting days' had to be returned. It was Mr Matthews who brought news in October 1944 of Brother Aubert's beleaguered family in Holland. He had received a letter from an army friend, stationed near Aubert's home, who had visited the family many times and was able to report that all was well. A couple of days after the dissolution of the fire watch, the 'blackout' was relaxed, and news of the release of the internees in France was received. These were all firm indications that the war in Europe was drawing to a close, but it was not all good news.

Reports from Heston told of V-2 flying bombs, more lethal than the V-1s, now hitting the capital. And as late as the 27th December 1944 a flying bomb blew off the gates and the lodge roof at Rossington Hall and shattered the windows in the main house. News was also received that the college at Autreppe had been burnt to the ground, and that the Belgian novices at Thy-le-Château had been taken to Germany as prisoners.

By the start of the new school year in September 1944, the number of soldiers had decreased and the school had regained two of the big refectory tables that could seat a total of 24 pupils. This was exactly the number of boys that started the new term. As soon as their three-day retreat was finished they were sent out to collect blackberries to augment the jam ration. In October Mrs Rodgers, the cook, made more than 200 pounds of jam with the blackberries and apples. The sugar must have boosted the boys' energy levels for they then won all their football games in September and October including one with 'the army team' which they won 4-1, and another with 'a REME team' which was won 7-1. After this game they were sent out berry picking again, collecting 30 pounds to fortify them in the following months. But it was not good enough to prevent them being beaten by the staff team 3-1 and by the REME 3-1 in November. The REME team were jubilant, but their fellow soldiers were not so happy for many of them had bet on the Priory to win, one of them losing 30 shillings, which was about two weeks wages. Maybe his faith and his pocket were rewarded when the Priory beat the REME 7-3 in their next match.

Accommodation Problems

The Allied invasion of North Africa in December 1942 released the students and priests who had been detained there by the occupying forces. The group included Fathers John Robinson and Joseph Murphy who had been ordained during their enforced detention and now joined the Priory staff. The others went to St Columba's to continue their theology studies.

St Columba's was bursting at the seams for it now housed schoolboys, philosophy students and the North African theology students with Father Howell as Superior of the whole community.

The previous year's theology students had been sent from Scotland to the Birmingham diocesan seminary at Oscott because of the overcrowding. The situation was considerably relieved in July 1943 when Rossington Hall was returned to the Society though in an abused and dilapidated state. By September it had been sufficiently refurbished to accept the philosophers and theologians from St Columba's, as well as the students who had been at Oscott.

In September 1943 it seemed that St Columba's would, at last return to its original function as a junior school, but this was to be for only a year. The students who had been interned in France had to face a novitiate year when they returned in September 1944, and St Columba's was to be the place. The junior school pupils were transferred in September of that year to the Priory, in the expectation that they could be accommodated, but the army did not finally leave until the end of November, and the Boys' House did not become habitable until January 1945. St Columba's continued as a novitiate house, and was not reopened as a school until 1948.

The liberation of North Africa meant that contact with the Mother House could be resumed and new appointments made. In 1943 Father Brown was appointed rector at Rossington Hall and relinquished his post as Regional Superior to Father Bernard Gaffney, who had been appointed Pro-Provincial Superior while still serving with the First Army as a military chaplain. Gaffney had accompanied the invasion troops to North Africa, and had been consulted by the commanders on the topographical details of the Algiers and Tunis regions with which he was familiar.[123] He came back with the released students on an empty troopship, and after the war was sent a bill for first class travel![107] On his return he was released from army service and was able to attend to his Provincial duties. His appointment signalled the recognition of Britain as a self-sustaining Province. It now had the physical, financial and manpower resources for the comprehensive training and education of brothers and priests for the Society, and also a centre for promotions work. Its autonomy was further emphasised on the 1st January 1944 when English was used for the first time for the official records.

The Army Leaves at Last

On the 20th November 1944 the REME left for good, but before they left, they repaired the goalposts and the long fences around the football fields. A Royal Signals detachment and some RAF personnel left a few days later. The REME soldiers returned in mid-December 1944 for an informal visit and to lose another game of football. They were now stationed at Gosport as part of a larger unit and returned in March 1945 with a stronger team. The game finished with five of their players and one Priory player having been carried off injured. The game seems to have been played on the understanding that if you want to play rough, we can play rougher. With superior numbers, if not with skill, the school won 6-0. A complaint was later received from Gosport suggesting that the Priory had fielded two amateur international players! *HMS Mercury* was the next up to be beaten 3-1. Then the Queen's Own Regiment was defeated 6-3. A game with the local Combined Cadet Force in between times was won 13-0. The score could have been higher and the game was described as a farce. Another farcical game was against the Colden Common Youth Club, beaten 8-0. The school was used to playing against adult teams, rather than schools or youth teams when similar high scores were the result. The only side to beat the pupils (2-1) in this season was the staff team, which included the three smallest pupils.

In 1946 and 1947 the school continued to play army and navy teams. The results against school, youth club, village and parish teams, continued to be embarrassingly high in favour of the Priory. But they were no match for the staff (and student priests) 'international' team, which resoundingly defeated them in October 1946. The international team was Bruls (Holland), Brothers Boyd and Paul Anthony (Scotland), Coghlan and Robinson (England), van den Hout (Holland), Tolmie and Murphy A (Scotland), Lavallée (France), D'Arcy (Ireland), and Ralloffzen (Holland). The German prisoners of war could also field a good team and beat the Priory 5-1 in May 1947.

A garrison officer visited on the 28th November 1944 to inspect the buildings that had been vacated and to say that the school was derequisitioned. However, no official statement was received, so the Society could not occupy the empty buildings, except for the three rooms that they had previously been given permission to use. The military had again left the central heating system out of order and the drains broken. The heating system could not be repaired until the army gave permission, so oil stoves had to be used in the dormitories, classrooms and study hall in what was proving a bitter November. The school was very damp and cold, and one boy had to be admitted to hospital with pneumonia. The drains were a health hazard and workmen were called in to repair them. An exchange of letters brought a Brigadier along on the 21st December to find out what was happening and he seems to have authorised repossession, but it was not until after Christmas that any repair work, other than on the drains, got under way. The heating system was eventually fixed at the end of December.In January 1945 workmen unexpectedly came and erected scaffolding at the front of the Fathers' House to repair the damage caused by enemy action. What seemed prompt action by the army was in fact a commendable response by the local authority.

After classes on Christmas Eve 1944, there were singing rehearsals and manual work. After a few hours sleep the boys were up at 11.30pm for the first Midnight Mass since 1938. They were up again at 7.30am on Christmas morning and sang another High Mass at 10.30am. Mrs Rodgers worked on Christmas Day to prepare a splendid lunch and in the afternoon the students presented a play attended by 20 parishioners. They rose the following morning at 4.15am and were taken by Southdown motor coach to London for the start of their Christmas break at home.

The fathers spent the Christmas holidays 1944–45 scrubbing the floors of the Boys' House and generally cleaning the building, which had been left in a deplorable state, especially the classrooms that had been used as workshops. Father Robinson repainted the bedsteads and lockers, Father Coghlan laid lino on the floor of the Fathers' House, and Father Andrew Murphy replaced and re-seeded the surface of the grass tennis court. When the boys returned after Christmas two of the classrooms had to be used as crowded dormitories until the main dormitory could be properly cleaned and the walls repainted. It was not until the 17th May 1945 that the dormitory could be used again.

Italian and German Prisoners of War

From 1943 until the end of 1947, Italian prisoners of war attended Mass in the Priory chapel separately from the boys, and they also came from time to time to play football against the school team. They were in a nearby camp on the Winchester Road and were able to walk over. There were 75 of them, all captured at Tobruk and El Alamein, and they worked on the surrounding farms. They first came to Mass on the morning of the 13th June 1943 and returned in the afternoon to play football. In May 1944 the Italian prisoners were told that they were free to join the fighting units in Italy, but they did not avail themselves of this offer. They could not help but be aware of the local bombing and destruction, and that it would certainly be worse wherever they were sent. They stayed in their camp, but were free to move about the district, two of them coming to help restore the Priory gardens in 1945. There were also two German prisoner of war camps nearby, one at Droxford and one at 'Waltham'. Mass was said at their camps, but from the beginning of 1946 some of them came to Mass at the Priory. It was one of the German prisoners who repaired the chapel organ in 1946.[124] All the German prisoners remained until 1947 because the Prime Minister, Clement Attlee, had controversially prevented the repatriation of prisoners of war in 1945 so that they could continue working on farms and clearing bomb damage in the towns until enough British manpower was available.

The 8th May 1945 was VE(Victory in Europe) Day. The school was decked with flags and bunting, and in the evening a huge bonfire was lit around which the boys sang well into the night. They watched the searchlight displays and could see other bonfires twinkling in the surrounding countryside. The 13th May was a national holiday to celebrate the end of the war in Europe, and the Priory day started with Solemn High Mass followed by the *Te Deum* and *God Save the King*. There were big congregations at all the Masses at the Priory and in other parishes where most of the fathers were out on supply. VJ (Victory over Japan) Day on the 15th August 1945 occurred during the holidays and was not celebrated so solemnly or enthusiastically.

7

Sick Men at the Helm

The first term after the end of the war in 1945 started with 30 boys. It was not until September 1946 that the school resumed, to a large extent, its pre-war life with almost 80 students. The timetable, however, was modified: the rising time was changed from 6.15am to 6.45am, the early morning 45-minute study period was abolished, and six class periods were introduced by changing the study-class-revision system to the English system of classes during the day and study (prep) in the evening. Wednesday and Saturday afternoons were spent in organised sport or working on the farm or in the gardens. The end-of-term holidays were extended to give the boys a longer time with their families: the summer holiday was increased from six to seven weeks and the Christmas holiday from two to three weeks; the Easter break was spent at the school and varied in the coming years between three days and a week.

Now that the war was over, priest students from the continent reappeared for studies at the universities, teacher training colleges, or to improve their English. From the 20th January to the 16th September 1946 there were five of these students lodged in the boys' recreation hut. On the 17th May they went off to see the King and Queen who were visiting Winchester, and a few days later they met up with 25 Dutch White Fathers who, with 75 other missionaries, sailed on the 21st May from Southampton for Africa on board the aircraft carrier *HMS Fencer*. When they themselves left in September, they were replaced by three others: Fathers Bruls, van den Hout and Ralloffzen. Bruls had presumably come to improve his English for he was given the job of teaching Latin to the two lower classes until he left in July 1947.

A noteworthy first appearance in October 1946 was that of Mr John Heath. The choirmaster asked him if he would 'lend a hand with the singing' and he did so for the next 17 years in a dedicated and exceptional manner.

On the 27th June 1947 Father Howell was appointed Provincial Superior of Great Britain while he was attending the General Chapter in Algiers as the representative of Britain – confirmation that Britain was now a fully-fledged province. His predecessor, Father Gaffney, was assigned to Uganda.

Father Moran Takes Charge

In October the Priory Superior, Father Lea, was taken ill during the night and, after a dash by ambulance to the hospital, an operation was performed on his stomach at 4.30am. Surprisingly, the school was allowed to continue for a year without a superior, but even after that lapse of time Lea was still too ill to resume his duties and remained in a nursing home. In September 1947 Father Tom Moran took charge.

7.1. Father Thomas Moran, Superior 1947–51.

Moran had not been properly fit since his wartime internment when he had contracted tuberculosis, and his condition was not helped when he again took up smoking cigarettes. He always looked slightly unwell and cold with his burnous wrapped around him like an Arab in a sandstorm. Although he had been at the school since 1945, he had not been teaching but convalescing and, during his better periods, helping out in parishes around the diocese. He continued being unwell and went at intervals during his term of office for x-ray scanning at the hospital in Winchester. He also went off for 'rests', sometimes for a fortnight. In December 1950 he collapsed and this resulted in him spending time in a London hospital followed by some months in a Manchester nursing home.[125] He returned on the 9th May, and the car bringing him back was stopped at the school gates by the pupils who towed it up the drive to the front door with rousing cheers. This signal honour was usually reserved for eminent and highly regarded figures, but in this instance it indicated affection for Moran and pleasure at his return. Towing a visitor's car had replaced the French pupils' tradition of building a floral arch, and seems to have been based on the old English tradition of unharnessing carriage horses and enthusiastically pulling an honoured figure for the last stretch of his journey. Others to whom this tribute had been recently paid were Bishop Holmes-Siedle in March 1947 and, in May 1947, Father Côté (by then Provincial Superior of Canada) accompanied by Bishop Cabana.

Because, presumably, he was feeling below par most of the time, Moran was not an energetic man. Persuasion rather than the big stick was his way of encouraging the boys, and he generally succeeded, especially with the more headstrong. The pupils liked him rather than admired him, and his slight Lancashire accent gave him an endearing quality. His laid back attitude made for a happy and cheerful school but did not provide the impetus for academic achievement. Some of the teachers could be martinets but it was the superior, more by his demeanour than by regulation, who established the climate of behaviour. It was one in which the pupils felt they could move along at their own pace rather than striving for higher objectives.

Amazingly, considering his health, Moran played two games of football for the staff team in November and December 1947 when they defeated the St Mary's (Bitterne) school staff 6-3 and the Montfort school (Romsey) staff 6-1. The staff team also continued to beat the pupils. Several of the staff could well have played football professionally, especially Andrew Murphy, Bernard D'Arcy, and even Tom Moran.

Despite feeling unwell most of the time, Moran travelled a lot in a small Austin Seven car acquired during the war years. It could be very unstable at times, so Moran usually required two boys to sit in the back to act as ballast when he travelled locally. It was probably the most familiar car in the district to the AA patrolman, who greeted Moran with a sigh and 'Hello Father' as he resignedly set about yet another roadside repair. This was the second car owned by the school. In December 1925 there was mention of *l'auto de maison*, which must have been acquired in addition to the high mileage motorcycle and sidecar.

7.2. The Fathers' House in the 1940s.

St Columba's Reopens as a School

In September 1948 St Columba's College resumed its original function as a junior school, and the Rudiments class (now split into two years known as Lower Figures and Higher Figures} with more than 30 pupils was transferred there. Father Andrew Murphy was appointed rector, and was replaced as the Prefect of Discipline by Father James Tolmie. All this was possible because earlier in the year it was decided to transfer the novices from St Columba's to an international Novitiate at 'sHeerenberg in Holland.

At the start of the 1948 school year the Priory had 50 students in four classes, one boy arriving two days before the start of the term through error, not enthusiasm. After their three-day retreat the boys were put to work during their free periods picking over 100 tons of potatoes in the Long Field. Brother Patrick raced up and down between lines of boys holding sacks, first with a plough and then with a very large trailer on to which the full sacks were heaved.

In September 1949 there were 70 pupils distributed between the four classes. The main dormitory could only accommodate 60, so the classroom next to the infirmary was converted into a dormitory and the class of Rhetoric moved into the recreation hut. The students included a couple of military veterans who had come for a year to improve their Latin and French. These were Tom McKenna from the navy, who was ordained a White Father, and Peter Gilmore from the RAF, who became a Cistercian monk. From 1950 onwards, older entrants did not attend the Priory but went instead to Campion House (a college for late vocations at Osterley, Middlesex) to acquire the prerequisite academic qualifications for higher studies.

Earlier in 1949, on the 12th July, Archbishop Arthur Hughes had died suddenly at the early age of 46 while visiting England. The boys were unable to stay for the funeral because arrangements had been made for their holiday travelling. They left on the morning of the 15th July, the day of the funeral. Archbishop Godfrey, the Apostolic Delegate and future Cardinal Archbishop of Westminster, officiated at the ceremony, the staff sang the Requiem Mass, and a wreath from King Farouk of Egypt was placed on the coffin, which was borne to the little school cemetery for interment.

Pupil Numbers Continue to Rise

The new school year in 1950 started with 90 pupils. It had been hoped that having the lower classes at St Columba's would alleviate the overcrowding problem, but the numbers there had risen too. Whereas earlier superiors had rejected applications when numbers exceeded the school capacity, Moran was accepting them. But where to accommodate so many students in a building designed for 60, which was the maximum originally expected in Britain? It seems that one of the more fortunate investments made in the past was the purchase of the recreation hut, for it was again brought into service. Part of it was used as a dormitory and part as a classroom and study hall, and elsewhere it was a case of all bunching up.

In the late 1940s and early 1950s, some of the boys regularly cycled home to the north of England and to Scotland, travelling distances of 260 to 500 miles. They would set off at 2pm and cycle continuously for 24 hours arriving at Liverpool or Lancashire destinations by 2pm the following day. Those cycling to Scotland would continue northwards and stay the night at a youth hostel in the Lake District. It was only when the weather was very bad with rain and wind that they would stay in a Midlands hostel. In July 1951, after the push bike cyclists had left for home, they were followed by Fathers O'Sullivan, Dickson and Duffy on their bicycles with newly fitted 'cyclemasters' – small 50cc petrol engines fitted on the rear carrier and driving the back wheel to give a speed of about 10 mph and delivering 150 miles to the gallon. In 1950, a group of boys, instead of heading for home, cycled to Rome without the aid of engines, where they spent a week, and then cycled to their homes in England and Scotland.

Those not inclined to cycle set off in motor coaches. The coaches were regularly hired from Southdown Motor Services and then from the Glider Coach Company of Bishop's Waltham not only to take boys to and from London and for local group travel, but also to take them to the north of England and Scotland at holiday times. Until January 1933 journeys to and from Bishop's Waltham were entirely by train. Father James Smith recalls that in his time as a student

> ... you could go to any railway station in Great Britain and ask for a ticket to Bishop's Waltham. Although you would certainly have to change trains on the way, the various companies seemed to work together to make sure that you did not have interminable waits, and no matter how late your train might be in the Southern Region the 'Botley Express' was always to be relied on; it would wait for you to arrive before setting out on its four-mile trip, and when it deposited you at Bishop's Waltham there was only School Hill to negotiate and there you were at the Priory.[89]

When passenger traffic ceased in 1933, the line from Botley continued to carry goods until 1962 so luggage could still be delivered by rail.[126] The small puffing steam engine, sometimes with a single carriage, hurrying along the valley four times a day was a sight that was strangely missed. From 1933 arriving passengers took the train as far as Winchester, then a public service bus to Bishop's Waltham. From 1944 onwards coach travel proved quicker and cheaper.

A surviving 1948 school prospectus shows that the fees at this time were £50 per term, books seven shillings per term, and sports expenses two shillings and sixpence per term. Parents, some of them widows, who could not meet these modest fees, were asked to contribute what they could. All parents, however, had to bear the full costs of travelling, and medical and dental expenses.[127] The Society was willing to bear the full expenses of those who were without any financial support, and this had been the case in the 1920s when some of the boys had come from an orphanage. (They included Owen McCoy, the future Prefect Apostolic of Oyo in Nigeria, and James Smith the future Priory Superior and professor of Greek.) It was again necessary in 1961 when 'some boys' were reported as paying no fees.[128] Cardinal Lavigerie was in the same situation as a boy when his well-off father refused to pay the fees of the local diocesan seminary. Lavigerie was only able to continue his studies by being recognised as a bright student and given a free place at the junior seminary in Paris – a long way from his home in Bayonne.[1]

During the Second World War and for several years after it, only a minimum list of clothing and bed linen was required of each boy. Parents were reminded that 'This is the minimum outfit, a number of articles required is purposely omitted on account of the difficulty of [clothing] coupons'.[127] During the summer holidays all the clothing coupons, and often those of parents, were used to renew the school uniform and other necessary clothing for the term ahead. Clothes therefore had to last. Most of the boys, like sailors and soldiers, had their personal sewing kit with needles, cotton and wool. It was not an unusual sight at this time to see boys expertly patching tears and darning their woollen socks. Clothes rationing ended in 1949 but, maybe from habit rather than necessity, sewing kits continued to be used for the next few years.

'If you want an egg, go home!'

Tom Moran remained until 1951. He had been popular, kindly and fatherly although still a comparatively young man of 39. However, his health and his temperament were not up to running a tight ship.

7.3. Father Patrick Donnelly, Superior 1951–53.

In September 1951, Father Patrick Donnelly awaited the boys as Superior. The difference in character between the two men could hardly have been more apparent. Donnelly's background had not prepared him to deal sensitively with boisterous schoolboys; he had spent most of the previous ten years teaching theology and he was a rigorist who did not bend rules. His first talk to the pupils included the remark 'I shall be strict, but not severe', but when one boy tentatively complained about the standard of the food, he was told 'If you want an egg, go home!'[129] His first duty was to get a grip on a school that had been without an effective headmaster for a long time. Within a week three boys were advised to leave. In March two boys were severely caned and summarily expelled for smoking. The prefects were told to attend to their responsibilities rigorously, and the Prefect of Discipline must have been similarly instructed for caning came back into fashion. There was no trace of Donnelly's boyhood Glasgow intonation and he set about eliminating it from the speech of Glasgow boys in his care, with public rebukes where necessary.

He reckoned an injection of culture was required and took boys on visits to cathedrals and museums, and to tea with the Mayor of Winchester. He also started cultural general knowledge quizzes in the study hall at which all had to be present with him presiding. In a liberal gesture he occasionally allowed the boys to visit the Bishop's Waltham cinema to see films that were subject to his approval. They included *Odette*, *King Solomon's Mines*, and *Cry the Beloved Country*. Films were still shown occasionally in the gymnasium, and one shown before his arrival seems to have prompted the nickname he was given. On the 5th February *Tom Brown's Schooldays* had been screened and, thinking his manner resembled that of Cedric Hardwicke's Doctor Arnold, the boys had immediately christened him 'Doc Donnelly', so that henceforth he was known as 'the Doc'.[129]

Classes Renamed as Forms

In May 1951 during his Provincial Visitation before Donnelly's arrival, Howell had told the staff that a new structure of studies had to be put in place for the 'general schools examination' – the about-to-be-introduced GCE (General Certificate of Education), which would replace the matriculation examination. He also wanted the classes to be renamed Forms I to VI and standards improved for he considered that the students were not working as hard as they should be, especially the Syntax and Poetry classes.[130] New textbooks were hurriedly purchased and the class names were changed to form numbers ready for the start of the new school year, but the old-fashioned teaching methods did not change as quickly. Little more could be done before the arrival of the new superior who, like the two superiors that were to follow him, came with no experience of secondary school teaching. It was all starting a little late to prepare adequately for the new style of examination in the following June. There seemed to be little understanding of the GCE requirements, besides which some of the teachers were short-term foreign visitors who had no knowledge of the English education system or its new examination requirements. And the frequent long absences of the previous superior had not helped. The teachers had previously relied on their own experience of matriculation examinations to coach pupils, but now all were venturing together into the unknown with little preparation and on the assumption that it would be easier than the matriculation examination. Even Donnelly referred to the new type of examination as the 'slacker's charter'.[131] The five-year education programme stayed in place, but the A-level programme could not be completed in this time and pupils were going on to study philosophy without doing A-level work. There were exceptions: for example, Francis Tortolano in 1953, and Michael Fitzgerald and Eugene MacBride in 1954, mainly through self-study, sat their A-levels at the same time as their O-levels.[132] On his appointment Donnelly had suggested to the Provincial Superior changing what he considered, rightly, to be an inadequate curriculum, especially the lack of science[129], but no changes were introduced until two years after his departure in 1953. Nevertheless the school was officially applauded. In December 1952 a government inspection took place. Mr Collins, HM Inspector of Schools reported that he was 'extremely pleased with all he saw and admired the spirit among the boys'.[133] The only area he commented on for improvement was the sanitary arrangements. Nothing appears to have changed as a result of his visit and no other government inspection was ever recorded after this.

In January 1952 Donnelly introduced the dialogue Mass as a means of concentrating attention and increasing devotion. Although the dialogue was in Latin, it pre-empted the Second Vatican Council by more than a decade. He also arranged for the Easter Vigil to be celebrated for the first time on the 12th April 1952, and this was done every year afterwards, starting at 10.45pm and finishing at 1am on Easter Sunday morning.

Closer Relationships with the Town

The Coronation of Queen Elizabeth II in June 1953 provided an opportunity for closer relationships with the town. Donnelly offered the use of the gymnasium for the celebrations, and it was used in March 1953 for two concerts in aid of the Coronation Fund. In return, he and some of the fathers were invited to a play performed in the local school in aid of the same fund. The local Coronation Festival Committee must have felt that sufficiently friendly relationships had been established for them to ask the

Priory to provide guards for a few nights to help patrol the festival site in the grounds of the Bishop's Palace. A marquee and some smaller tents had been set up in preparation for the Coronation festivities, but vandals had mischievously cut some of the guy ropes. It was ironic that two Irishmen were chosen to do the patrolling: Father Bill Halligan and Brother Patrick.[102]

On the day itself a group of the boys provided entertainment in the marquee with a 'Black and White Minstrel Show', and in the evening all the pupils gathered around the communal bonfire outside the school gates rather than having their own within the grounds. The only separate celebration during the day was a Mass and prayers for the new Queen. Father Donnelly had been invited to join the Anglican Rector and Congregational Minister for a common religious service, but in those pre-ecumenical days he felt he had to decline.[134]

Until this time there had been little contact between the townspeople and the school. There were brief encounters during football and cricket matches, but otherwise the only interactions with local people were on a business level through the Father Procurator or on farming matters with the brothers. These relationships were very cordial, but understandably brief. In other boarding schools, the boys would visit the town, and the staff, especially if married, would often live out and become part of the town's social life. The Priory, virtually self-sufficient, employing a minimum of local people, with a monastic-like austerity and no socializing outside its grounds, must have seemed forbidding and faintly suspicious. It seems it would only require a foreign war to harden those suspicions. However, one of the results of the 1939–45 War was that, because the staff worked happily with the military and were involved with townspeople in civil defence, the apparent suspicion that it was a foreign institution disappeared. (This was not the case in Scotland, where St Columba's College was suspected of harbouring spies.[107]) The school was probably still an unknown and invisible entity as far as most of the townspeople were concerned, but this state of affairs was changing.

The fathers were already responding to invitations to give talks based on their experiences. In January 1953 Father Tolmie gave a talk on Tunisia in the local youth club. This was the first time any

White Father had been invited to speak publicly in the town since Father Travers spoke at a meeting on the 11th November 1918 to celebrate the end of the First World War. In February Father Tryers, a strong personality, an admired teacher and fine speaker, gave a talk about the Gold Coast where he had spent many years and where he was to end his life. This set a precedent and over the next several years many of the fathers happily responded to invitations to give talks, and succeeding superiors encouraged the public use of the gymnasium, probably the largest hall in the area and with extensive car parking. The gymnasium had always been available to parishioners and, from the war period, it had been available to any local people who wished to use it for large meetings or concerts. Towards the end of the Second World War and for a couple of years just afterwards, the most frequent users were the Bishop's Waltham Growmore Club and the Farmers' Union. From January 1947 it was licensed for public performances, Father Moran going to the Droxford Magistrates' Court to obtain the first licence for a play in aid of the Soldiers' Welcome Home Fund, which was attended by about 200 members of the public. The most regular users after the war were the parishioners who used it for socials and whist drives. It was at a whist drive in March 1954 that Brother Patrick won first prize – a tea set!

Father Donnelly appeared briefly at the start of the September 1953 term, but had to retire on sick leave. He was by now a popular head and an able one, but his health had been bad for some time and was worsening, so Howell was forced to replace him after only two years with John Cassidy who had been in charge of the students at St Andrews. Like Moran, Donnelly had been trapped overseas at the start of the war. He was ordained in Tunisia, but had to stay there because of its military occupation, and was immediately put to work teaching theology on which he thrived. He continued teaching theology when he returned to Britain. From the Priory he was posted to Marienthal in Luxembourg, and on his return was responsible for students studying at the university and colleges in London and was again at his best. In later years he gained a praiseworthy reputation as a counsellor and spiritual director, for which he was in great demand until his death in 1997.[135]

The Garden Fête

John Cassidy served for an even shorter period than Donnelly – 15 months. It was during his period of office that the first Garden Fête and Fair was held on the 10th July 1954. It was organised by the parishioners in aid of the parish building fund with the pupils providing most of the manual labour to set up the stalls. It was open to all who wished to come and proved a huge success with people turning up in large numbers, apparently to the disadvantage of the Swanmore Flower Show which was held on the same day.[136] A band was hired and it marched through the town up to the school, where it continued providing music. Besides the usual sideshows, roundabouts, pony rides and prize draw, the fête continued in the evening with dancing on the lawns. It proved a popular event on this occasion and in the following years until the school closed. 'It was the village event of the year.'[137] Large crowds turned up each time, and the dancing attracted many of the younger people in the evening, except when it was held a month earlier in June 1957 and it rained all evening. By January 1959 the local newspaper was able to report 'Their Christmas pantomime, carols in the village, and summer fête are established events in the town's social calendar'.[138]

7.4. Garden Fête 1962. L to r: Mrs Rodgers, Fr Moreton, Fr Duffy, Fr Geraghty, Fr Moloney, Mrs Stubbington.

Pilgrimage Walks

Beginning in June 1954 the custom arose of a one-day pilgrimage to a local shrine of Our Lady. It took place either on the last day of April, the feast of Our Lady of Africa, or on May Day. It was usually a walk to the chapel of Our Lady of Winton in St Peter's church, Winchester, but sometimes the pilgrims would walk to other churches dedicated to Our Lady such as that at Bursledon about 10 miles away.

There would be High Mass, a sermon by the Father Superior, a picnic lunch, Benediction at 3pm, then a walk back.[139] Boys and fathers would set off at 8am after Mass and breakfast and, if it was the May bank holiday when the kitchen staff had the day off, the Fifth and Sixth Forms would follow on after washing up the dishes. On the 30th April 1958 the walk to Winchester took two and a half hours via Morestead.[140] On May Day in the previous year the pilgrims seem to have walked the 11 miles in double-quick time or set off at an earlier hour, for the first two groups arrived by 9.45am. Mass was in the side chapel at 11am where 'there was absolute stillness as the procession of celebrant and ministers made its way slowly to the Lady Altar ... [and] the plainchant echoed down the empty nave'.[141] The pilgrimages had ceased by 1964 probably because the senior forms were now attending school at Southsea.

Cassidy's appointment seems to have been a holding exercise for he was sent to the missions in December 1954 and was replaced by John Egan in January 1955. This was a more unsuitable appointment than the previous two. Egan had been teaching philosophy and had been a novice master. His personality and previous experience did not recommend him as one to have charge of schoolboys; he was known as a severe and 'unbending' novice master[142] and, more tellingly, he was a sick man. He seems to have been moved to what was perceived as a less demanding role because of his ill health, but he was in Guy's Hospital, London, in May, and was forced to retire within eight months of his arrival. And so another year passed without an effective head.

8

Changing Times

Fortunately the next Superior proved himself an able, healthy, and accomplished school head. This was Father Francis Moody who had been teaching at St Columba's, having previously taught at the Priory, and before that having acquired a degree in science at St Andrews University. His first moves as Superior were to introduce a sixth form and to set up a science course throughout the school taught by himself and Father John Fowles. The first members of the Sixth Form were Richard Calcutt, Michael McDonnell, Edward Creaney and Brian Foley. In August 1954 another able teacher, Father Patrick Fitzgerald who had just completed his degree course at London University, had joined them. From this time forward there was a noticeable and continuing upturn in the school's academic attainment.

8.1. Father Francis Moody, Superior 1955–58.

The number of pupils had remained above the design capacity for many years and in September 1956 there were 71. Every attempt had been made to house them in the main buildings, but once again the recreation hut had to be used as a dormitory and small study hall, and this arrangement had to continue until 1964 while the numbers remained above 70. 'Hut' was an inappropriate term for it was a long substantial building with steel trusses supporting the roof and divided into several large rooms by partition walls. Barrack room stoves, and later electric radiators, provided the heating. It was considered a reasonably comfortable place to be, especially after Mr Attridge redecorated the interior and the fathers the exterior in the summer of 1956.

The long-serving Brother Patrick was not around for the start of the 1956–57 school year for he had been appointed to St Augustine's College of Philosophy at Blacklion in County Cavan. This college had opened in 1955 to replace Broome Hall, which had been re-designated as a Novitiate House. It was the White Fathers' first establishment in Ireland, and was part of the British Province until 1971 when the Irish Province was established with Father John Jones as the first Provincial Superior. There had been at least one previous attempt to open a house in Ireland. In March 1944, Father Gaffney, the Pro-Provincial Superior, reported that he had found exactly the house he wanted, but unfortunately the local bishop would not give his approval to a foundation. It was another 11 years before permission was granted and 28 years since Howell made his first promotional visit in 1927. However, it was in July 1916 that the newspapers reported the first sightings of a 'White Father' in Ireland. It was a rogue who had succeeded in getting hold of a white habit and gone about impersonating a missionary and collecting money. He was condemned in Dublin to nine months imprisonment with hard labour for numerous offences.[143]

Looking Outwards

In August 1958 Moody was appointed to the missions. He died tragically in Lubumbashi, Zaire, in January 1978[144] when he was killed in a motorcycle accident. Father Patrick Fitzgerald, the Latin master, succeeded as Superior.

8.2. Father Patrick Fitzgerald, Superior 1958–61.

From 1959 onwards changes were introduced which recognised that the social climate had changed and that a more outward-looking attitude had to be adopted. Special privileges were accorded the top form: they were provided with *The Daily Telegraph*, *Punch* and the *Illustrated London News*, and this concession was extended to the whole school in 1961. Previously, the boys had not had access to newspapers unless they were sent from home, although *The Times* had always been delivered regularly to the staff library. Allowing the pupils access to newspapers and periodicals contrasted pointedly with the Provincial instruction issued eight years earlier: 'A list of periodicals for suitable boys' reading should be drawn up and submitted to the Provincial for approval. Comics, 'bloods' and newspapers to be forbidden henceforth. Time was lost on these things and a low tone maintained in literature.'[130] In the refectory the Sixth Form could enjoy the company of their own classmates at table where before a senior boy sat at each table and ages were mixed.[139] Perhaps more appreciated by the students who shaved was the availability for the first time of hot water in the washbasins. The first television set owned by the school arrived in November 1960 – a gift from former pupil Bernard Windscheffel-Chancellor, but viewing was strictly rationed to programmes such as *Panorama*. In a more significant break from the past, the boys were allowed to visit the local towns more frequently and to find amusement at public venues, so that the rector was able to say in 1961 'The boys are not shielded in any way. You can find them at the swimming baths, the ice rink, the cinema.'[128]

In 1959 Father Fitzgerald offered the services of the boys to help prepare the route through the town, which the Queen and the Duke of Edinburgh were to pass along. They put up bunting and flags, and for their work they were paid a handsome tribute by the chairman of the parish council.[139] And in an enthusiastic show of loyalty to the Crown they turned out on a wet 8th June to cheer the royal couple as they drove through Bishop's Waltham on their way from opening the new council offices in Winchester to open the restored Guildhall in Portsmouth. In the same year 36 of the students were stewards at the Bishop's Waltham Agricultural Show and the same number of them continued to act in this capacity in the following years. The students also provided entertainment at the Merry and Bright Club, the Youth Club and children's parties at the British Legion Club. The choir was also making guest appearances in the town and giving carol concerts conducted by Mr Heath. Fathers Fowles, Sweeney and Dickson gave occasional talks and appeared at different times on the local *Any Questions?* panels. In 1961 Father Moloney was on an *Any Questions?* panel in Gosport organised by a branch of the United Nations and he also took part in a debate arranged by the Southampton University students. There were also visiting speakers. In 1961, for example, they included Commander Pierce RN of the School of Navigation, Warsash; Professor Scullard from Portsmouth; Mr Paul Norris, history teacher at St John's; and Commander Kane RN.

An attempt was made to foster relations with the French Apostolic School at Bonnelles in France, and on Easter Sunday 1960 a coach took a group of boys there for two weeks. It is remarkable that it had never happened before, nor that were ever any exchanges with similar schools in the other European countries. Surprisingly, the trip was not repeated in later years and there was no official return visit by the Bonnelles pupils, although three of them came in July 1961 for a short holiday.

Not only were the social attitudes changing, but so too were the liturgical forms and attendances at religious services. The Sixth and Fifth Forms were separated from the younger boys for spiritual reading. The rosary was no longer said as a community in the chapel, but individually whenever a student wished – this was intended to cultivate personal conviction. And whereas previously two Masses had been attended each Sunday, Low Mass at 7.30am and High Mass at 10.30am, now it was only required to attend High Mass at the new time of 8.30am, and at all Masses the epistle and gospel were read in English.[139] On Palm Sunday 1962 Mr Williams, a lay teacher, read the Passion in English. Previously this was sung in Latin by the priest, deacon and sub-deacon. By 1962 the Priory appears to have been pre-empting the decrees of the Second Vatican Council. This was partly due to the boys at St Columba's coming under the influence of Father Camille Dufort who came to teach there in 1958. His outlook, thinking and liturgical practice were of the *avant garde* continental persuasion. The boys who proceeded to the Priory over the next few years therefore came with a different liturgical experience to those anywhere else in Britain. One of them was Peter Johnson, who was later to become the Lord Abbot of Our Lady's Abbey at Quarr. He founded the Society for Liturgical Renewal at the Priory in 1962, and adapted an English translation of the *Salve Regina* to plainchant in 1963. Mass with dialogue in English and an offertory procession soon followed.[145] By 1963 the Sunday evening compline was being sung in English, parts of the Mass said in English, and the Society's formula for morning and night prayers had been discarded in favour of the traditional prayers of the Church and the psalms.[146] This was all taking place well before the Second Vatican Council decree on the liturgy, which was not published until the 3rd December 1964. The Priory seems to have been ahead of other Catholic schools, and even ahead of the British bishops and theologians who were not adequately prepared for the debates of the Vatican Council, nor aware of the direction that the Council would take.

On the last day of the Christian Unity Octave on the 25th January 1962, the Superior – Father Duffy, in an unprecedented ecumenical gesture, invited the rector of Bishop's Waltham – Rev Frank Sergeant, and the local Congregational minister – Rev Frank

Ockenden from Shirrell Heath, to a unity service and afterwards to lunch, which they happily accepted. The services were repeated each year and were followed by an 'ecumenical supper' until January 1966 when the new Rector of Bishop's Waltham – Rev Christopher Biddell, the Congregationalist Minister – Rev Mr Werder, and the Methodist Minister ('who did not touch the wine') attended. Just when the Priory ceased hosting these occasions, they started to become popular elsewhere in the country.

8.3. The Father's House in the 1950s.

Farm Closure

A momentous and understandable change at this time was the closure of the farm. It had become a liability rather than a beneficial asset. Farming on a small scale was proving costly and, since the mid-1950s, food could be obtained more cheaply on the open market. The decision to close down the farm was made in May 1959 when Father Richard Walsh (Assistant to the Superior General), Father Andrew Murphy (Provincial Superior) and

Father Francis Briody (Provincial Treasurer) met with the staff council. In July Father Briody and the new Provincial Treasurer, Father Patrick Walsh, returned to discuss disposal of the farm property with Father Superior, Father Procurator and local agricultural contractor Mr Colin Underwood. Cultivation ceased immediately and on the 25th March 1960 the Long Field was rented out on a yearly tenancy to Mr Underwood at £40 per annum, increased to £60 per annum in 1965.[147] By early 1960 all the animals had been sold. Some amusement was provided at the time by a handwritten telegram received the day that some pigs were sent off to Fareham market. It read 'One of your five pigs reclassified as a bear'. It should, of course, have been a 'boar'.[148] The farm buildings, except for the byre, were demolished. The Fifth Form was entrusted with 'the congenial task of demolition' and immediately set about their task with sledgehammers, nobly led by a perspiring rector (Father Patrick Fitzgerald).[149]

The brothers who ran the farm departed: Brother Aelred in 1959, and Brothers Casimir and John Ogilvie in 1960. The only brothers resident after this were Brother John Mennie who taught mathematics from 1960 to 1961, Brother David Kelley who was procurator from 1960 to 1962, Brother Albert Gardner who was studying at the Hampshire College of Agriculture at Sparsholt from 1964 to 1965, Brother Michael Kelly who was studying architecture and serving a year's pupillage at a Winchester firm of architects from 1966 to 1967 before continuing his studies at Edinburgh University, and Brother Thomas More who came for a few months in 1962 while on leave from Africa. The new thinking was to have a group of brothers in the province who could be assigned to where they were needed for specific projects rather than attaching them to a particular house.

The farm had gone, but home grown produce continued to be supplied from the vegetable garden which, from 1961, was maintained by the boys themselves.

The substantial brick byre was used for storing bicycles when the cows departed, but in the last few months of 1962, it was converted into a fine recreation hall. Not an easy job, for all the metal stalls had to be removed and the sloping concrete floor and gully broken up and levelled. It had also to be fitted out with a ceiling and wooden floor, plastered, rewired and decorated. A visiting team of brothers was called in to do the job and also to dismantle The Hut, the long wooden building that had served so well for more than 40 years as recreation room, dormitory, classroom, study hall and soldiers' barrack room.The team were Brothers Richard (John Cecil della Porta), Arthur Carte, Colin Conisbee, John Murphy and John Cummins. The new recreation hall was blessed and officially opened by Father Superior, Bernard Duffy, on the 11th January 1963.

The ambience of the school was considerably lightened in 1960 and 1961 by the removal of the thick invasive ivy, which had covered the walls for decades, and by felling most of the trees, especially the very large and gloomy pine trees that lined the Boys' Drive creating an almost impenetrable shade. At first the whole area had a rather naked look, but the daylight was able, after many years, to get through to the south lawn and the cemetery. The result was a brighter and airier environment.

It was not only the trees that were being thinned out. By 1960, the demands of the expanding African missions left very few priests available for teaching work and no brothers on the staff to maintain the property. Brother John Mennie was brought from Sutton Coldfield to teach maths from early 1960 when Father William Lynch departed for Africa. Mennie continued until July 1961 when he left to assist the Provincial Treasurer and, later, to teach at the Ujiji Seminary in Tanzania. He was replaced by Father Moloney who arrived from London University. In September 1960 Daniel Williams, a recent convert and former Baptist minister, was invited by Father Patrick Fitzgerald to teach History and English. He proved an outstanding success in what must have been a strange environment for him. The small dormitory next to the infirmary in the main school building was provided as his quarters, but of pecuniary reward there is no mention. He was probably less interested in money than in reflecting on a priestly vocation for he left in 1962 to study at the Beda College in Rome and was eventually ordained priest for the Menevia diocese in Wales. His further contribution to the school was teaching some of the staff to drive in his Hillman car, which was towed by the pupils to the school gates as a special mark of esteem when he left in 1962.[150]

Schooling at St John's College

In July 1961 Father Fitzgerald, after seven years at the school – three as Superior – departed for studies at the Gregorian University in Rome, and 38-year old Father Bernard Duffy took his place. Duffy had rejoined the staff in January 1961 having recently returned from Tanganyika. Despite the occasional bout of malarial fever he proved a strong and capable head. One of his first tasks was to implement an arrangement made by Fitzgerald for sixth formers to attend St John's College, Southsea, for full time schooling.

8.4. Father Bernard Duffy, Superior 1961–63.

The shortage of staff was still causing many of the pupils to move on to their philosophy course without taking A-levels. This situation could not continue. If sixth form teaching was to be had, then the only option was to seek it elsewhere. On Thursday 14th September 1961, therefore, two of the boys, Sean McGovern and Andrew Coyle, began commuting to St John's College, Southsea, to pursue their sixth form studies. In the event the experiment was a success. The two boys did outstandingly well and completed their A-level studies and examinations in one year instead of the usual two. At the 1962 prize giving in the Portsmouth Guildhall, McGovern carried off the Classics Prize and Coyle was awarded the History Prize and English Prize. Both then proceeded to their philosophy studies in Ireland.

In 1962, the Fifth Form began attending St John's, thus releasing more priests for their primary purpose – missionary work in Africa. Only the Third and Fourth Forms continued to be taught at the Priory. Students intending to go to St John's were interviewed and assessed by three of the college masters. All were accepted and did not fail to make an impression when they got there. One of the teachers writing in 1966 had this to say.

> A crop of new faces … would have aroused no comment were they those of the very young, but obviously these belonged to young men: adult and more than razor-familiar.
>
> Moreover, a priest, other than the school chaplain, was seen as often as any regular member of the staff. Masses could be attended at lunch-time and a group of these mysterious newcomers were observed to stay on for devotions long after anyone else and with apparent attachment to the Blessed Sacrament unprecedented, in such a number, in the history of St John's …
>
> Only during the past two years have I come into contact with their interesting personalities … For the poetry prize, more interesting entries came in from this group than from the rest of the school. These poems showed some interesting stresses, conflicts and probings revealing, in some cases, rich interior lives … One, leaving all competitors behind, won the public reading prize, another showed prowess in games, another excelled in athletic events; so the strangeness wore off: here was not an aloof, pious clique, catapulted into an alien environment merely for academic convenience, but warm living folk whose one desire was to integrate and contribute …
>
> Generally, their presence has immensely enriched the school. This is undoubted; they are joyous, they see things fully, sometimes with sympathy, sometimes with pity … Their standards are different … Every member of Staff, without one dissident voice, says that the school would be the poorer if, for any reason, 'Bishop's Waltham' has to be withdrawn.[151]

It had been a long day for the first boys that attended St John's, and it was an uncomfortable one in winter and on wet days. They left the Priory at 7.15am in their St John's uniform, which they had to acquire in addition to their Priory outfit, and cycled the four miles to Botley. They then took the train to Fratton and walked the remaining distance. They returned at six o'clock in the evening to follow the Priory regime.

When the two upper forms were attending St John's, they were taken each day in a van driven by one of the fathers. This saved on train fares and speeded up the travelling time a little though they were still out of the house for more than 10 hours each day. However, the van was too small, old and unreliable for regular journeys, so a small bus was hired from the Priory Motors Garage and later a coach from Glider Coaches. Eventually permission was obtained from the Provincial Treasurer to buy another vehicle, and in August 1963 a second-hand, worse-for-wear, 32-seater coach was bought to ferry the boys to their lessons and sporting venues. Although bigger, it was no more reliable than the previous vehicle until the ever-dependable Len Ponds replaced the engine with one from a written-off lorry. The boys tried to live down the embarrassment of travelling in it by maintaining it had classic qualities and remarking that 'they don't make them like that any more'.[152]

The boys settled very quickly at their new school and were energetically involved in as many school activities as time would allow. Many served as prefects over the years, following in the footsteps of Fathers Patrick Fitzgerald and Tony Maguire who had been school captains. The only challenge to their competing loyalties was when they were selected to play football or cricket for St John's against the Priory. This was occasionally the situation and until 1964 the Priory was the team of their choice, but otherwise they played for St John's. Besides sport, the only extra-curricular interest they pursued at Southsea was, after some training, preaching on the sea front. They were members of the Catholic Evidence Guild and spent many hours 'proclaiming to seagulls and a sizeable humorous crowd'.[153]

Public speaking, or 'speeches' as it was called, was part of the Priory English lessons. Individual pupils were required to speak on a subject of their own choosing. The subjects were as varied as 'Britain's Socialist Government' (the speaker being accused by the teacher of having the makings of a mob orator[154]), 'Mungo Park', 'La Belle France', and 'Westmorland Wrestling'. This, and the experience of public reading in the refectory, provided the self-confidence for standing up and speaking before an audience or congregation. It was particularly useful training for when students were exposed to public disputation at 'mercurials' at the College of Philosophy. Mercurials were Wednesday evening meetings in the lecture hall when a student would be required to present a thesis to the student body and staff and then defend himself against questions from the floor. It was debatable whether this was a more gruelling experience than standing on a soapbox on Southsea promenade dealing with questioning and humorous abuse from the public.

Golden Jubilee

1962 was the golden jubilee year of the foundation of the Priory. The ceremonies and celebration were arranged for Monday 16th July. Archbishop King, Bishop of Portsmouth, celebrated Pontifical High Mass on the lawn with Father Andrew Murphy (Provincial Superior), Father Bernard Duffy (Priory Superior) and Bishop Thomas Holland (Coadjutor Bishop of Portsmouth) assisting him; and an impressive sermon was preached by Father William Burridge. The Mass ended at 12 noon and lunch was served at 1pm in a marquee on the playing fields. After lunch there were speeches by Father Provincial and the Archbishop, Father Duffy read a letter from the Superior General, and John (later Judge) Baker QC, representing the old boys association, spoke on behalf of the former pupils. Several of the guests then left but many stayed behind and filled the gymnasium for a concert at 3.30pm. They were entertained with *Hiawatha's Wedding Feast* under the direction of Mr Heath and, after an interval, with a performance of *Box and Cox*. The celebrations ended with Solemn Benediction in the chapel at 7.45pm.

A special edition of *The Pelican* school magazine also marked the occasion. It was filled with contributions that reflected the happy relations between the staff and pupils, recalled joyful schooldays, and expressed confidence in the future. The future, however, was to be shorter than was enthusiastically envisaged.

9

'A Little Novitiate'

In 1918, the General Council, apparently defending the St Laurent school against possible closure by the government, declared that it was 'a little novitiate for the missions and not an ordinary secondary school'.[155] This pretty well defined what the Priory was. It was a seminary for preparing youths for an adult missionary life in Africa. It was also preparing them for many years of rigorous training that was required after their schooling and before final acceptance by the Society. Each of those years became progressively more difficult, intellectually, psychologically and physically, and it was at these later stages that the majority decided to pursue other callings.

Today, allowing a boy, maybe only 12 or 14 years old, to choose to live a quasi-monastic and, consequently, materially difficult life, may seem rash. But until comparatively recently this was the accepted age for boys to make such decisions and to pursue adult lives. It was usual for boys to join the Royal Navy and go to sea at the age of 12, and even earlier, many of them rising to very senior rank. One calls to mind immediately Horatio Nelson[156] and Francis Austen (Jane Austen's brother) who became Admiral of the Fleet.[157] Even King George V went to sea aboard a battleship at the age of 12. Boys started at the Royal Naval College Dartmouth at the age of 13 with no thought of university but only of going to sea. It was little different in the army with its boy soldiers, often expected to lead troops in early youth. General John Slessor, for example, was commissioned at the age of 16 in 1794, and his brother William embarked for India as a cadet aged 14.[158]

It was with a contemporary view of teenaged youths as young adults that the Council of Trent in 1563 proposed that boys could begin training for the priesthood at the age of 12, and as a result junior seminaries were established. This proposal in fact raised the starting age. In the early monastic schools boys started very young. The Venerable Bede, for example, entered a monastery at the age of seven[159], and boys entered Winchester College at the age of eight and a lot was expected of them: the third clause or rubric of the Founder's statutes laid down that all entrants, even at the age of eight, must have been already grounded in Plainsong as well as in reading Latin.[160]

The Priory was continuing a tradition of nearly 400 years, although its purpose and spirit were those of the White Fathers Society. This spirit was expressed in a circular letter of Lavigerie's dated the 11th November 1874.

> I beg you, my dear children, to temper your zeal with prudence, patience and charity ... I want to see you united together in one large family, having a true *esprit de corps* in the Christian sense of that expression ... You should be more than joined together, you should be one ... I have told you that I will never keep a single one of you who does not include in an equal love all members of the society, no matter to what nation they belong. Keep that brotherly affection – more than ever, if that be possible – in every danger, in every hardship, and in death itself.[161]

The boys, of course, were not members of the Society, which one entered as a novice after successfully completing philosophy studies, but they felt part of it with the same loyalties and ambitions. The sense of brotherly affection is strong in the Society and was fostered in the school, so that there was always a bond of mutual respect and affection between pupils and teachers. The Priory, consequently, provided more than schoolroom learning; it was a confraternity imbued with the Lavigerean spirit; it was spiritual, spartan, team-oriented, adventurous, brotherly and happy. The loner or introvert, no matter how clever, would not take to the way of life – 'the discipline of the common life' as it was called. The outgoing team player with little academic ability was more likely to be absorbed into it.

Lavigerie's letter of 1874 spoke of mutual support; another of his letters in 1875 addresses what lies in wait for the individual.

> No thought of gain or glory impels you. You will be without bread or shelter, you will die unknown to the world, perhaps under some terrible torture. This is all I can promise you. But you know, and it is all you need, who it is that can reward those who serve Him, according to their merits.[162]

The boys, even at an early age, were well aware that they were signing on for a difficult and challenging life, and this was an attraction in itself. Future adversities and vicissitudes were never minimised; on the contrary, the boys were reminded of them daily. They knew they were being trained for hardship. All were familiar with stories from the missions that included cultural changes, unappetising food, physical exhaustion, debilitating illness, the demands of celibacy, administrative difficulties, and violent death. All knew the story of Lavigerie writing 'endorsed for martyrdom' across the letter of a young priest applying to join the Society.

Writing in 1960 Father Patrick Fitzgerald, the Superior, reminds parents and others that the boys '... while infinitely blessed in having accepted a noble and austere ideal, [they] are nevertheless perfectly healthy and normal young men, who share the activities and interests of their contemporaries in the world.' He goes on to say '... So great is the emphasis on success in examinations today that ... vigilance is needed if first things are to keep their priority. With us those first things must clearly be the formation of character and the strengthening of a love for the missionary vocation ... A great deal of activity [must be] devoted to the spiritual, missionary formation of the students.'[149] He also said elsewhere 'We believe that the boys who have the idea that they want to become priests should be given the opportunity to test that deep and genuine desire – but there are no commitments on either side. If after three or four years they say 'this is not the life for me' – well, we look upon that as quite a normal feature of our life here.'[128]

Schoolwork

The education in terms of schoolwork was far from being in the premier league, although it came close to it in the late 1950s and the 1960s. The public examination results were in general very good, and by 1965 the school magazine was reporting 'outstanding academic successes'.[163]

Although university entrance level was the required prerequisite for further studies, a university education was not the aim. 'Formation', a word that appears continually in reports and instructions, was the primary purpose of the school – the development of holy, self-reliant and knowledgeable priests able to exercise their ministry in foreign and hostile circumstances. Prayer, work, learning and austerity were the basis of the education; the surrender of family life, home and native culture was the expectation. Higher studies, with continuing formation, were provided in the Society's own colleges by their own professors who had obtained doctorates or licentiates in philosophy, theology or canon law at Catholic universities abroad.

The course of studies, after the departure of the French pupils, was much the same as that in an English grammar school. However, the pupils on the whole did not think of themselves as schoolboys for, until they went to St John's, they never felt that they went to school. They rather saw themselves as young adults participating in training camp activities, some of which required attendance in a classroom.

From 1912 to 1952 there were five classes: Rudiments, Grammar, Syntax, Poetry and Rhetoric (the top class). The class names were based on the medieval university trivium ('three ways') of grammar, dialectic and rhetoric. The names were now simply identifiers, and were otherwise meaningless. Each class had its own room and master, but different teachers taught the different subjects. The system coped satisfactorily with the matriculation examinations but eventually had to give way to the English system of Forms I to VI with the introduction of A-level examinations in the 1950s. The original class names indicated not only their origin, but also the limitations of the curriculum. The education provided was 'classical' and related almost exclusively to the humanities. The principal subjects were English, Mathematics, Latin, French and History; a pass had to be achieved in all of these subjects to matriculate. Other subjects were Geography, Greek, Scripture and Biology, but no other science subjects. Physics and chemistry, for example, did not make an appearance until Father Moody introduced 'science' as a classroom subject in 1955, but by 1959 they were being taken at A-level. Any other subject had to be pursued as a hobby.

The number of subjects was very limited, but this was little different to many public schools. Even at Harrow the education was described as 'narrow, mundane and inept', its curriculum of classics being 'a device to regulate entry into a governing elite'.[164] But despite these apparent shortcomings it produced an impressive list of prime ministers, viceroys, generals, bishops, ambassadors and high court judges.

Some pupils had successfully taken the London University matriculation examinations prior to 1924, but the school curriculum had not been geared up for it. It was not until June 1924 that pupils, who had been prepared, were entered for the examination. Even then Bernard Brown and William Malone had to go home to take it, while William Brencher and James Smith went for four days to Southampton. Brown and Smith did particularly well with First Division passes. Thereafter the matriculation examinations were sat every year except for a period during the Second World War when the school was evacuated, and until the General Certificate of Education replaced them in 1952. Until 1954 the pupils had to travel to Portsmouth or Southampton or go home to take the public examinations, but in June 1954 the GCE examinations were taken for the first time in the Priory, which had been approved as an examination centre by London University.

Pupils who wished to go on to higher studies within the Society had always to make an application, but from June 1954 onwards, they were also required to sit an entrance examination for the College of Philosophy in addition to the public examinations. The suitability of the applicants was assessed by the staff council and references prepared. The Rector of the College of Philosophy reviewed their notes and conducted interviews with each of them, and it was not unusual for candidates to be refused or advised to reapply at a later date. In 1954, for example, four students were rejected, and in 1960 three were not accepted and two were advised to reapply later. Those that were advised to try again, often, but it must be said not always, took it as an indication that they were on the wrong track and went elsewhere. This rejection must have been a blow to a pupil who had spent several years working towards this moment. Rebuffs also occurred in the later stages of training: either outright rejection or advice to reapply later, so perhaps rejection at an early stage could be considered a benefit.

Clubs and Societies

Although the academic curriculum was restricted, the interests of the students were not, but any wider interests had to be pursued in the boys' own time.

The evening recreation period, especially on Sundays, was a time for societies, supervised by a priest or brother. The societies (sometimes called clubs or groups) varied over the years depending on the current interests of the boys and staff. They included, amongst others, debating, science, art, photographic processing, nature studies, and liturgy. Skills of a more practical nature were learnt by doing them; this included, as the need arose, painting and decorating, cooking, milking, vegetable gardening, woodwork and metalwork. In the mid to late 1950s, pupils were enthusiastic enough to attend evening woodwork classes in the local school and, in 1962, 15 of them cycled regularly to Swanmore Secondary School to attend Mr Gannon's woodwork classes. Metalwork was taught by Brother John Mennie and was put to practical use on at least one occasion by making a large metal frame to enable the tractor to tow a big roller for the sports fields.

As with most schoolboys there had always been an interest in animals, especially farm animals and birds. In 1947 a Naturalists' Club was formed. Bird-watching and ringing migratory birds was the initial interest, but the club soon took over the small orchard between the Boys' House and the farm, and filled it with small animals. Rabbits, white mice, guinea pigs, bantam hens, geese, ducks, squirrels, homing and wood pigeons, owls and kestrels appeared with bewildering rapidity.[165] From 1957 to 1961, the interest of the members was principally in breeding budgerigars.

The Debating Society always appealed to impassioned schoolboys who were prepared to set the world to rights and to give their strongly held views on important matters of the day including nuclear disarmament, immigration, and the Common Market. In 1960 the society became the Current Affairs Society giving it, maybe unintentionally, more of a political leaning. The political bias became more apparent when Sean Hughes joined the group and even more so when he became chairman. He introduced a House of Commons procedure and invariably represented Labour views in what was becoming a politically charged atmosphere.[149] He later arranged visits to the Houses of Parliament as guests of Prime Minister Harold Wilson whom he was to succeed as MP for the Huyton-Knowsley South constituency. At the same time the society's newsletter, *The Comment*, came in for some criticism for its Labour Party views especially as expressed in the editorial.[152] What was becoming a hot house of political argument, was restored to being a more general debating society with fewer politically contentious subjects in September 1964. In the reformed society, speakers' names were drawn out of a hat to support or oppose burial without a coffin, ambiguous smiles, and similar light-hearted subjects. If nothing else it introduced more fun into the proceedings.[163]

In the 1950s an Arts Society sprang up with fairly wide interests including painting, music, films and drama – especially French drama.[149] About the same time the Science Society made an appearance. Besides the usual programme of speakers on scientific topics, films and visits to industrial concerns, the members busied themselves with practical projects such as the construction of radios and photographic equipment.[149, 152]

The Liturgy Study Group was boosted by the Second Vatican Council, which provided more than enough material for study and debate and also seems to have prompted a change of name to the Society for Liturgical Renewal. All the students were encouraged to study the reports of the Council as they appeared. The reports were discussed by the Liturgical Renewal group and disputed in the Debating Society, the 'Progressives', who favoured the use of the vernacular, always being in the majority.[152, 163]

Music & Singing

Music was another subject that had to be pursued as an extra curricular activity. Learning to play a musical instrument depended entirely on the motivation of the individuals. Singing however was something the boys were immersed in. All were required to sing as an essential part of the liturgy, and this required an ability to read the music in the *Liber Usualis*, the *Westminster Hymnal*, other hymnals and sheet music for voices. There was thus a universal, if limited, acquaintance with musical notation. The boys were proud of their singing: plainchant, polyphonic, or popular. Every boy seemed able to sing. There must have been some who were tone deaf, but none that can be remembered. Journeys by coach were always spent singing, teams were supported from the sidelines by singing, and at Christmas and celebratory meal times, anybody could be called upon by popular acclaim to sing – this included the staff, who could all do their party pieces with funny songs and monologues. The Irish boys seemed to be given mostly to melancholy airs, the Scots to urban folk songs that were generally unknown, the Welsh to faintly recognised traditional melodies, and the English, reputedly from a nation without traditional songs, had their own large repertoire. French songs, learned mostly from the French Canadians, were popular with all, and so too were traditional student songs sung in Latin.

There was daily singing in the chapel even if it was only the hymn at night prayers, but often it was much more as required by the liturgy. Until the 1960s the Tridentine liturgy was the norm with its great sense of worship, reverence and solemnity. The religious ceremonies, conducted entirely in Latin, were always impressive. On Sundays and red letter days, during Holy Week and for funerals the full ritual was enacted with priest, deacon, sub-deacon, master of ceremonies, acolytes, choir, and the entire male congregation singing the plainchant Mass or office of the day. Everybody knelt, stood and sat in unison and with military timing controlled by the sound of a clapper in the hands of a second master of ceremonies at the back of the congregation. Nothing but the best was considered appropriate for the worship of God in the little chapel.

9.1. The chapel in 1946.

The music that accompanied the Latin prayers had been written with church and chapel spaces in mind, so that polyphony or plainchant resonated gently and beautifully and immersed the community in an atmosphere of prayer. It was not music to relax to, which unfortunately is the way commercialised versions are marketed today; the music fortified the words of the prayers directed to God as worship, love, and repentance. One of the hymnbooks had on its title page *Cantare bis Orare* (to sing is to pray twice); for the Priory boys this could well have read 'thrice'.

Their liturgical repertoire and singing ability were never recognised outside the school, except for one radio broadcast on the 11th July 1957. It was a Solemn High Mass that had been recorded two weeks earlier and it went out while the boys were on holiday. Mr John Heath was the organist, Father Hugh Monaghan the choirmaster, and Father Agnellus Andrews, OFM, was the producer.

Many boys could play the piano, the organ and, until about 1930, the violin. They seem to have been diligent pupils for many of them achieved a high level of expertise despite apparently few lessons. Efforts were made to provide regular piano and organ instruction but, except for Father Prentice, they depended entirely on the availability and generosity of lay people. Mr Arthur Gilbert, who lived in Winchester Road, Bishop's Waltham, gave lessons three days a week in 1918 and maybe for some years afterwards for in October 1920 the pupils gave a concert featuring piano and violins. Their fingering may have been affected on this occasion for they had spent the previous period harvesting mangel wurzels in the cold weather. Father Prentice, who was choirmaster from 1921 to 1924, gave piano lessons and maybe more for he staged musical concerts at which the pupils demonstrated their singing and instrumental abilities with the clarinet, violin and harmonium as well as the piano. It was another five years before further lessons are mentioned. In March 1929 Professor Guilbert was giving harmonium lessons to eight of the pupils on Tuesdays, Wednesdays and Thursdays. (It is probable that Mr Gilbert and Professor Guilbert were the same person, for the records, written in French, occasionally used French spellings for English names and vice versa. Gilbert/Guilbert may perhaps have been giving lessons continually from 1918 to the 1930s for Mr Arthur Gilbert was still living in Winchester Road in 1936.[166]) From 1959 to 1962 Mrs Doreen Heath, the wife of John Heath, gave piano lessons to small groups of pupils, and she was followed by Miss Wylie, organist at a nearby Anglican church, who gave organ lessons until about 1965.[145]

Entertainments

A play, musical show, concert or pantomime was presented at the end of each term and at other times whenever there was an opportunity. There was a big and usually ambitious production in July and a concert or pantomime on Christmas Day afternoon. The feast day of St Cecilia (the patron saint of music) on the 22nd November never passed without a musical concert, no matter how few boys were in the school. Shows generally veered towards the light-hearted, but the St Cecilia concerts were presented with more gravity and included choral, solo, and instrumental excerpts from such works as *The Messiah*, *St Matthew's Passion*, and *The Dream of Gerontius*. Parishioners and others were invited to most of these productions, but sometimes they were private affairs to entertain a distinguished visitor or for a special family occasion. Such an occasion was Father Travers' 50th birthday in November 1924, when he was entertained in the recreation hut with a concert of singing, monologues, recitations and 'orchestral music' with piano, two violins and clarinet.

Presumably the monologues at least were in English, but until this time visitors such as Voillard, who came in December 1920, were entertained entirely in French.

All these events were produced, directed and played by the boys, who also wrote many of the scripts and made the scenery and costumes. Some of the costumes were, at least on one occasion in 1951, cheekily borrowed when Jim Wallace went to a naval tailor's in Portsmouth and asked to borrow an admiral's and a captain's uniforms circa 1880 for a performance of *HMS Pinafore*. Surprisingly, the owner let him have them on condition that he and his wife received invitations to the performance.[167]

In July 1948 the first Gilbert and Sullivan opera – *The Mikado* was produced. It was one of the more ambitious shows staged at the school and was produced and directed by pupils John Baker and Jim Wallace. *The Pirates of Penzance* and *HMS Pinafore* followed in the next couple of years, and an even more ambitious *Mikado* was staged in 1951. The shows continued to be directed by Jim Wallace with musical direction by Mr John Heath and striking scenery painted by Michael Bolan. Each year the outstanding performances of the players attracted considerable attention in the local press and earned requests for further showings at the Priory and, in 1951, at Wickham. Full houses were assured with people coming from the surrounding area, friends and families from further afield, and coaches turning up from Portsmouth, Southampton and Dorking. But popularity was not the gauge used by the Father Provincial. In 1951, he expressed satisfaction at the cultural values of the operas and plays and felt that the pupils were well trained thereby in music and elocution, but he considered them sentimental and not very manly. Changes were therefore to be made in the coming year.[130] In 1952 and for several years afterwards plays and musicals were banished in favour of something more 'manly' and choral concerts became the norm. After the 1951 visitation, Mr Heath started his monthly 'gramophone concerts' in the evening recreation period after supper. The concert would include an analysis of, for example, the *Pastoral Symphony*, and a comparison with similar pieces of music. The staff could hardly believe that often 50 boys would turn up voluntarily in their recreation period to hear talks on, and music by composers such as Bach, Beethoven and Handel, and then ask for more. Listening to classical music continued to be encouraged especially by Father Garvey and Father Moreton; and in their time concert-going became popular, the pupils attending symphony concerts in Southampton, Portsmouth and Winchester. In the 1960s the Arts Society reintroduced gramophone concerts, but this time contemporary composers such as Gian Carlo Menotti were included.[145]

Plays were reintroduced in 1959 with *The Crucible*, followed by *Twelfth Night* and *Murder in the Cathedral*. The performances were of a high standard so that Father Fitzgerald was able to say after a performance of *The Crucible* at Christmas 1959 'If the quality of a school is reflected in its stage productions then the Priory's must surely be at the flood'.[168] An outsider's view came from Brother Bernard Mahon of St Mary's College, Bittterne. He had this to say about the 1965 Christmas play.

> The seasoned playgoer knows that where schoolboy dramatics are concerned he must often make extravagant concessions ... I made my way to the Priory and its rather small roll-call of pupils to sit in at their rendering of Jean Anouilh's difficult play *The Lark*. Recollection of other school productions, still wincingly remembered ... [but] one became suddenly involved. It was compelling drama ... Throughout, the production was bold in its simplicity ... Above all, of course, it was the way the actors interpreted their parts which made this a performance to remember ... a very distinguished performance. I liked the production immensely.[169]

The first film show in the school was on the 24th January 1929 when Mr Bob Symes of Bishop's Waltham set up his 'cinematographic apparatus' in the refectory to show examples of its potential. Bouniol and most of his staff were unable to see this exciting advance in technology because they were in bed with flu. Mr Symes came again on the 8th December and then on Mardi Gras every year until 1934, for a '*séance de projection*'. Some withdrawal symptoms must have been experienced after 1934 for in December 1936 Father Rijkers bought a 'Kodak cinematograph' in London and made his projectionist's debut on the 6th January with the film *Pickwick Papers*. When Father Burridge was the projectionist he would put his hand over the lens if he considered part of the film was showing too much flesh; this did not endear him to the boys.[102] During the war years and for a while afterwards the boys were subjected to Ministry of Information films – hardly entertainment, but they were probably free and provided a reason for being indoors on a wet evening. Films continued to be shown several times a year in the gymnasium and later in the new recreation hall.

The first recorded visit to a cinema since the French boys were at the school was on the 30th June 1932 when the pupils were allowed to see *Trader Horn*. But they must have been to the cinema in previous years for Brother Patrick recalls as a pupil going to see silent films in the Bishop's Waltham cinema where a pianist sat in a corner of the hall and played throughout the performance.[102] It was not until 1952 that permission was given to visit the cinema more than a couple of times a year, and then only to see films approved by the Superior.

A permanent television set was installed in November 1960, but viewing was strictly controlled; it was limited in general to news programmes and big sports events. Previously a television set had been borrowed to watch international football games.

One-day holidays usually meant sports, or camping, or 'outings'. Outings were group bicycle rides to places in Hampshire, Sussex or the Isle of Wight until 1951 when two coach outings were arranged. In March 1951 more than 30 pupils went on what seems to have been a whistle-stop marathon tour of London for 7s 6d each. In one day they managed to visit the House of Lords, the House of Commons, Westminster Abbey, a model railway exhibition at Central Hall, the Science Museum, Brompton Oratory, Westminster Cathedral and Madame Tussaud's. Heston provided them with a substantial lunch, and a late meal on the way home. All agreed that the lunch alone was worth much more than 7s 6d. A few months later there was another trip to London; this time to a single, but very large, venue – the Festival of Britain. Coach outings became fairly frequent, and a popular annual trip was to Wembley to see England playing in the schools international football competition. Other football matches that were often attended were the home games of Southampton FC. This support for the local professional team started in March 1914 with Father Coutu and the French boys. Hampshire Cricket Club was another team that had the regular support of the pupils.

The Pupils

No entrance examinations were required for entry to the school. An 'eleven-plus' examination pass, or equivalent, was expected, but a sound Catholic family background, a strong physical constitution, a reasonable level of intelligence, an expressed desire by the boy to be a missionary priest and the consent of his parents and teachers were the basic requirements. An interview with a peripatetic White Father from the promotions team and a letter written by the boy to the Superior explaining why he wished to be a missionary priest were used to judge the candidate. In the absence of any entrance testing and, for the most part, the lack of qualified teachers, it is surprising that so many did well in the public examinations. The small classes doubtless helped, but the untrained teachers would probably not have been acceptable to an inspector of state schools.

The boys were on the whole extremely fit – physical and mental robustness were prerequisites of entering and continuing at the school. Nearly all proved to be strong, and many were outstanding athletes. Physical condition was tested daily by the austere living conditions, manual work and sporting activities. Most were average learners; some were brilliantly academic. Tests in all academic subjects took place each month, and examinations at the end of each term decided whether a pupil would move to a higher class or not or move from St Columba's to the Priory.

In addition to the usual demands on a schoolboy, much importance was attached to the spiritual life, which included daily Mass, evening services, communal prayers, weekly confession, an annual three-day retreat conducted in silence, and a monthly retreat. When not studying or praying, the pupils were expected to be involved in some communal activity or doing manual work. Idleness, hanging around, wasting time was never an option. Nobody was allowed into the dormitory during the daytime, unless it was to clean it, or into the study hall during recreation periods. Even desultory reading was considered malingering.

Monthly 'notes' were written about each boy, and at the end of the academic year each pupil was assessed by the staff council on his academic progress, his health, and also on his 'conduct and manners' for which he received a rating ranging from 'fair' through 'good' and 'very good' to 'excellent'. Father Superior then interviewed the pupils over several days and gave them their 'remarks' (appraisals), and all was included in the school report that was sent to parents. Some of the boys were required to leave because of lack of academic achievement, some because of ill health, and a small number because of their conduct. Many of those that left early did so because they were advised, or became aware, that they did not have a vocation to be missionaries. Many went off to pursue secular lives and a good number entered other religious societies or studied for the secular priesthood.

The Teachers

All the teachers (or professors as they were known – retaining the French nomenclature until about 1960) had received higher education in philosophy and theology, some of them to the highest level; for example, Francis Walsh had a doctorate in philosophy and a doctorate in theology obtained at the Gregorian University in Rome. But it was not until the 1950s that staff started to appear regularly with British or Irish university degrees in secular subjects.

The teachers were fluent in French and Latin, and in one or more African languages if they had returned from the missions. Some knew classical Greek; others had an extensive knowledge of history and the English classics. Until the 1950s, their knowledge of mathematics, science, geography and other subjects was principally what had been retained from their own school days. Although many of them had studied pedagogy as a theoretical subject, none had been trained as teachers, although some attended the Institute of Education in London after graduation in the 1950s. They were aware of their shortcomings, but brought to the classroom enthusiasm, camaraderie and well-prepared lessons. Teaching schoolboys in England was not what they had trained all those years for, but they seldom appeared weary or bored with their lot, probably because they were never there long enough to suffer from ennui.

The problem of short-stay staff with sometimes little interest in teaching was not a new problem. At the Society's General Chapter of 1912, it was proposed that the school at St Laurent should be closed as it was not providing a good enough level of education, but this was out-voted. Instead it was decided to improve the school by raising the standard required of new entrants and of the staff. The new guidelines included 'putting stable and capable staff in place, and not sick missionaries or those in transit'.[5]

The guidelines carried over to the Priory, and for the years up to the start of World War II there were long serving superiors and a fairly stable teaching staff. The war, however, upset this equilibrium when staff and pupils were dispersed. Although the school came together again, the old problem of transient, sick, and insufficient qualified staff again occurred and was never fully resolved.

The turnover of teaching staff was rapid and would have been totally unacceptable in any other school. It could be expected that in the years a boy spent at the Priory the teaching staff would have changed completely. Some of the teachers were there for a term, others for a year, and very few for more than four years. Frenchmen, Canadians, Germans, Belgians and Dutchmen turned up on leave from Africa or to improve their English and were put to work teaching for the duration of their stay. To the boys this was the unremarkable norm; and it was always exciting to have men who were back from Africa – sometimes on sick leave – with their fascinating stories of lives in the bush and the desert. The boys also welcomed young newly ordained priests, usually waiting for their overseas appointments, for they could strengthen the class or house sports teams.

Even the superiors did not have long tenures. Fathers Travers and Bouniol served as rector for 12 and 11 years respectively, but these were exceptional terms of office. Father Smith served for six years (1937–43) and Father Moran for four (1947–51), but others held the position for only two or three years, Father Cassidy for just over a year, and Father Egan for less than eight months. Many of them were already serving on the staff, or had done so, before being promoted and so there was some sense of continuity. Others were brought in from elsewhere; for example, Patrick Donnelly (1951–53) had spent most of the previous ten years teaching theology, John Cassidy (1953–54) supervising university students at St Andrews, and John Egan (1954–55) teaching philosophy and being a novice master. Tom Moran (1947–51), although he had been at the school for a couple of years before being appointed Superior, had not been teaching but recovering from tuberculosis and remained an unwell man throughout his term of office. One questions the wisdom of these appointments, no doubt driven by expediency.

The priority of the Society was to put men where they should be – in Africa. The school was siphoning them off, as it were, for secondary duties. School staff jobs, although important, were usually a staging post for men on their way to somewhere else. It was nobody's inclination to wish them many years in office for it was the ambition of every White Father to be in Africa. These conflicting demands were an ongoing problem. It involved not only placing men as schoolmasters, but also as teachers in higher educational institutions. They all responded generously, but longed to be away. They seldom saw the fruits of the work they had begun whether it was preparing boys for university examinations or making a new tennis court. This situation was to lead eventually not only to closure of the Priory, but also of St Columba's, and of the colleges of philosophy and theology run by the Society in Britain.

Overall the academic level was not what it could have been, judging from the achievements of those who continued their studies elsewhere. Those who did particularly well, especially in the early years, seem to have been successful because of their innate ability rather than because of superior teaching. Besides the reluctance of most boys to learn anything, one of the drawbacks was that many of the staff, especially the foreign staff, were not familiar with the English education system or public examination requirements. Another was that some of the teachers were not sufficiently experienced in their subjects or they were not cut out for the job. This could put them at the mercy of the brighter boys. They themselves were aware of it and readily admitted that they learnt from some of their students.[170] Even at Greek, the boys could have the advantage. A pupil of the 1940s tells of how some of them were always ahead of the teacher and caused him much trouble for which one of them felt obliged to apologise when an adult.[171] When the teachers were experienced and knowledgeable the success rate was high. For example, Mr Daniel Williams and Father Alan Thompson could get their students through the A-level examinations in one year, and so could the staff at St John's. Father Murphy in the 1920s and Fathers Moody, Thompson, Fitzgerald, Garvey and Fowles in the 1950s and 1960s were noted for successfully getting all their students through the public examinations by proper preparation.

The first teacher to obtain a British degree was Father Thomas Keane who was awarded a BA by London University in June 1931 without apparently having attended any lectures there. He took the examinations within a year of arriving from North Africa and during most of that year he was teaching Latin, English and History. But it was not until the early 1950s that priests with British or Irish university degrees in secular subjects started to appear more regularly beginning with Father Francis Moody in 1953 (science degree from St Andrews). Those appointed to teaching posts were now generally, but not always, sent to a British university after ordination. This must have seemed a disappointment after seven years of higher studies and expecting to be sent to Africa and, in Francis Moody's case, having been interned in France for four years. Some came with a degree obtained prior to joining the Society. Such was Father Pierce English (engineering at University College Dublin) who, after many years in Africa, arrived in September 1959 to teach science. Others having taught for several years at the Priory went off to university. One of these was Father John Fowles who obtained his Bachelor of Science degree after having taught physics for six years to A-level and having set up a school laboratory with second-hand equipment. In the late 1950s the teachers were appearing with MAs starting with John O'Donohue in 1958, followed by Brian Garvey and Frank Nolan who collected theirs from Oxford in 1965, having also studied at the Institute of Education. The formal academic qualifications would of course be useful for teaching in the missions, but teaching, even in Africa, was not the primary purpose of the Society. It did set up, staff and administer many secondary and higher educational establishments, but being a missionary and not a teaching society, it could not supply a continuous stream of qualified teachers in Africa any more than it could in Britain. Local people or teaching congregations were expected to take over once the pioneering phase had been completed.

Lay Teachers

The shortage of available White Fathers to teach – sometimes nobody being available – required the superiors over the years to look for laymen or other clerics to provide assistance. Qualified lay teachers were welcome, but the reality was that they could not be paid a salary to match their skills. Professional teachers understandably did not come cheap, and the Society could not even afford cheap, so when some very talented people provided teaching assistance it was out of kindness, for they received a very small remuneration or none at all. Many gave generously of their time and talent, and none more so than Mr John Heath.

John Enos Heath was not so much a teacher as musician almost-in-residence. He was director of music, choirmaster, organist and musical coach. He lived with his wife at Coppice Hill House in Bishop's Waltham and generously gave a huge amount of his free time to the school for 17 years. He was a manager of an animal food processing company by profession, but a gifted musician and choirmaster by nature. His musical talents he put entirely at the disposal of the school with no material reward. From 1946 to 1963 he formed, rehearsed, produced and conducted choirs, concerts and musical entertainments, sacred and secular. His rehearsals in the early years were particularly remembered when he would be seen playing the

9.2. Mr John Heath, Director of Music 1946–63.

piano, conducting and singing all at the same time with a cigarette permanently stuck to his upper lip. He also played the organ at High Mass on most Sundays and always for big occasions. He and his wife had their own personal grand pianos in the drawing room of their home, but they must have had little time to play together for he spent so much of his time, including Sunday mornings, at the school. The plainchant singing was organised and conducted by the Father Choirmaster, and he or Mr Heath tested all new boys for their singing ability, and those with the required talent were drafted immediately into the choir. In July 1961 he and his wife were deeply touched when a special celebration was arranged for their wedding anniversary at the Priory. The boys were given a day's holiday, and there was High Mass in the morning followed by a festive lunch, speeches and presentation of gifts. Mr and Mrs Heath moved to Twyford in 1959, but John continued with his musical work at the school often staying overnight, especially for the Holy Week services and Easter vigil. He retired after years of unparalleled zeal and devotion in July 1963.[172] The pupils and staff held him in the highest esteem and affection, and in June 1965 when the old boys association held a reunion at the Priory he was made an honorary member. He died in February 1987, aged 79, and was buried in the Twyford parish churchyard.

The Brothers

The school could not have been established, nor could it have survived the early days without the brothers.

The brothers are non-ordained members of the Society who apply themselves to aspects of work that a priest with his preaching, teaching, and sacramental role would not have the skills or the time for. Although not teachers in the academic sense (there were exceptions), the brothers were teachers by example. They were hardworking, holy, often jovial men. To the boys they were a kindlier species than the priests; they were not taskmasters, not examiners, not disciplinarians, not preachers, not demanding. They were the mainstay of the place, always there, working hard, praying fervently, sharing jokes with the boys, respected by the fathers and admired by all who knew them.

The first brother assigned to the Priory was Brother Camille (François Viel) who was nominated by the Mother House to purchase the place together with Fathers Travers, Chollet, Coutu and Falquières.[173]In the event neither his name nor Coutu's appeared on the deed of purchase, but both were amongst the group that first occupied the house. The other brothers in this group were Jean, Max and Egbert.[174] Aubert joined them in 1913. It was these brothers who with their own hands made the three beautiful altars and pews for the chapel, produced furniture for classrooms, study hall, refectory and Fathers' House, and established a farm. Thereafter three brothers were assigned to run the farm and maintain the property, although others came from time to time for short periods.

Different teachers influenced the boys in different ways, and many were remembered with fondness. But there were three men for whom there was universal admiration and affection. They were the long-serving Aubert, Modeste and Patrick. These brothers became almost part of the school fabric; they were known to generations of boys and left a lasting impression of goodness, hard work and devotion with all who knew them. Aubert and Modeste went about their daily duties without fuss or bother, always ready for a joke with the boys. In temperament they were very dissimilar, for Modeste was inclined to be serious whereas Aubert pretended that nothing was to be taken seriously, himself least of all. Patrick was big, jovial, and a dynamo who never seemed to stop.

9.3. Brothers Aubert and Modeste.

They were humble and self-effacing, but humility did not prevent Aubert from having a keen eye for a young quality animal that he would buy to rear as prime beef, or from having the respect of those who knew him. He used to go to the local cattle markets, especially the Bishop's Waltham livestock sales where he was well known and liked. Despite his retiring disposition, his kindly features and gentle humour attracted people to him. He was always greeted at the sales with shouts of 'Hello Brother!' One of the farmers was once heard to say: 'Bloody parsons! I ain't got time for them. When I be a-dying I'll send to the Priory for Brother Albert!'[102] Aubert was 'temporarily' appointed in 1913, but it was to be where he passed all his missionary life. Brother Patrick recalls that 'It was he who began our modest farm; he erected the various sheds for the accommodation of the livestock, the hay barn, the grain store and the once famous slaughter house.'[175] The author remembers when the frail, sandy-bearded Aubert was confined to his bed just prior to his death in 1950, and it was then discovered that his mattress was filled with stones. He tried to imitate his Saviour even in his suffering. He died on the 28th June 1950 in hospital at Winchester. That evening the local policeman, Police Constable Smith, came to take a statement about what appeared to be a suspicious death. It turned out that a few days before, Aubert, by now deaf and blind, had taken phenobarbitone tablets thinking they were soda mints, both having been prescribed by the doctor. He passed into a coma and never recovered consciousness. Father Tolmie said the Requiem Mass in the absence of Father Moran (the Superior), and Father Howell conducted the funeral service. Unusually for a humble religious brother many local people and farming friends attended the funeral.

Modeste was a thick set man with a powerful chest and a fine square cut beard. His sojourn at the Priory was not entirely uninterrupted. He went to Maison Carrée in March 1921 and returned in April 1923. In 1931 he joined Fathers Francis Walsh and Balthazar Drost to form a community in Scotland. They rented a house in Melrose to promote the White Fathers and to explore the possibility of a foundation. A site was found at Newtown St Boswells, Roxburghshire, in 1934. The small community moved into the farmhouse on the site, and then established a postulancy for aspirant brothers who were set to work on the site for a new college. The foundation stone of St Columba's College was laid in 1935, and Modeste, the postulant brothers and, later, a group of German brothers set about building the college which opened in 1936. Modeste then returned to the Priory, where he remained until his death. He celebrated his golden jubilee as a brother on the 2nd November 1954 and died on the 22nd February 1956 aged 83. Father Patrick Fitzgerald recalls the circumstances of his death. 'It was a bitterly cold month and Moddy was in bed with pneumonia. He heard that it was freezing outside and he became worried about his precious bottles of 'beer' in his hut. Unknown to any of us he slipped out and went to the hut where he spent some time in freezing cold temperatures. This worsened his condition and he died a couple of days later.'[176] He was buried on Saturday the 25th February after a Solemn Requiem Mass said by the Very Reverend Father Côté.

Patrick, the youngest of the trio of brothers and a big powerfully built man, is especially remembered calling in the cows for milking each evening, and for the times spent working with him haymaking, potato picking, milking, clearing fields of flint stones, felling trees and fencing the pasture. He now lives in Ireland where he continues as an active member of the community although nearly 90 years of age. He travels the length and breadth of the country collecting funds for the African missions and still finds time to run a small engineering workshop and keep bees.

9.4. Brother Patrick in later life.

Postulant Brothers

The arrival in April 1918 of Samuel Rogerson, who wished to be a missionary brother rather than a priest, marked the start of a brothers' postulancy, that is, a probationary period before being accepted for the brothers' two-year novitiate. The postulants were instructed separately from the other pupils, but they attended some classes in French and Latin. Thirty prospective brothers were accepted between 1918 and 1935 when those that remained were transferred to Newtown St Boswells in Scotland. In September 1941 four postulant brothers who were at St Boswells came to the Priory because of their cramped living conditions and were able to provide much needed help on the farm and in the kitchen for 12 months. They moved in September 1942 to a new house at Sutton Coldfield near Birmingham. Six other pupils decided to train as brothers and went directly to the novitiate.

From January to July 1923 Arthur Herbert Johnson, a convert, was a postulant brother. In the July he went to Maison Carrée to enter the brothers' novitiate, but did not complete it, and returned in early 1924 retaining his religious name of Brother Alban. He joined the staff as a Brother Oblate following a simplified religious rule, but not being a member of a religious congregation. He left in June 1926, but what he did was not specified.

Domestic Staff

The brothers did the cooking until the beginning of 1918 when a male cook with the Christian name of Clement took over. In April 1919 Mrs Cooper, known as Ma Cooper, was engaged to run the kitchen. She retired in 1933 and then received a pint of milk a day from the farm in appreciation of her services.[177] A long line of local people who looked after the kitchen followed her. But, generally, the cooks and their assistants seldom stayed for long, and there were intervals when domestic staff was not available and the brothers again attended to the kitchen duties. This was particularly true from 1940 until the mid-1950s when there was a lot of coming and going, and some cooks tended to leave abruptly. In May 1941, for example, Mrs Butler, the widow of a dentist, whose son lived with the students, departed suddenly with her son in May 1941, and Mr Tilbury took over for a few months.

From September 1941 to September 1942 the postulant brothers from Newtown St Boswell's did the cooking, then Brother Cuthbert was borrowed from Scotland until January 1943. He was followed by Brother Terence from Algiers until July when Mrs Rodgers took over. In January and February 1944, when nobody else was available, Father Kingseller did the cooking; and in 1948 when Mrs Brewer suddenly left leaving a note saying she was not coming back, Mrs Rodgers returned.

Mrs Norah Rodgers was an exception to the short-stay staff for she remained, with some breaks, for 18 years. She lived with her family in 'the bungalow' (a former First World War army hut acquired by Bouniol) next to the coach house. Her daughter Patricia, who was born there, had the honour of being the only child born at the Priory during the White Fathers' occupation. (It is also worthy of remark that the father of Mrs Rodgers, Thomas Byrne, won the Victoria Cross at the Battle of Khartoum in 1898, and her husband, Arthur, was awarded the British Empire Medal for bomb disposal work.[178]) When Mrs Rodgers was required to spend time looking after the common rooms and the oratory in the Father's House at the start of 1955, her sister, Mrs Lilian Smith, a professional cook, took over the kitchen. She remained (with a two-year break) until December 1961 when she left to join her family in Australia. Mrs Smith and her children occupied the 'bungalow' vacated by the Rodgers family. All the ladies on the domestic staff were considered 'more friends and helpers to the fathers, brothers and boys than employees'.[179]

Mr Wheeler, affectionately known as 'Pop', was the unofficial catering manager, recruiting occasional staff and looking after the refectory in the late 1930s and for some years after 1945.

Len Pond was the general handyman and mechanic in the 1950s and 1960s after the departure of the brothers. He could turn his hand to most things: changing the engine in the school bus, repairing the central heating, driving the fathers by car to London, or painting the vast exterior of the wooden gymnasium.

The School Year

The school year started in September with a three-day retreat given by a priest from outside the community. The quality of the preachers, whose talks were the focal points of each day, varied from the boring to the uplifting and motivating with no punches pulled. Besides the usual prayer times, daily Mass and evening services, there were additional periods of prayer, meditation, reflection, examination of conscience, confession and spiritual reading. Except for two periods of recreation each day, the entire time, including manual work periods, was spent in silence. For the adolescent boy walking into the school for the first time, this was the short sharp basic training he was hit with. It was a taste of what was expected of him. It was demanding, but the boys were stimulated and encouraged to what now seems like heroic levels of virtue. Despite this sudden immersion, there were never any dropouts at this stage except for one boy who left after five days in September 1964. There was also a monthly half-day retreat given by one of the staff, which usually finished with a preparation for death. One boy recorded in his 1951 diary a particularly memorable monthly retreat that was devoted entirely to 'Death'. He remembers it to this day with a certain fascination.[154]

The first term finished on Boxing Day, 26th December. Christmas Day was spent at school until 1958, so that the full solemn liturgy could be celebrated. It was a marvellous festival, everywhere warm, brightly lit, cleaned, polished and decorated. Christmas Eve was spent in preparation and then about 11 o'clock at night began the liturgy leading up to the highlight of the occasion: sung Solemn High Mass at midnight. The ambience appeared golden: the vestments, the candlelight, the shining brasses, the reflecting polished floor and furniture – all contributed to the aureate glow. The splendour of the little chapel became immediately charged as the first plainchant phrases of the Introit rolled out and were taken up by the whole community: '*Dominus dixit ad me: Filius meus es tu, ego hodie genui te*'. ('The Lord said to me: Thou art my son, this day have I begotten thee.' Ps 2, 7.) The Mass was followed by carols, then a party meal and singsong in the refectory. High spirits, laughter, jollity, brotherliness and a general amiableness marked the occasion. To bed about 3am, then up early for the ceremonies of Christmas Day, followed by a concert in the afternoon. Boxing Day was spent travelling home for the holidays.

From 1918 the pupils could spend their Christmas holidays at home, though not all chose to do so. A surprisingly large number, every year until 1950, preferred to remain in the school. Often more than half stayed behind in the 1920s and 1930s, and the school captain with a group of the boys would visit the Fathers'

House to wish the staff a happy New Year. In December–January 1933–34 an astonishing 40 boys out of a total of 65 decided to spend their vacation at the school, and in 1934–35 37 boys out of 67 stayed at the school. It was not until 1938 that more than half went home regularly for the Christmas vacation, and from 1950 to 1958 between six and twelve each year still chose the school to home. Those that remained behind often spent time with the brothers working on the farm and helping the fathers to repaint classrooms and hallways. It is perhaps indicative that the school was more home to them than their family homes where they would lack compatible companions and outlets for their energy, and perhaps find themselves beset by boredom and frustration.

From 1958 the boys left for home on the 22nd December, rising at 4.15am as was usual on these occasions, so that they could spend Christmas Day with their families. This was thought a good idea by staff and parents, but according to the school magazine the boys were not so enthusiastic for they were denied a very jolly time.[139] The only other years the pupils had left for home before Christmas Day were 1918, 1919 and 1920.

The spring term, which started in January, also finished on a high note – Easter Sunday. The preceding Holy Week was observed with all due solemnity, including fasting (but not for the boys) and abstinence from meat and Modeste's 'beer'. The religious vestments were purple, the statues were draped in purple, and the general mood was purple. All of which made Holy Saturday and especially Easter Sunday so much the brighter and more welcome. A short holiday period followed and was spent in the school. The school rule still applied during the Easter break: rising and lights-out times remained the same, daily Mass and other religious duties were adhered to, and so was the grand silence. However, there were no classes or manual work, so the days were completely free for outings or other recreational activities.

The summer term was also the cricket season, which seemed to introduce a slower tempo into school life until the annual sports day. The only blots on the horizon were the end of year school examinations and the university entrance examinations. After these testing periods, the senior boys went camping and farm working for two weeks until the end of term in mid-July. They spent their time about three miles away under canvas at Galley Down. They did all their own cooking and although the food was plentiful, Brother Patrick, who joined the boys for meals, considered the cooks were not always up to scratch.[102] However, the Jubilee Inn was always available, but mostly for liquid refreshment to which, surprisingly, a blind eye was turned by the staff. During the evenings there would be music, songs and stories around the campfire after Patrick had roared off on his tractor to the Priory.

After a holiday at home, those that had completed the matriculation or school certificate examinations departed in August for the College of Philosophy. Until 1924 they went to Kerlois at Hennebont in France, except for an experimental period of one year in 1920–21, which was spent at the Priory. From 1924 until the outbreak of war in 1939, they went to St Mary's at Autreppe in Hainault, a French-speaking area of Belgium. The war prevented travel out of the UK after the departure of the group in 1939, and the farmhouse at St Columba's was hurriedly requisitioned for the philosophers, then Rossington Hall in Yorkshire from 1944 to 1948. From 1948 to 1955 philosophy was taught at Broome Hall, near Dorking in Surrey, and from 1955 to 1971 at St Augustine's, Blacklion in County Cavan.

Daily Routine

The sleeping accommodation was one long dormitory almost the length of the building. The beds were simple iron bedsteads acquired at army surplus auctions. Beside each bed was a locker four feet high and in this was stowed all that one was allowed to possess other than schoolroom materials that were kept in a personal desk in the study hall. Nobody ever complained of lack of space. At one end of the dormitory was a cubicle occupied by a duty member of staff. He would come to bed much later than the boys, and either he or another member of staff would wake the boys in the morning by walking up and down the dormitory clapping his hands or banging his breviary and calling out '*Benedicamus Domino*' to which the boys were required to reply '*Deo Gratias*', in as heartfelt a manner as they could blearily manage, and thus prove they were awake.

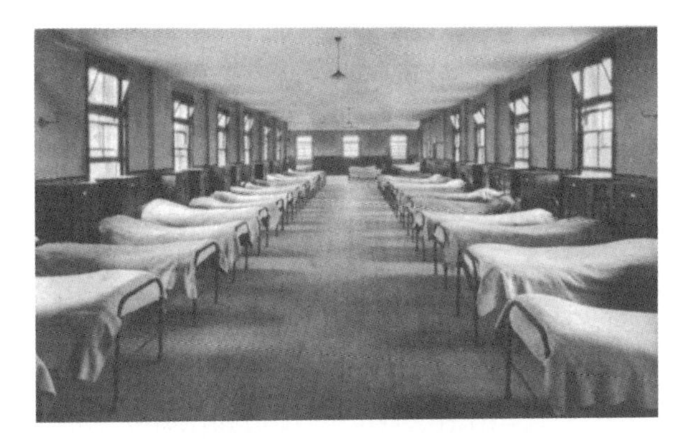

9.5. The dormitory in 1946.

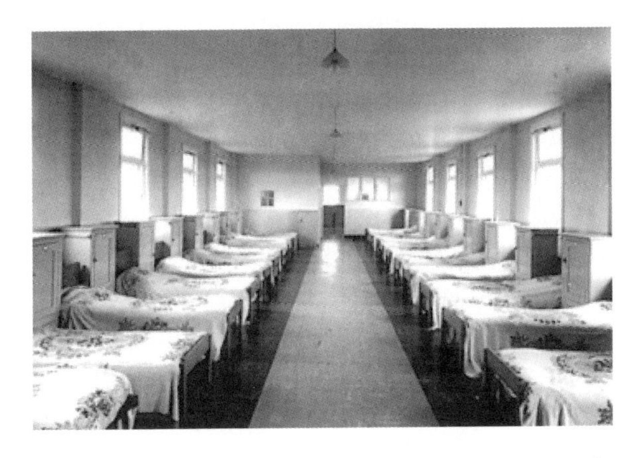

9.6. The dormitory in 1961. Still no curtains on the windows.

The winter cold was the most memorable part of those early mornings. There was central heating, but often the boiler had not been fired up long enough or the procurator thought that the temperature was not low enough to turn on the heating. The bare floor and the absence of curtains or blinds on the windows were no help in conserving the warmth even when it was available.

The first morning duty, after bedside prayers, was to dash to the 'lavabo' (washroom) with towel and toilet bag to attend to what were known as ablutions. Until 1960 there was only cold water available, which was a trial for those that shaved. After dressing, beds were made and, still in silence, everybody would go to the chapel for morning prayers. The rising time moved in stages from 5am in 1912 to 6.45am in 1946. Until 1946 the pupils had a period of study after morning prayers, followed by Mass. After Mass there was breakfast, usually at 8.30am, where the Father-in-Charge stood at the door of the refectory inspecting personal appearance. Unpolished shoes, badly combed hair, or deranged clothing resulted in a miscreant being sent back to the dormitory two floors away to put things right with the risk of missing at least part of breakfast. It was all done in good humour. It was at breakfast that talking could be resumed after the long silence. After breakfast there was a short break to collect books from personal desks in the study hall and go to the appropriate classroom for the first lesson of the day at 9am.

There was a fifteen-minute break at 11am without snacks of any sort, then lessons resumed until 1pm when lunch was served. Afterwards there was a recreation period followed by a half hour of manual work, then tea. After tea there was a long study period in the study hall until the evening service and spiritual reading, which were followed by supper and recreation before night prayers at 9.15pm or 9.30pm in the summer. The top form had a half hour of additional study after night prayers. Every Wednesday and Saturday there were classes in the mornings and study in the evening but the whole afternoon was free for sports, cross-country runs or long walks. In 1957, Wednesday evening studies were brought forward to the afternoon, and the recreation period was after tea; Saturday manual work was transferred to an earlier time in the afternoon leaving the rest of the day free.

On Sundays there was an hour of letter writing between breakfast and High Mass in the morning and another hour of letter writing or reading in the evening before compline, benediction, rosary, and spiritual reading. Until 1948 there was a lesson and a period of revision between the end of High Mass and lunch.

Very early on, even before the school opened, the Superior was instructed by the Superior General's council to give a *lecture spirituelle* in the evenings that would encourage the boys 'as good students, serious Christians and apostles'.[36] This *lecture*, known as 'Spiritual Reading', was given every evening in the chapel to all the pupils. It was a mix of short homily, briefing, advice, exhortations, warnings, information and news. It included subjects from the sublime to the mundane, from the thoughts of St John of the Cross to the results of an international game played that day at Wembley, from attitudes for meditation to the monthly house points tables. For the boys it was principally a welcome channel of information. It was almost the only means of discovering what was about to happen in the school and what was happening outside it; there was no radio until the 1950s – and then only for evening recreation, and no newspapers were available until the 1960s. It could be considered in today's emotive terms as a closed environment with controlled access to the media. It was indeed a semi-closed community, that was what it was intended to be, and in the thinking of the time not dissimilar to other organisations of the period. There is no record or indication of any boy or parent ever complaining about this situation. It was what they signed on for and were happy to trust the methods of their mentors; they were free to leave whenever they wished and many did so.

9.7. The study hall in 1961.

At night prayers, the hymn *Sancta Maria, succurre miseris* was sung. This beautiful prayer, beseeching the intercession of the Mother of God, with its lovely melody and sung by male voices in an echoing dimly lit chapel was supernal. It seemed like a staged performance. It was quiet and dark outside; the lights were dim because of the economy low wattage electric bulbs, and the red sanctuary oil lamp glowed softly, barely illuminating the white altar cloth with the words *Deus adest et vocat te* (God is here and is calling you) in a large red script across the front of it. The echoing sound was helped by the chapel being half empty (the part allocated for parishioners being unoccupied), and the rich vibrant resonance was created by the voices of the entire community rising in unison. In the mid-1950s the lighting was improved, but many of the lights remained switched off during night prayers.

Meals

The main meals of the day were *diner* at midday and *souper* in the evening. These words continued to be used even when the entire staff was English-speaking. Inevitably they were eventually pronounced 'dinner' and 'supper' before becoming lunch and supper in the 1950s. All meals were taken in the refectory. Lunch and supper were community meals at which all staff and pupils were present. At breakfast and afternoon tea only the Father-in-Charge sat at the high table, the other members of staff taking these meals, if at all, on the hoof. Because the fathers and especially the brothers took these meals at very irregular times, part of covered quadrangle, with access from the Fathers' House, was partitioned off in April 1949 to form a staff dining room for breakfast and tea.

The refectory furniture comprised a long table for the staff and, at right angles but well separated from it, several 12-foot (four metre) long tables each of which accommodated twelve pupils. The tables all had scrubbed deal surfaces. The staff sat on chairs, the pupils on long benches the same length as the tables. There was a tendency for at least one of the benches to fall over with a deafening thud on the bare boards as the boys stood up at the end of a meal. In 1950, as a concession to modern living, the tables were sawn in half to seat six pupils. The tabletops were covered with pale yellow wipe-clean plastic, which certainly reduced the manual labour required to clean them, and the benches were replaced by tubular steel-framed chairs, putting an end to the always unexpected heart-stopping thuds of toppled benches. Places at each table were assigned at the start of each term, maintaining a mix of classes and ages. This changed in 1959 when boys sat at table with others of their own age group.

Grace was said standing, before and after every meal, often in Latin. After the pre-prandial grace at community meals all sat still and in silence while a few verses from the gospel were read aloud by one of the boys standing at a lectern. Another book was then taken up and read, and the meal was eaten in continuing silence. A passage was read from these books each day, and one rather looked forward to the next episode. They included such titles as *The Life of Miguel Pro*, priest and martyr in Mexico, *The Kon-Tiki Expedition* by Thor Heyerdahl, and *The Ascent of Everest* by Sir John Hunt. The readers changed half way through the meal so that one could hurriedly eat while the other read. The end of the meal was signalled by the Superior pressing a desk bell in front of him. The reader then changed to reading a verse or two from *The Imitation of Christ*, then all stood for grace. The bell was something one did not want to hear during a meal because it usually meant that the Superior's eagle eye had spotted some offending boy who would then be chastised publicly.

On Sundays, feast days and other special days, the Superior, or Father-in-Charge, would announce *Deo Gratias* after the gospel reading. This was the signal that talking during the meal may take place.

The Imitation of Christ was listened to every day, so that it became as familiar as the gospel narratives, and many of its verses could be repeated by heart: 'He that followeth Me, walketh not in darkness, saith the Lord. These are the words of Christ ... Let it then be our chief study to meditate on the life of Jesus Christ'; 'I would rather feel compunction than know how to define it'; 'What doth it profit thee to dispute about the Trinity if thou be displeasing to the Trinity?' These and similar sentiments influenced the lives of many, and the book itself continues, if not as the daily reading, then as the frequent recourse of a good number of former pupils.

After a community meal the fathers and brothers processed in single file from the top table to the chapel reciting Psalm 51 aloud in Latin, '*Miserere mei, Deus, secundum magnam misericordiam tuam ...*'

('Have mercy on me, O God, according to your loving kindness ...') In the chapel the names of deceased members of the Society whose anniversary occurred on that day would be read out and prayers said for the repose of their souls.

A boy from each table brought the meal from the dumb waiter to his table, and the diners then helped themselves. At the end of a meal the dishes were piled at the end of the table ready to be collected and returned to the kitchen below on the dumb waiter. On Sundays and public holidays when the kitchen staff had time off, the dishes were returned to the scullery where they were washed by a team of boys.

The meals were described in the school prospectus as being 'plain but substantial'. That was fairly accurate. Sugar and condiments, except for salt, must have been considered extravagances for they never appeared on the table. The daily bowl of porridge was flavoured with a liberal sprinkling of salt, and tea came in very large brown enamelled pots with milk and sugar already added. There was always plenty of soup, vegetables, potatoes and bread, but butter or margarine was minimal and had to be divided accurately from a small block by one of the boys at the table. Accuracy was guaranteed; the boy who did the dividing took his share last. Nothing was to be wasted and nothing taken for granted. The meat allowance was reasonable, and fish was always provided on Fridays and days of abstinence. Puddings were the usual English school fare: semolina, tapioca, steamed pudding, and something known as 'dead baby' the constituents of which nobody ever discovered. Apples from the orchard, sometimes pears, but hardly any other fruit, appeared regularly. In the absence of margarine or anything else to spread on bread, apple sandwiches were regularly made. Hungry boys were even known to spread salted mashed potato on their bread. For many years individual pasties containing mincemeat were served on Wednesdays. These were so popular that they were the currency of wagers.

A bet could range from half a pasty to a large number of them so that a loser could go all term without the main part of his Wednesday midday meal. As well as obvious betting on sports results, many were placed on 'dares'. One, the author recalls, required boys to jump from an upper floor classroom window on to the path below; another dared three boys to have their heads closely shaved so that they appeared bald. The dares usually took place unknown to the staff, but the head-shaving could not but be noticed by all. The bald boys won lots of pasties, but they were banned for a term from leaving the school premises, and so too was the barber who presumably received a percentage of the pasties. In the 1960s 'Arctic roll' (ice cream inside a roll of cake) appeared once a week at supper. This was the boys' favourite pudding, and was the new currency for wagers. During Lent it disappeared from the menu, thereby curbing the appetites for food and danger.

Sweets were seldom ever eaten. They were not available on the premises until 1947 and then were only available with ration coupons. On the rare occasions when sweets were bought during the ration period, the deal was that British boys supplied the sweet coupons and the Irish boys provided the money. The wartime rationing of sugar remained in force until 1953. Sweets, writing materials, shoe polish, and similar items were all bought at 'The Shop', which was a room in a corrugated iron hut near the quadrangle and, later, in a room in the Boys' House. It was open on Sundays for a couple of hours and occasionally at other times. It was run in the early days by one of the fathers, but from 1943 one of the boys was appointed to that particularly attractive duty. Any profits went towards the purchase of sports equipment.

During the food-rationing period the boys had to surrender their ration books to the procurator so that he could feed them, and when at home on holiday each had to apply for an emergency ration card in his home town by applying personally with his National Registration Identity Card, the first of which were issued on the 29th September 1939 and the last in February 1952. The identity number on the card became additionally important in the late 1940s when it became a person's National Health number and had to be produced to obtain treatment. Mid-May was the time for boys to complete the forms for new ration books. More foodstuffs were rationed after the war than during it, bread being one of them, and rationing did not finally end until 1954. The scarcity of food affected everybody, so it was not an unusual burden for the boys to have little bread at this time. Potatoes tended to make up the shortfall, which was just as well for the procurator only had one shilling and seven pence per day to feed each boy in 1950.

Meals improved from 1955 onwards. The wartime and post-wartime austerity periods had passed. A greater variety of food was purchased to relieve the home farm's excellent but monotonous provisions, and the cooks were able to produce appetising food and more of it. The school diary remarked in 1955 that 'there is a vast improvement in the food: in quality and quantity. The standard has never been higher.'[180] In 1962 there was a reference to food being left after meals: 'Ten years ago that would have been unthinkable'.[181]

On Wednesdays, Sundays and feast days 'beer' was served with the meal; a 75cl bottle between six. It was known as 'Moddy's beer', being a cider produced by Brother Modeste in what he called his 'factory' – a long hut where he kept all his apples in serried ranks on slatted shelves. He maintained that his beer was made from ash leaves, and nobody was ever able to disprove this remarkable claim.

The meals that were enjoyed most of all, were those that were cooked by the boys themselves when they went camping, which is what they invariably did whenever a day's holiday was declared. On these occasions groups of about half a dozen boys were formed and each group was given all the raw ingredients of what they would otherwise consume in the refectory that day. This could be supplemented by snaring rabbits at the campsite. This proved dangerous on one occasion in 1952. When the boy went to the wire trap, the animal in it was still alive and snapped at him taking a piece out of his Wellington boot which, fortunately, he was wearing. He had caught a wildcat.[182]

Discipline

A German university professor, Dr Schmidlin, writing in 1913 said, referring to the White Fathers,

> These missionary priests who dress like wandering Arabs have a compact organisation, and an almost military discipline. Steeled

> and hardened by long years of systematic training, they attain a high degree of personal self-control, which enables them to acquire an amazing influence with the desert Arabs ... Their society is as remarkable for its elasticity as it is for initiative and motive power ... In the union of external activity with thoroughness in spiritual matters lies the secret of their success.[161]

This training started as soon as an aspirant entered a White Fathers' establishment, whether as man or boy. Understanding the purpose of the training and the long time it would take (seven to nine years after the Priory) were made abundantly clear. The discipline was a combination of monastic school tradition and outward-bound training. Learning, prayer, manual work, sports, timeliness, acceptance of regulations, smart appearance, few possessions, properly made beds, tidy lockers, cleanliness, inspections, camping, team spirit, walking long distances, and self-reliance, all within a mitigated version of the Society's rule, imposed a military cadet style of discipline.

Many of those who later served in the military found no hardship in the demands of service life; on the contrary, it was in many ways easier and more comfortable. The food was generally better, the accommodation was superior, the physical demands were no greater, obedience to the most demanding orders was a normal way of life, lack of entertainment was not noticed, absence from family and friends was the norm, and facing death was something the boys had always been exhorted to prepare for. Even those who served in the British Parachute Regiment and the United States Marine Corps, saw their service as a continuation of school life with added benefits. 'I spent most of my time with the marines who reminded me of Priorians at their best: cheery, sturdy and steady, uncomplaining under hardship and glad to be what they were.'[183]

It is remarkable that after sports and camping expeditions, what some past pupils remember most vividly were the canings they received, usually because they felt they had been unfairly delivered. One of the masters had the title Prefect of Discipline. He could have been an awe-inspiring or terrifying person, but generally he was not, the holder of the office usually being a respected and friendly priest. Offenders were sent to him, and queued up outside his door in the evening recreation period. He was the only one allowed to administer physical punishment and he made the final decision on what it would be: it varied from a mild lecture to 'six of the best' with a cane. In those days of physical punishment the office of Prefect of Discipline was a safeguard that prevented a teacher, perhaps driven to rage, from administering punishment in the heat of the moment. However, there was at least one occasion when the Superior caned a boy, and that was in 1944. The boy was questioned about the content of one of his letters (outgoing letters were censored by the Superior), and this resulted in punishment 'not for what you have written, but for your attitude'.[184]

Lawrence Geraghty writing in 1962 says 'Throughout my years at the Priory [1947–52], one figure loomed larger than any other, and that was the figure of the Master of Discipline, at that time Father Tolmie. It was only afterwards that we learned how foreign to his nature was the sternness which his office demanded of him, but we certainly had a healthy respect for him, and it was largely due to him that an atmosphere was created in which order prevailed and in which real education could take place.'[181]

A severe Prefect of Discipline could be at risk when he played football. Some of the more disgruntled boys would set out to hack him down or perpetrate some professional foul on him. Sarcastic remarks in front of others were just as likely to ignite a smouldering sense of revenge. A boy staggering late into a lesson with several stitches in his leg was greeted with: 'Where have you been?' 'To the doctor's, Father.' 'No doubt to have your head examined. Sit down!' Or to a hesitating Latin pupil: 'You wouldn't recognise a subjunctive if it was served up to you on a silver platter.' Such sardonic comments were no doubt the currency of many schoolmasters, but most of them did not engage in physically competitive field sports with their pupils.

Teachers could administer penances, which varied from losing a few days of annual vacation to sentencing an individual to manual work during recreation periods for a day or several days – a sort of community service. A most agreeable penance was doing chores on the farm. No penance was considered really burdensome unless it prevented participation in an important match or it meant having days deducted from holidays at home. The latter punishment was last inflicted in December 1964 when two boys were not allowed home until four days after the others had left for the holidays. This was the penalty for going to Eastleigh by themselves rather than in a group of three or more. Caning was abolished in the school by 1954[185], but we find two Priory boys reporting that an irate teacher at St John's had caned them on separate occasions in March 1966 for the trifling offence of talking during a study period.[186] Other than noting the incident, it seems that the Priory staff took no action and made no enquiry.

Lack of discipline could also result in deduction of house and class points, which was felt keenly because it let down one's fellows and could earn their displeasure. It was not unusual therefore for class meetings to be called by boys who wished to ensure discipline in the classroom and protect points by agreeing that there would be 'no more mucking about in the maths lesson'.[154] Hands in pockets was an offence well into the 1950s; this was punished by having to sew up the pockets for a week or longer and losing points.

A school captain and prefects, elected by the boys at the beginning of each school year, had a responsibility for monitoring discipline, but not for administering any physical punishment. Other than attempting to correct misbehaviour on the spot, their only alternative was to bring an alleged offender before a prefect's committee to explain himself and then either to administer a penance or report the matter to the Prefect of Discipline who could in turn report to the Superior for his decision. Expulsion was the ultimate punishment, and some superiors did not hesitate to implement it, sometimes for what today might seem to be trivial reasons.

Most of those that were asked to leave were considered not to be up to the mark; those required to go because of their behaviour were comparatively few; others were given their marching orders for transgressing school rules. Smoking was a major misdemeanour and could result in dismissal; surprising, since smoking was a common adult pastime without any moral overtones – many of the staff smoked. Such a harsh decision depended entirely on the Superior at the time. Eating in an out-of-bounds café could result in being gated for a whole term. As late as 1965 'boys seen in cafés are being dealt with'.[187] Shopping in Bishop's Waltham was forbidden even in 1963 when Father Duffy on seeing three smartly dressed boys in uniform coming out of a shop, which they had approached by a roundabout route using back lanes, was literally hopping up and down with anger and astounding passers-by.[188] As for meeting with girls in the neighbourhood, even when of an innocent nature, expulsion was the immediate reaction of the Superior unless he could be persuaded against the odds to abandon such a ruthless decision. Father Moran was so persuaded in 1950[182] and so too was Father Duffy in 1962 (after exhibiting near apoplectic rage)[189] by the school captains. But Father Donnelly could not be dissuaded from expelling two boys for smoking in 1952 despite appeals by the captain and vice captain to him and to the Prefect of Discipline.[131] Sexual misbehaviour was unknown in the school and almost unknown outside it. In these days some may find this difficult to believe. Strictures, physical and moral, were in place to protect the boys, but no strictures could be completely effective especially beyond the school precincts.

Dismissals or expulsions were recorded, but the reasons were not always clear for Latin or French circumlocutions were sometimes used rather than precisely identifying the nature of the offences.

In 1920, a pupil was sent home because '[he] does not have the right spirit'.[190] In 1923 two boys were requested to leave because 'They have not given satisfaction and do not have the moral qualities required to make good priests'.[191] Another was sent home in 1924 'for violating the rules'.[192] Three boys were sent home for 'indiscipline' in 1925.[193] A new boy was considered 'not intelligent enough' in 1928 and sent home within two weeks of his arrival.[194] In 1933 a pupil 'who does not give satisfaction' departed quickly.[195] In 1935 three boys, while on vacation, were asked not to return because of 'a lack of intellectual capacity'.[196]

Some expulsions were for more serious matters or for what appear to be more serious matters. In 1919 the good name of the school was brought into question when a local man came with his daughter to complain that on the previous Monday evening one of the pupils had insulted her. The following day a policeman came with two young girls from the town with the same complaint. In the absence of the Superior, Father Bouniol visited the families of the three young ladies to apologise. The pupil in question, who should not have been out of the school grounds, was dismissed immediately, the police and the girls' parents seemed satisfied and no further action was taken. The nature of the 'insult' was not specified.[197] In 1926 a pupil was sent home for 'passing a fraudulent letter'.[198] In 1954 a boy was expelled for taking money from the Superior's office.[199] In September 1965 a boy who had only been at the school for two weeks was expelled for being out of the dormitory from 10.15pm until after 11.15pm.[200]

Smoking on special occasions was allowed in the early years, but unauthorised smoking or smoking at all in later years was considered a heinous offence. On the 1st November 1921 (All Saints Day), for example, the pupils were given permission to smoke. This seems to be a surprising authorisation for schoolboys, and it seems harsh that in the following month two pupils were severely punished for smoking and one of them was expelled. Earlier, in 1915, the punishment for unapproved smoking was not so severe. In January of that year many boys had bought cigarettes during the Christmas break and were smoking while out on walks, in the attic above the dormitory and in the bike shed (the French boys did it first!). Presumably if large enough numbers offended then the sanctions had to be of a general nature. In this case all the pupils suffered: all meals were taken in silence, the use of bicycles was prohibited, and walks outside the school had to be in groups accompanied by one of the fathers. In 1924 a boy was expelled 'for smoking and for being incorrigible'[201], but in 1928 'a pupil caught smoking is punished severely' and was only allowed bread and water at supper 'to serve as an example to others'.[202] The severe punishment may have been caning, for he was not expelled. The pupils continued to be given permission to smoke on special occasions, the last recorded occasion being St George's Day, the 23rd April 1935. Illicit smoking was never completely stamped out, but very few were caught. One pupil in the late 1930s, who was to become an eminent member of the

Society, had a unique place for avoiding detection and that was at the top of a very large tree where he could not be seen and where the smoke went imperceptibly upwards.[203] It was known that older students smoked when at home where it seemed to be no more offensive than drinking coffee, and no thought was given to the likelihood of addiction or disease. But it continued to be punishable in the school.

The staff required permission to smoke up to 1939. During the war and for several years afterwards there was a more liberal attitude as far as the staff were concerned. A few of them smoked in their recreation room in the evenings, but it then seems to have gone out of fashion rather than to have been forbidden. A further relaxation for the staff on feast days was coffee in the fathers' recreation room after lunch.

Until the mid-1950s, except for holidays at home, there was almost no contact with people, young or old, outside the school. Sports meetings and occasional approved visits to the theatre, cinema or circus provided some of the few occasions for mixing with others. In the early days there would have been little contact with others even during vacation times. It was recommended in 1912 that the annual vacation of the pupils at St Laurent should be reduced to eight days, and before going on to study philosophy they should not have more than 15 days vacation. This was so that they 'would not be exposed to dangers that threatened their virtue and vocation in irreligious surroundings'.[5] The French Priory boys before 1918 spent only the 15 days annual holiday of their final year at home, and several of those days were taken up with travelling.

One would perhaps expect the school to become an introverted community with the intense irritations and strong feelings of an isolated closely confined group, but this was not the case. The men that established the Society, and the members of it, were well aware of the dangers of emotional inclinations; they had studied psychology and moral theology, they were well acquainted with human behaviour and failings in Europe and Africa, they were rigorously self-disciplined (although failings were not unknown), they were generally more worldly wise than would be expected, and, importantly, they were subject to a discipline that clearly identified the potential problems of close relationships.

A cardinal rule enunciated very early on was *raro unum, nunquam duos, semper tres* (rarely one, never two, always three). White Fathers operate in groups of three or more and this rule applied to schoolboys as well. The rule was reinforced by forbidding 'particular friendships'. When emerging through a doorway to start work or recreation a boy had always to take up with whoever followed or preceded him. This applied to boys and staff, so that it was no uncommon thing to see boys and staff working, walking and playing together. This integration of staff and pupils meant that the strengths and weaknesses of each were quickly identified by the other. Aggressiveness and timidity were quickly noticed; both were channelled into community activities, particularly sports, and attempts made to persuade the aggressive types that their inclinations should be cultivated as leadership qualities.

It was all further reinforced by the 'grand silence'. This forbade anybody in the community to speak from night prayers in the chapel until breakfast the next morning. Further, nobody was ever allowed to be unoccupied. Boys had to keep moving. There was no television until 1960 and that was in the Fathers' House for approved viewing, and there was one faulty old radio in the recreation hut, which could be listened to with difficulty during evening or Sunday recreation periods. Few boys ever bothered, they were all far too active. Dry evenings, cold or warm, were taken up with games on the sports field, or walks up and down the long pine-lined driveway known as the Burma Road, often speaking French with one of the fathers. On wet evenings the recreation period was spent playing billiards, chess, cards, boxing and table tennis. Quizzes, musical evenings and whist drives took place from time to time, and occasionally there was an old-fashioned lantern slide show or an old film run on a whirring 16mm projector. Rehearsals for choir, concerts, music and drama were recreational activities, so too were obligatory cross-country runs and any form of sport; these activities were not allowed to interrupt the curriculum. Exhaustion seemed to be the objective, but there is no record of any boy ever suffering from that particular malady.

In the 1960 edition of the school magazine, lay teacher and former Baptist minister Mr Daniel Williams wrote:

> Most [Nonconformist] ministerial students are what Catholics would call 'late vocations' … and are quite mature … [However] too much stress is laid upon examinations and obtaining degrees. Apart from a brief morning service there are no spiritual or devotional exercises. This is left to the individual student. It is up to him to find the means of nourishing his spiritual life. Unfortunately he can without proper guidance find himself in a theological maze. There is little or no discipline. Apart from fifteen or so lectures, the student's time is his own. Indeed any attempt by the authorities to impose discipline is met with stiff resistance … This lack of discipline very often has unfortunate consequences. When the student is faced with opposition in his ministerial life he is ill-equipped to deal with it, as he has never learned the hard lesson of obedience. In short, life in College is too soft and relaxed. Here at the Priory the ethos is altogether different. The boys are much younger and naturally discipline is strict without being severe. If accepted in the right spirit, the discipline is a wonderful help to the formation of Christian character and braces the seminarian for the hard and exacting life of the priesthood. To run a junior seminary is not easy and requires great wisdom on the part of the Fathers. This they exhibit, for they themselves have learned that only those can rule who have first learned to obey.[204]

Despite the rigorous training, old boys to a man look back to a rose-tinted past. James Holmes-Siedle, Bishop of Kigoma, Tanganyika, was one of those who put it into writing

> Few religious societies had a seminary system so pleasant and varied as the White Fathers ... It started at the Priory, it took us across the Channel to Belgium where we learned some philosophy and quite a lot besides ... then a year in Algiers, which to us resembled the Thousand-and-One-Nights, to finish up with four years in that delightful Carthage.[92]

Another who put his memories on paper was Alfred Howell. He wrote of the wonderful atmosphere in the school while he was a student there. He wondered if it was the enthusiasm of a new foundation. He went on:

> Yes, I think so, but above all I think we were entranced by the simple, affectionate relationship inspired by Father Travers between the fathers, brothers and students, a relationship which, while astonishing us, delighted us. During that first summer term, we used to go out all together – Superior, most of the staff and all the students – on bicycles, which the French boys had left behind. Titchfield-on-Sea was the favourite rendezvous, only ten miles or so from the Priory, and there we bathed to our hearts content. I also recall a bicycle trip to Quarr Abbey; we picnicked in the grounds, and the Abbot led a procession of monks, all carrying rice pudding for our dinner.[2]

Succeeding generations of boys remembered the same affectionate relationship and camaraderie, and the same bicycle rides to the same places.

Manual Work

A period was set aside every weekday for manual work by the boys. Besides saving the expense of maintenance staff, it instilled an appreciation of labouring work and taught self-reliance.

At the start of a term each boy was allocated a work duty. The tasks included cleaning the dormitory, chapel, corridors, windows, gymnasium, recreation huts, washrooms, showers and lavatories; polishing floors, chapel vessels, candlesticks and furniture; tidying the quadrangle; weeding lawns and gravel drives; working on the farm and in the gardens; attending to the central heating boiler; peeling potatoes until a machine was installed; cutting bread for the next meal; maintaining the fathers' and pupils' libraries; and generally doing what maintenance staff would do. Members of a class were responsible for cleaning their own classroom during recreation periods; this was worth class points if it passed inspection. Grass cutting was done with scythes until 1950 and Brother Modeste showed the boys how to use a scythe for the lawns. Jim Wallace nearly cut his foot off the first time he did it, but soon became expert and did it regularly.[205] From the 1940s field grass was cut by one of the brothers using a tractor, and from 1950 the lawns were trimmed by one of the boys or fathers with a mechanised mower. Rolling the cricket pitch and tennis court was something the pupils did in their own time. On Sundays and public holidays a team of boys with a senior boy in charge washed the dishes by hand. This was far from onerous; it only occurred about once or twice a term for each pupil, and the occasion was spent with noisy banter and singing.

Four of the appointments included work in addition to the manual work periods. These were the bell ringer, the barber, the sacristan and the infirmarian. The bell ringer rang a large hand bell to signal the start and end of the many periods throughout the day; he also rang the belfry bell for the Angelus at midday and in the evening. Haircutting was done (very well it must be said) during the manual work period and during the recreation periods if there was a call for it. In the early days Father Robert and Brother Modeste performed this duty, but from the 1930s onwards it was the responsibility of one of the senior boys, who was expected to pass on his skill to an assistant. This was their school job so no payment was given or expected. The sacristan and his assistant cared for the sacristy and all that it contained including the sacred vessels, vestments, and liturgical materials; he was on duty whenever there was any chapel service. The pupil infirmarian cleaned the infirmary, served meals to the patients, prepared the room for Holy Communion, and slept in a small dormitory next door to the infirmary in order to attend to emergencies. The Infirmarian proper was one of the Fathers, who, if necessary would call on the local physicians.

The 'school doctors', who were very much friends of the school, were: Dr Whittindale from 1912 until his death in 1924, Dr Dodd until about 1929, Dr Mitchell from 1928 to the mid 1950s, and then Dr Steel until the school closed. Dr Hemming also served the school: he was a General Practitioner for 63 years and always lived in the Bishop's Waltham house in which he was born. Doctors Mitchell and Steel were particularly intimate with the school and occasionally came to lunch or supper, and had the fathers to dine in their homes.

There was no laundry in the school. Once a week each boy changed his bed linen, prepared his laundry list and sent his filled laundry bag off in a van to a nearby commercial cleaners. The sacristan and infirmarian saw to the chapel linen and infirmary linen.

The brothers spent most of their lives doing manual work, but the priests were never averse to getting their hands dirty. The Superiors themselves were often out with sleeves rolled up. Father Bouniol's work on the playing fields has already been mentioned. Father Moody, bathed in perspiration, regularly undertook the extensive lawn mowing. Father Fitzgerald worked in the vegetable garden, where his expertise, especially with the rotovator, was worthy of published comment when he produced enough cabbages in one season to feed the community for three years.[141] And Father Duffy, when Superior, was on more than one occasion mistaken by visitors as a servant.[152]

Others of the staff built tennis courts, did painting and decorating, picked potatoes, brought in the harvests, weeded gravel drives, and generally seemed to relish hard work. Regrettably, it was while working on the main drive that Father English had a heart attack and died early the following morning, 1st April 1960, in hospital. Archbishop King presided at his funeral Mass, which was celebrated by Father Provincial, and he was buried in the school cemetery.

The Farm

An attractive, even enjoyable, form of manual work for teenaged boys was helping on the farm. This they had done willingly and happily since 1912. One of the first acts of the newcomers in that year was to set up a smallholding on part of the three acres of land that came with the house. There was very little money and it was necessary to supply as much food as possible from their own little piece of land.

In 1913 two meadows totalling 9.7 acres, and adjacent to the school grounds, were purchased for £600 from the West family of Brooklands Farm.[206] These meadows were later to form two football pitches, a large orchard, the site of the farm buildings, and an area of pasture. In the late 1940s, a half-acre vegetable garden with a large garden shed was established at the edge of this field alongside the Boys' Drive.

In 1923, 12.6 acres, known as the Long Field, to the north of the farm buildings were also bought from the West family.[207] It was in the Long Field that Brother Patrick was nearly killed by a bull. He came out one evening in 1948 to take the bull elsewhere. As he was leading it, it pulled itself free, ran off for several yards, then turned, pawed the ground and headed at full speed for Patrick, who by this time was running for his life to the far side of the field and into a thick copse that formed a hedge. The bull hit an ash tree at speed, leaving a scar across the trunk that was still visible for decades. The bull remained enraged until it was corralled the following morning and taken for slaughter.[61]

When Brother Patrick arrived in 1934, the seven-acre Lower Field (also known as the West Field), between the football pitches and the Botley – Bishop's Waltham railway track, was rented for pasture from Mr Alfred West, the local butcher. The cricket pitch and a small pavilion were established on part of this field.

As soon as the school buildings were completed in 1913, Brother Aubert erected timber farm buildings on the recently acquired land. He built a huge hay barn, pigsties, fowl houses, cattle byre, slaughterhouse and granary. He also built a carpenter's workshop and erected a bicycle shed – both of them long spacious buildings, which were also used as storerooms.

In 1913, the procurator (Father Bouniol) bought a couple of cows and two pigs, which were the start of the dairy herd and a successful pig farming venture. He must also have bought some hens, for in 1918 Modeste was selling eggs at Fareham market for fivepence a dozen, which was the maximum price fixed by the government. He suffered a setback a little while later when a fox took 15 of the hens and it cost £2 to replace them. About the same time Aubert sold three heifers and bought a cow for £32. A year later he sold 17 pigs for between 36 shillings and 43 shillings each. By comparison, in 1944 the pigs were selling for £12 each. So by rearing and selling livestock, the farm was quickly providing a useful source of income.

The large orchard of nearly an acre was planted in 1915 when Father Lassoumery was the procurator. He ordered a large quantity of apple trees from France and the boys were put to work planting them.

Horses were used to work the fields until 1941 when a bomb-damaged lorry was purchased. Brother Patrick repaired it and attached a hay sweep to throw the hay up into an adjacent cart, so saving the back-aching pitching. This was one of Brother Patrick's many inventions. During the harvest season the brothers rose at 3am and scythed the hay or corn before meditation, Mass and breakfast. They then returned to their work and continued until the light of the long summer days faded. The work was long and laborious. It was relieved considerably in July 1944 when Brother Patrick was able to borrow Mr Brooks's tractor for the mowing and sweeping, and in 1945 he was able to use Mr Carpenter's tractor. In return the brothers and fathers helped their neighbours to bring in their crops. It was obvious that a tractor had been necessary for some time, especially as Aubert and Modeste were now past their prime, and in February 1947 the farm acquired its own Fordson tractor, and this was later replaced by a Ferguson.

9.8. Brother Patrick bringing in the last of the harvest at Galley Down in 1950.

Mr Carpenter has already been mentioned for offering the use of a cow and a horse in 1913. He also offered to help in other ways, and he and his son assisted with the haymaking until the early 1930s. After them, Ernie Apps, who lived in Albert Road, provided help on the farm and in the vegetable garden, often spending his weekends in later years helping Brother Patrick when Aubert and

Modeste were too old and frail to do heavy work. Generous help also came from Colin Underwood, a local agricultural contractor, who used to thresh the oats and barley at Galley Down and also bale the hay and straw. Charlie Morgan of Waltham Chase was another who was always ready to help and lent his ex-army trailer each year to take the bales home from Galley Down.

The farming people were always very neighbourly, not only with their practical support, but also in dropping by to chat and regale the brothers with stories of yesteryear. They included Major Kemp, ex-Indian Army; Mr Bailey, who had started his naval career on sailing ships; and Mr Haughton who came to sharpen his sickles and billhooks, and who as a boy was caught smoking by his father when celebrating Queen Victoria's Diamond Jubilee and ran away in fear of his life – but told in more colourful language.[208]

During both world wars the farm was run efficiently and productively for the wartime governments had necessarily encouraged food production and to some extent subsidised farming. During World War II, Brother Patrick received additional petrol coupons for farm vehicles and even a sugar allowance for feeding the bees in the spring. (Bee-keeping was promoted to encourage the production of honey and to assist in the pollination of plants.)

In 1948 the wooden cattle byre was replaced by an impressive modern brick building for the increasing dairy herd. It was built by Mr Pink, the local builder and undertaker.[208] It was a large airy building with a dairy at the east end and a storeroom at the west end, and it had the latest type of milking machines and milk cooling and sterilising equipment installed. The Guernsey herd was bovine TB tested before this was a requirement and was in the top seven herds in Hampshire for milk production. It was a successful commercial venture and earned valuable income for the school. The area around the byre was improved considerably in April 1951 when Brother Patrick took on the onerous task of concreting the whole of the extensive farmyard.

On Lady Day (25th March) 1947, the Priory acquired the tenancy of Galley Down through Austin and Wyatt, estate agents of Bishop's Waltham. It was on the Corhampton road about three miles away and had a wood and three meadows. It yielded generous crops in the very first year: the first haymaking was finished on the 26th June in glorious summer weather, the barley was brought in early in September, and the potatoes were picked in October. Brother Patrick considered it a 'godsend', for it helped to provide sufficient produce to feed the boys and earn an income.

> There were about 50 acres of land part of which was used for growing potatoes and barley while other fields were reserved for cattle or hay. There were also about 40 acres of woodland where badgers and foxes had a quiet home with plenty of rabbits for company. There were many nightingales in the hedges and they could be approached quite closely with a torch.[102]

Father Jim Wallace, when a pupil, recalls being awakened in his tent by Brother Patrick who was calling the boys out to hear a nightingale, but he preferred to turn over and continue his sleep. 'I have regretted that decision ever since for I have never heard a nightingale.'[209] The three large fields were hedged and one of them was in a long valley with extensive woodland hangers on the steep hillside. The hedges have now been grubbed out to form one huge prairie-like landscape, the field in the valley has been fenced off, and the woodland has passed into the hands of the Forestry Commission.[210]

9.9. Camping at Galley Down, 1961. L to r: F Smith and T Russell (standing); A Coyle, E MacBride, P Martin, P McKenzie.

To the boys, Galley Down was not so much farm land as a huge camping site and play area that was used almost immediately after acquisition for two football matches on the 2nd April, reviving the tradition of 'Downs' on Wednesday afternoons. It seemed that one could roam for miles, and there were often several different groups of boys camping there at the same time without being aware of each other. Their camps would be in different parts of the woods, in a distant part of a field or in the copse between the valley field and the other fields. Each group of about half a dozen would set off to walk to the down with their provisions and pans in rucksacks. Rabbits would be trapped for dinner, and chopped nettles and wild herbs added to the pot.

The farm supplied the school with vegetables, milk, butter, eggs and meat. The meat included beef, chicken, pork, homemade sausages, black puddings, bacon, and rabbit during the Second World War and for a couple of years afterwards. In 1941 a rabbit warren had been established to supplement the meat ration. Other meats were bought locally. Often potatoes were bought, which is surprising since potatoes were grown on the farm and at Galley Down. The orchard produced bumper crops of apples, some pears and a few nuts, all of which Modeste harvested and carefully stored in his long hut. All this was supplemented by Modeste's soft cheese and secret formula beer.[61]

At times all the available boys, and very often the priests as well, were assigned to help on the farm or at Galley Down when the workload was heavy. This was particularly the case when bringing in the hay, barley or potatoes, and when planting potatoes in April. The boys also helped on local farms, including Mr Carpenter's, Mr Brooks' and Commander Wynne Owens', in exchange for the assistance those farmers provided. The times spent on the farm are lovingly remembered by the old boys, but perhaps not always with delight. The author particularly recalls having to wring the necks of all the chickens that were to be prepared for a Christmas Day dinner. It was the one time he felt no appetite for what was later set before him. The author also well remembers Modeste slaughtering pigs by holding each one squealing between his legs, then inserting a long thin knife into the lower part of its throat and pushing downwards to the heart.

There was hardly any blood. In those apparently less hygienic days, the school diaries record no instance of food poisoning; flu, pneumonia and scarlet fever – yes, but never an upset stomach.

It was in the 1950s that the three brothers, who had run the farm for generations, departed. Aubert died in 1950, Modeste died in 1956, and later in 1956 Patrick was appointed to Blacklion in County Cavan to set up the farm at St Augustine's College. Two young brothers, Eugene Leonard in 1955 and Peter Biewer (Brother Aelred)[211] in 1956, replaced them. In 1959 Peter Biewer, much to his joy, was appointed to Mwanza in Tanganyika where, in a bitter turn of fate, he was murdered on Christmas Eve 1969. In March 1957 Brother Casimir Warszylewicz, a burly Pole, arrived to manage the farm. He had been condemned to hard labour in the Siberian salt mines during the Soviet occupation of his country – an experience that damaged his eyesight and his temperament.[212] He remained until 1960, when the last of the animals had gone and the farm finally closed.

Sports

The first field games were croquet on the lawns, tennis on the existing court, and football on the downs. Football was taken up with enthusiasm; it was through the French boys that the Priory first made a name for itself in local football circles – a name that it always proudly maintained. There was no flat field within the grounds, so matches were played on the downs or on other teams' pitches.

> For a long time the downs served as the training ground for those who were to introduce soccer to various parts of West, Central and East Africa. Every Wednesday, immediately after lunch, all went up to the dormitory, changed into football togs and slung their football boots around their necks; they then trotted off to the downs, played a pre-arranged game of football, trotted back again, and then changed to arrive breathless in the refectory for tea.[89]

However, to ask visiting teams to trot a few miles to play a game (although it might have proved advantageous to the home team) would have meant no visiting teams at all. For the benefit of visitors, the rare home games were played on a nearby neighbour's meadow that had less of a slope than the Priory fields. After the departure of the French students it was not until 1921, when there were more than 20 pupils, that a regular first team could be put together. They played their first game on the 1st April in Bishop's Waltham and beat the home team 8-0, and on the 16th April they cycled over to Swanmore where they won 12-0.

The increasing number of competitive football games necessitated a proper home pitch, so work on levelling part of the 10-acre meadows into two huge terraces, each planned as a football pitch, started in 1928. It was a massive undertaking with pick, shovel and wheelbarrow. Progress was assured with many penances being allotted to this field of endeavour. The first terrace was completed in 1929 after exactly 12 months of hard labour. When the second terrace was constructed between late 1935 and 1936 the wheelbarrow phase was mechanised with a length of railway track and a large wheeled truck to roll along it. The truck was pushed until it was travelling under its own momentum, whereupon the fillers jumped aboard for a strictly illegal ride. The speed was controlled by a piece of timber that was applied to the wheel as a brake. On one occasion the brake broke, and the truck left the track and careered over an embankment. Fortunately the riders avoided injury by jumping clear in time, but earned themselves a good number of additional penances.[102]

9.10. Football 1st XI 1927–28. Holmes-Siedle is in the back row, far left.

Bishop Holmes-Siedle reckoned his year (1927–28) had 'the best [football] team of all time'[92], but that claim would have been contested by later teams. In 1951–52, 1954–55 and 1964–65 the First XI did not lose one game; for four years between 1946 and 1950 the Second and Third XIs did not lose one game; in April 1960, the only time the school entered the inter-schools competition for six-a-side football, they reached the final round, but were beaten by Toynbee School; and in April 1931 the Priory won the cup final of the Portsmouth Area Catholic Football Competition when the other final round team was noted as having an average age of 22, while the Priory team age probably averaged less than 17.

The school continued with outstanding performances year after year. Even in 1943–44 with only 12 boys in the school they did very well. They could not muster two teams to play against each other, so they played the army about once a week and the Italian prisoners of war on most Sundays. They won all the recorded games except for two: they were defeated 4-1 by the REME in March 1944 and 3-2 by Montfort College in April 1944 after the team had cycled to Romsey with all the Scotsmen wearing kilts.

9.11. Football 1st XI 1950–51. L to r: back – A McGarry, P Menzies, C Robinson, P O'Brien, F Dillon, P Finn; front – T Bradley, R Clyde, J Morrissey, D Fitzmaurice, P Farrell.

Holmes-Siedle recalled that in his day the first [football] team had to club together to hire an ancient bus to go to away matches and off they would go with team and supporters singing their battle song 'Hushabulla, hushabulla, rah, rah, rah!' His cricket memories, other than of the actual games, were of Father Howell as one of the better batsmen; of Father Hughes, who had 'an encyclopaedic knowledge of all things connected with first-class cricket' but never played the game, and of Mr Primmer of Bishop's Waltham, the acknowledged local authority on cricket whose word was law in the town and in the school. Holmes-Siedle tells of the Priory hitting its biggest score off Mr Primmer's bowling, but despite his team's calls for him to come off, he refused to do so – to the Priory team's delight.[92] Another cricketing friend of the school was Mr Bill Matthews, who in older age walked his dog daily through the grounds and never tired of telling how on one occasion, when playing for the town against the Priory, he took a wicket with his first ball.

Bill Matthews owned the corner shop in Albert Road and had known the school since its infancy. He would recall how, from earliest times, boys paying illicit visits to his shop would remind him to tell no one. He regularly cheered on the Priory teams from the sidelines even when playing against Bishop's Waltham, and he was not averse to heckling a referee when decisions were not in favour of the Priory. He could recall the teams when the French boys played and how those who returned as teachers played as boys.[213]

The first mention of a cricket match was on the 17th June 1922 when there were sufficient pupils to form a team, but neither the teams nor the scores were recorded. The only ground available for cricket was the sloping meadow.

> Cricket, during the period when the slope of the playing fields did not differ much in gradient from the School Hill [Victoria Road], was a real thrill for the adventurous, an ordeal for the enthusiast and a grave danger for all. Any batsman at the bottom end would have preferred standing up to a Larwood or a Voce than to any bowler coming down the hill. It was quite a change to meet the local team at the Chase or at Upham where the wicket was usually in excellent condition.[89]

When the Lower Field was acquired in 1934 for pasture, that part of the field between the lower football pitch and the stream was also used for cricket. It was a big field with a very modest incline, so that only the centre needed levelling to form the wicket. A small roller requiring two boys to pull it was regularly used on the wicket and a huge roller pulled by a tractor was used on the outfield. In April 1955 a new cricket pitch was made on the far side of the stream and closer to the Botley road, and a wooden pavilion was built.

Many of the cricketers came from Scotland and Ireland and had never played the game before coming to the school, but they were natural sportsmen and proved themselves better than much of the competition. There was never a bad season, and in 1951 only two games were lost: to St Peter's School, Southbourne, and to the Naval School of Navigation at Warsash; and in 1957 there was only one defeat – again by the School of Navigation. Cricket matches at Southbourne usually included a swim in the sea before or after the match, or sometimes both as in 1951 when it compensated for losing the game.[154]

In the football season the cricket field (except for the wicket and practice nets, which were fenced off) was used for pasture, and in the cricket season the football pitches were given over to the cattle. During the holidays the cows had uninterrupted occupation of both.

Tennis had been played from 1912, when a grass tennis court had been part of the acquired property. The court was at the bottom of the front lawn near the entrance gates and where the present Catholic church now stands. Apart from putting some protective wire fencing around it and re-seeding or relaying the turf, it remained essentially the same. Brother Patrick constructed a hard court in 1944 using broken concrete (from the bases of the abandoned US army tents) and a borrowed concrete mixer.[203] This was replaced in 1955 with another hard court built by the boys and Father Alan Thompson using 900 cubic feet of rubble brought from the Eastleigh brickworks by Mr Len Pond in a borrowed lorry. The rubble base was covered by six inches of brick dust rolled by a hired steamroller.[214] In May 1960 the surface was replaced with tarmac.

The other perennially popular sport in the summer was swimming, first in the sea and later in the very cold Durley millpond. In 1944 the Scivier family, who owned the mill, gave permission for the boys to use the millpond whenever they wished, except on Saturdays. Their first swim was on Whit Sunday 28 May 1944, and the pupils continued with this privilege until they were allowed to use the public baths, which were out of bounds until the late 1950s.

Boxing competitions until 1951 were popular, but then disappear from the sports reports in the school magazine. They always figured as part of the annual sports days, and tournaments were staged for visiting dignitaries, the last such tournament being in March 1947 to entertain Bishop Holmes-Siedle. The two sets of high quality boxing gloves used on that occasion were a gift from Canon Mullarkey, the Parish Priest of Winchester who, with his curates, was a regular visitor. The bishop was also treated to a gymnastics display, was entertained with a concert, sat round the stove in the recreation hut with the boys chatting, and confirmed 21 people in the chapel. Professional boxing championship bouts were followed avidly. There was an exchange of banter between the French staff and the boys when the French boxer Carpentier defeated the British idol Joe Beckett in 73 seconds on the 5th December 1919. In later years some of the fathers would rise about 3.30am to listen to the radio when bouts in America were broadcast, as they did on the 17th May 1955 to listen to the Cockell-Marciano fight. The results of these fights would be announced at breakfast to cheers or boos.

The absence of boxing appears to have generated a greater interest in billiards. In February 1951 the covered quadrangle was redecorated, the concrete floor covered with lino paint, and the lighting modified to provide a large billiard room in which the billiards table from the staff recreation room was installed. This signalled the start of what Father Tolmie referred to as 'misspent youth' for the table was in constant use during recreation periods.

An equally popular indoor activity was table tennis. The school never competed at billiards, but it did enter a table-tennis competition in February 1955 and won the district championship. Some of the fathers were hot-shots at billiards, but table tennis was more popular with some of the visiting bishops and provincial superiors, especially Father Maguire, who also liked to play basketball when he made a visitation. The French students had made an outdoor basketball court in May 1913, and they played the game until the last of them left, but it was not revived until 1954.

There were several attempts to introduce rugby: the union game being popular with those coming from southern schools, and the league game with the Lancashire contingent. Probably because there were so many Scotsmen who were primarily interested in soccer, and very few others from rugby playing backgrounds, it was not until early 1962 that the first school XV was formed. There was enthusiasm, but little tactical knowledge until Father Brian Garvey, who had played at Oxford University, arrived. The first game on the 11th April 1962 was against Swanmore who defeated the school 30-0. During the following season it started to come right, and the Priory team won as many games as they lost. By 1965 they were winning most games, but it was becoming very rough. Two Priory players were sent off on the 23rd October 1965, but the team still managed to win the game. They were given a severe talking to after the match and this seems to have prompted them to win the next game 47-0 against Winchester RFC 'B' without anybody disgracing themselves.

An unusual game played enthusiastically for a few seasons in the evenings after World War II was *Shlagball* – German baseball, which was taught by Father Adolf Eisele. Shinty was played in the late 1950s and early 60s, but it faded quickly as there were no other teams to play.

In 1957 students entered outside athletic events for the first time when they took part in the Eastleigh Athletics Meeting in June. They won several events, and Patrick Shanahan (100 yards), Paul Ashby (220 yards) and Peter Jackson (one mile) were selected to represent Eastleigh District in the Hampshire AAA (Amateur Athletics Association) Championships at Southampton on the 15th June. Shanahan and Ashby both won their events and broke the county records.

Prior to this the only athletic events in which the boys had been involved were the weekly cross-country run of about five miles and the school annual two-day summer sports. Prizes were awarded for the winners of all events on sports days and a *Victor Ludorum* (Victor of the Games) medal was awarded to the competitor who earned the most points. In an effort to be better citizens, the school sports were abandoned in 1957 and the pupils participated in local sports days at Bishop's Waltham, Swanmore and Curdridge from which many of the pupils returned with a considerable number of prizes. This participation in local athletic events continued until 1965 when Charles Savage broke the 100 yards record at Swanmore.

In the years following 1957 the students competed individually in the Hampshire Schools AAA championships and did extraordinarily well despite the lack of training or coaching. In 1960 the Priory entered as a school for the first time and won the Eastleigh and District Schools' Sports Competition; several individuals were awarded district badges for breaking existing records, and five collected district badges for equalling record times. As *The Pelican* report noted 'Considering the advantages of pupil numbers in the other schools, the equipment available to them and our absence of formal training, the Priory boys excelled.'[149] They continued doing well at athletic events winning medals and setting records, but some disappointment was expressed when they could only come second to St Mary's College, Bitterne, in the 1963 inter-schools competition.[152]

It was in March 1962, as part of a fund-raising show for the Hampshire branch of the AAA, that the pupils gave an exhibition of Scottish dancing at Eastleigh in the presence of the Mayor. The performance was by former pupils of St Columba's where Scottish dancing was encouraged. The writer of the report in the school magazine was concerned that 'Fr Travers must be turning in his grave', but the reception was enthusiastic.[215] This was in contrast to a similar exhibition for students from the College of Theology at Monteviot in Scotland who visited St Columba's in 1959. The visitors were mostly French, German, Dutch and Belgian students who expressed astonishment or sat bemused until the Superior explained the meaning and masculinity of the dances.[139]

The school had always been outstanding at soccer, but by 1959 its sporting emphasis had been transferred to athletics. A consequence was that in the 1959–60 soccer season the team faltered losing 12 of their 19 games. This in a school were even one game was seldom lost in a season. The decline started in 1959 when the First XI suffered 'two humiliating defeats'.[149] They were beaten for the first time in seven years by Montfort College in an away game at Romsey, and then by an international team of students, including former Priorians, from St Edward's College at Totteridge, North London. There was on the staff at this time a former Scottish schoolboy international, Brother John Mennie, but because of ill health he was unable to play and perhaps maintain the school's soccer reputation. It seems that athletics now occupied the interest of potential footballers.

The last year that the school entered an athletics team was in 1964 when they took part in an inter-school competition. The pupils attending St John's turned out for the Priory, and Sean Hughes won the mile.[216] From this time the Priory no longer took part in district, county and schools athletics events, and teams representing the school at other sports virtually disappeared. Since 1961 the Priory boys had been playing for St John's first teams and were unavailable to play for the Priory (unless it was a St John's versus Priory game), so that in 1963 the school diary frustratedly remarked 'Terrible football season – being regularly beaten'.[217] The pupils' commitment and loyalty were by now more closely associated with their daytime school. However, in 1964 those at St John's chose to play for the Priory on Saturdays so that things picked up again in the 1964–65 season: the soccer First XI football team was undefeated with 89 goals for and only 17 against, and the rugby First XV lost only one game.[163]

Houses

Competition at team level, rather than between individuals, was an important element of the education, encouraging group loyalty and spurring team members to greater effort. For competitive purposes the boys were divided into 'houses', each with a captain, one being the school captain. 'Teams' may have been a better word for there was no physical separation. Boys were allocated to a house on their arrival and stayed with it until they left, so that there was a strong sense of loyalty. Until 1962 there were two houses, Augustinians (St Augustine) and Xaverians (St Francis Xavier), but in 1962 they were increased to three, the new one being Claverians (St Peter Claver). Until 1962 there were also inter-class competitions, but these were abandoned when a third house was established.

Just about every sport or game was played not only for amusement, but also for house points. Even the indoor games of billiards, table tennis, whist and chess were played on a competitive basis. Points were awarded for exam results, monthly tests, inter-house games, sports-day results, and just about any activity where an element of competition could be introduced. They could also be deducted for misbehaviour. The exam and test marks of each individual were read out in public during spiritual reading and so were the house and class points tables. A silver cup and a half-day holiday were awarded to the house with most points in a term, and the winning class also got a half-day holiday.

School Uniform

So that the pupils would look more like English schoolboys, they were issued in October 1912 with 'little English round caps' that were blue-black with the initials WF in yellow. They had been bought for 1s.6d each. From the 1920s until 1940, prefects had the distinction of wearing a cap with a gold-coloured Maltese cross and tassel on the crown. In the 1920s the uniform was established as a dark blue blazer, grey flannel trousers, a plain dark blue cap, and a blue and gold diagonally striped tie. That is how it always remained, although many of the Scottish boys continued to wear their St Columba's College (Royal Stuart) kilts or clan kilts instead of trousers. An enamelled metal school badge was worn on the cap (replacing the WF initials) and a cloth version on the breast pocket of the blazer. In the 1950s a simpler, less cluttered, image was worn on the blazer.

9.12. The school cap badge.

Visitors

Visitors were many and the hospitality generous. There were continual comings and goings of missionaries from Africa, Europe and North America; diocesan priests and lay people came for retreats and holidays; European members of the Society stayed several months to perfect their English; and convert clergymen called to discuss their future vocations. District Commissioners from Africa often visited either alone or with their wives, and so did former pupils. As a rule visits by former pupils were only recorded with a mention of the visitor's name, but when Paul Wiseman, a diamond merchant living in Paris, visited in October 1958 his make of car was unusually remarked upon for he arrived in a very large Rolls Royce.

Other visitors included French White Fathers and seminarians serving in the armed forces, a Belgian refugee family in 1914, a bombed-out family from Portsmouth in 1941, bed and board for members of other missionary societies on promotional work in the area, and occasional visits by 'gentlemen of the road' who for a night's lodging and meals would work in the gardens.[218]

Many organisations around Hampshire, particularly parish groups, came for a day out to picnic and play games on the playing fields. And each summer, from 1933 until 1938, about 70 parishioners came from Heston by coach for lunch, tea, cricket, football and tennis.

Even during the school holidays and at weekends it was not a still place; on the contrary, the number of visitors often increased, especially during the summer when schoolboys and their teachers came for camping holidays.

Civic dignitaries never visited the school, but bishops from the missions often came by, including many native African prelates. When they travelled to Europe, usually for their duty visit to the Vatican or to the White Fathers' Generalate in Rome, they would almost invariably make a detour to visit the Priory, nostalgically spoken of by many of the priests that had taught them and baptised them. Bishop's Waltham, it seemed, was better known in Africa than in the United Kingdom. Other frequent visitors were missionaries from North America travelling to and from Europe and Africa by ship, which usually called at Liverpool or

Southampton. At least one bishop or African priest could be expected each year, and they would spend time informally with the boys in their recreation areas. This was a pattern throughout the life of the school. Some of those that came were Bishop Roy of Bangueolo in 1936; Bishop Kiwanuka of Masaka, in 1939, 1950 and 1958 – the first native African bishop of modern times; the patriarchal Bishop François Lacoursière of 'the Mountains of the Moon' Rewenzori in 1948; Bishop Owen McCoy of Oyo in 1949 and 1960; Bishop Msakila of Karema in 1959 – he had succeeded Bishop Holmes-Siedle, who was working as an ordinary missionary priest in Tanganyika having established the local church with its own native clergy; and Dr Laurian Rugambwa, Bishop of Rutabo, in 1956, 1957 and 1960. Dr Rugambwa was the first native born Tanganyikan to be raised to the episcopate, and in 1960 he had the further distinction of being appointed the first African-born cardinal.

9.13. Cardinal Rugambwa.

Sometimes there would be an influx of visitors as in May 1936 when a ship on its way to Canada called at Southampton. A group of five White Fathers, heralded by a warning telegram, and including Bishop Julien of Nyassa, came for a couple of days. Bishop Julien was a keen table tennis player and gave the pupils a few hard fast games in 1936 and on a later visit in 1944. (The telegram system was in general very efficient, but there were occasional concerns expressed when an unexpected visitor turned up ahead of his warning telegram, or when the telegram was not delivered at all which was sometimes the case. The first mention of a telephone (Bishop's Waltham 73) was in January 1932, although it may have been installed some years before. Until the late 1940s, however, distant priority communications, especially overseas, continued to be by telegram.)

The bishops of Portsmouth were frequent visitors, especially Archbishop King. He had also often visited when parish priest of Winchester and, as he mentioned at the golden jubilee ceremony in 1962, he sometimes walked the 11 miles from

Winchester accompanied by his curates Ibbett and Zollo. Canon Mullarkey, who replaced Canon King as parish priest at Winchester was also a frequent visitor. He too occasionally walked to Bishop's Waltham with his curate Father Pinkman, and later he and Father Zollo would cycle or come by coach with a football or cricket team.

There were also official annual visitations by a representative of the General Council or by the Regional Superior. Later the visitations were by the Provincial Superior, who was sometimes accompanied by a member of the General Council as in September 1950 when Father Henri Côté (a former Priory teacher) came with him. On at least one occasion, in November 1951, he was accompanied by the Superior General when Bishop Louis Durrieu came for a couple of days and was entertained by the boys with a concert of choral songs and solos. Episcopal visitors and the Superior General were publicly greeted with a short welcoming speech by the school captain – in French if the visitor was French speaking. The compensation for this demanding effort was that the reply always included a dispensation from schoolwork for a day, which would be noisily applauded.

The variety of visitors certainly indicated the universality of the Church, which the pupils would have been unlikely to experience elsewhere, and broadened their horizons significantly.

Relationships with other Religious Societies

One would have thought that there would be certain antipathies between the different missionary societies as they were all fishing in the same small pond for recruits. But the contrary was the case. Their common aim of producing priests and coadjutor brothers for the missions was never clouded by envy or jealousy. They all gave to each other and gave generously. Their relationships were marked by cordial friendship and mutual support that never slackened.

The White Fathers when visiting or recruiting in the London area before they had a house in London often stayed with the St Joseph's Missionary Society at Mill Hill. The Mill Hill Fathers likewise stayed at the Priory, and their Superiors General were frequent visitors, especially Bishop Biermans who visited on a number of occasions. In February 1920 Travers was invited by the Mill Hill Fathers to a ceremony at Westminster Cathedral for the departure of a caravan of missionaries to Uganda when Cardinal Bourne presided and Father Vaughan was the preacher. It was at Mill Hill in 1917 that Travers first met Father Parsons, Deputy Director of the APF, who was to prove a good and generous friend of the White Fathers in the years to come.

The relationship with the Montfort Fathers at nearby Romsey was very intimate. They had provided a warm welcome and accommodation before the Priory was acquired, and helped the White Fathers with solicitors and estate agents. They continued to provide brotherly support and affection, which was reciprocated to an amazing degree. Boys and staffs were constantly visiting each other for socials, concerts, sports competitions, and special anniversaries. They attended each other's festivities and funerals and brought their eminent visitors to each other's houses.

When the African Missionary Society of Lyons arrived in England it was the White Fathers turn to welcome and support newcomers. Visiting was more intermittent because of the distances involved, the Society of Lyons establishing itself first at Hastings and then in Monmouthshire. On the 21st March 1923 Mr Anderson called on his former colleagues at the Priory accompanied by two Redemptorist priests who wished to make a gift of their house and its 10 acres at Llancrwn in South Wales. This was the same house that was considered by Travers and Voillard in 1912 and rejected because of its remoteness, and because it was in need of considerable restoration. In 1923 the Society of Lyons acquired it and in October of that year, Father Laquarré, Vicar General of the African Missionaries of Lyons, came to the Priory to seek advice on setting up an apostolic school there. Father Travers returned the visit in June 1924 when Father Parsons took him by motorcar. Travers considered he had been right to refuse the offer for, although the main house was in a reasonable condition, all about it was in ruins, it was isolated and it was difficult to reach. Because of its remoteness, especially the difficulty of travelling to and from the channel ports, and the property maintenance burden, the Lyons Society did not continue there and returned to France.

There were always very close relations with the Christian Brothers: *Les Frères des Ecoles Chrétiennes* at Southsea, and *Les Frères de l'Instruction Chrétienne* (always known to the White Fathers as the Brothers of Ploëmel) at Bitterne. Being teaching orders, they were expelled from France in the latter part of the 19th century, and after many years of exile in Britain decided to found schools for English-speaking boys, and in doing so acquired Anglicised names. The de la Salle Brothers founded St John's College, Southsea, in 1908, and the Brothers of Christian Instruction moved their Novitiate from Bitterne to Jersey in 1922 and used the building to establish St Mary's College for boys. There was frequent visiting between the staffs, White Fathers regularly served as chaplains to the brothers, and the Priory Superiors were often invited to preside at the prize giving at both colleges. During the war years the Priory provided sanctuary for both congregations, and in February 1941 when Brother Maurice, the Superior at Bitterne asked for some provisions to feed the community, two pigs were immediately killed and taken with other necessary food by Father Kingseller in the car next day.

The Solesmes Benedictines at Quarr Abbey on the Isle of Wight were also great friends, and were fondly remembered for the welcome they always provided, for the beautiful grounds and farm, and for the liturgy in the great Abbey Church built by the monk-architect Dom Paul Bellot in 1912. The staff often stayed there for their annual retreats and the boys went there time and again for days out on their bicycles. The monks, however, being a contemplative community, never seem to have visited the Priory. The Abbots of Farnborough Abbey, a foundation of the Subiaco Benedictines who engage in pastoral work, did come to the Priory on particularly special occasions.

Good relations always prevailed with the Portsmouth diocese. Diocesan bishops could easily have prevented missionary societies setting up in their territories in case they drew off potential priestly vocations. But no, they encouraged them. In fact it was not unusual for students from diocesan seminaries to transfer to the missionary societies and vice versa. The Bishops of Portsmouth and their clergy had a tremendous affection for the White Fathers. Hardly a week ever passed without one or more of them coming to spend time at the Priory, often for a day, sometimes for several days and occasionally for long retreats. Priests even came from London and beyond (Father Field from Dunmow in Essex, for example, came regularly and so did Canon Parsons of Finchley). Bishop Cotter would invite the White Fathers to celebrate the Feast of the Martyrs of Uganda in the cathedral in the 1920s. The first time was on the 5th December 1920 when Father Châteauville, who had arrived in October, celebrated Solemn High Mass, Father Travers preached the sermon, and Father van Hissenhoven preached at Vespers later in the day.

The fathers were seldom in the house at weekends and during school holidays. They would be on supply (working in other parishes), serving as temporary chaplains, preaching retreats, and giving talks at conferences, exhibitions, schools, colleges, convents, youth clubs, and men's organisations. They also had to fit in their own annual one-week retreat or ten-yearly 30-day retreat at another of the Society's houses or at Quarr Abbey. It is remarkable how busy they were every weekend and during holidays, and how far they travelled to parishes, chaplaincies, and military bases in Hampshire, the Isle of Wight, and all parts of England, Scotland and Wales. Often there was only one priest on the premises. One weekend in 1960 all of them were at home, and this unique occasion was recorded as such in the house diary.

School Magazine

Much that occurred in the school and was known to the pupils was reported in the school magazine. Particular achievements, exceptional events, and special visitors were described; articles, comments and poems by the pupils appeared; and the results of every game and competition were reported. The team captains usually wrote the sports reports and were always sure to boast of their triumphs and quietly admit to their defeats. Every game had to be won; anything less would not be living up to the teams that had preceded them. The general impression from the magazines is of a fun-filled time, tremendous enthusiasm for everything, a love of God and his world, strong aspirations for the missionary life, and a longing to go to Africa.

The magazine appeared twice yearly at Christmas and in the summer until 1957. Thereafter it appeared once a year in the summer. The first issue of the magazine – *The Priorian* – was published at Christmas 1926. The magazine continued until the school closed, having changed its name to *The Pelican* in the Christmas issue of 1954. The change of name was occasioned by the decision to issue a single magazine for the Priory and St Columba's, which until then had had its own journal *The Columban*, and to include news of old boys. The students wrote and compiled the copy, but the final approval rested with the Superior. In the 1960s, editorial control and discretion were put completely into the hands of the students, and for the first time advertisements appeared. Local businesses, including pubs, made up the bulk of the advertising, and the rest were mostly national recruitment advertisements for army officers, the Midland Bank, and university scholarships. As the students were not in a position to respond to any of the advertisements, it was to be hoped for the advertisers' sakes that copies of the magazine were widely distributed in the locality and beyond.

Unfortunately, very few copies of the magazines have survived. They were very much the boys' view of their world, and those copies that are still extant depict a boyhood zest, a tremendous pride in sports results, little delight in academic achievements unless they earned house points, and a profound spiritual awareness expressed and implied. Reading them now one can hardly believe that robust schoolboys could be so religiously animated. One wonders how many in later life would recognise themselves in their boyhood writings. One fears that for many it would be a case of feeling, as Thomas Hood did,

... now 'tis little joy
To know I'm farther off from Heaven
Than when I was a boy.

10

The Final Years

The year 1962 had ended on an upbeat note. All seemed set fair for a smooth voyage, but contrary winds were to cut short this promising venture.

Seventeen months after the 1962 golden jubilee celebrations Father Duffy was appointed Brothers' Novice Master at Broome Hall, Surrey, and he left in December 1963. Father John Fowles, already on the staff, took his place as Superior in January 1964.

10.1. Father John Fowles, Superior 1964–66.

When Fowles took over, some changes were introduced as a result of the recent Second Vatican Council decrees. Most noticeably Mass was said facing the congregation for the first time in November 1964, and the first concelebrated Mass with Fathers Fowles, Garvey and Martin was said on the 7th April 1966. This was the second such Mass for Fowles, who had in January concelebrated a televised Mass with the new Bishop of Portsmouth, Derek Worlock, in the cathedral.

Restrictions continued to be relaxed. The students went home for the Easter break in 1965 and, when they returned, they were allowed to wear uniform without ties while in the school. In the following year the Priory uniform was discarded in favour of that of St John's, and the boys were allowed to wear casual clothes at weekends.

By this time the bonds had become perceptibly stronger with St John's and consequently weaker with the Priory, which was in effect serving as a hostel. In these circumstances a more liberal attitude to behaviour had to be adopted, but one cannot help but notice that the absence of a well-regulated life and disciplined common religious practice had a detrimental effect on the spiritual wellbeing of the students, which they themselves recognised. The editor of the 1966 issue of *The Pelican* felt obliged to say that 'It would be the lessening of truth if one were to omit to mention that spirituality has not been so obviously dominant as it might have been.'[219] The fact was that in a school where teachers and pupils pursued worldly success, the orientation of the students changed from an essentially spiritual and idealistic life to a material one with some religious practice.

On the feast of Our Lady of Africa, 30th April 1966 – a Saturday, there was no walking pilgrimage as there had been in previous years, the students went instead to a performance of *La Bohême* at Southsea. However, during the Easter holidays, from 1964 some of the pupils with Father Brian Garvey had been accompanying the Handicapped Children's Pilgrimage to Lourdes. The pupils had financed the costs of at least one of the children on each occasion with money earned by working on local farms during their free time.

The quality of the Priory staff had risen and was high both academically and in teaching ability, but there were not enough of them and it was proving difficult to assign others to teaching work. It was again necessary to look beyond the Society, and from 1964 to 1965 Michael Savage was employed as a resident lay teacher. He only stayed a year and then went to Africa where he studied for the priesthood and was ordained for the diocese of Mbala in Zambia.[220]

When Fathers Nolan and Garvey left in 1965 and 1966, none came to replace them. And when, regrettably, Father Fowles left the school and the Society in August 1966, Father Stanley Lea, who had been Superior in the 1940s, had to be hurriedly brought in to take his place. To him fell the unhappy lot of closing the school.

Since the St Laurent days, a continuing concern was the availability of teaching staff for non-African institutions and the effectiveness of those institutions, especially the apostolic schools. The Generalate wanted its men in Africa, and that was what the individuals themselves wanted. Moulding young men according to the precepts and traditions of the Society was considered an important and necessary investment, but the investment in property and diverted manpower was considerable. Savings needed to be made.

Using the more efficient teaching resources of St John's College had been a good start, and the arrangement was proving a successful venture academically. The boys were getting an education more suited to the national curriculum and fewer teachers were required at the Priory, but there was still a large and costly establishment to maintain and fees had to be paid for the pupils at Southsea.

In February 1963 Father Andrew Murphy, Provincial Superior, came to discuss a number of options. One was to send all the pupils to St John's if they could be accommodated; another was to buy a smaller house near Liverpool that would serve as a hostel for pupils attending a nearby grammar school. The number of students was still above 70 and there were about 40 at St Columba's, so placing them all in nearby schools was no small matter. However, from September 1966 all the Priory pupils were attending St John's College.

What to do with St Columba's was partly resolved in unfortunate circumstances. A devastating fire occurred on the 2nd November 1963 that made the place uninhabitable. Fortunately none of the boys or staff was injured. The immediate problem was what to do with the pupils. The Priory was asked to take them, but it was impossible to do so as it already had 11 more than it was designed for. With commendable speed – within a week – Danby Hall in Yorkshire was leased to house the unfortunate Columbans. They remained there until July 1966 when it was decided that from the following September they should follow the example of the Priory and attend a nearby school for their lessons. There being nothing suitable locally, they were transferred to a house in Ratho, eight miles west of Edinburgh and attended the Scotus Academy, Edinburgh, from 1966 to 1969. They then attended St David's High School, Dalkeith, from 1969 to 1977.[221]

A further significant move was made in 1965 when the Priory boys could elect to go home to study for their A-levels, and this is what some did.[222] The drift was obviously to a situation where the pupils pursued the whole of their academic education elsewhere, thus putting into question the need for the Priory. A grammar school education was now as available to Catholic boys as to anybody else, and had been for some time. It was therefore reasonable to question the continuing existence of the Priory as a school. But a further question was by this time being aired: Was the concept of an apostolic school contrary to contemporary life and education? The drift was becoming a strong inexorable current, which the Provincial Superior and General Council were not slow to recognise.

In July 1965 Father Murphy and his advisers met again to consider the future of the Priory and St Columba's College.[223] This had been discussed with Father Richard Walsh, Assistant-General, on his recent visitation. (Richard Walsh was a former Priorian who had the distinction of being the school captain for two consecutive years from 1928 to 1930.) Walsh was presumably conveying the concern of the General Council about the decline in the number of pupils reaching ordination and the rising costs for a lower return. He was also pre-empting the sentiments of the Second Vatican Council to be published in 1966, which called on religious communities to 'abandon whatever activities are today less in keeping with the spirit of the community.'[224] The French Provincial Council had already met in January 1965 and recommended that the Bonnelles school (which had succeeded St Laurent d'Olt) should be closed, apparently on the grounds of the beneficial reorganisation of French secondary education and the falling number of recruits.[225]

The British Provincial Council meeting began with a proposal to close the Priory, to keep St Columba's open for the four junior forms, and to send the Fifth Form and the Lower and Upper Sixth Forms to live in a hostel attached to a grammar school.

Some of the facts and opinions that emerged at the meeting did not bode well for the future. The low ordination success rate of 9.2% over a recent six-year period was rightly considered a waste of resources, and with only four applicants from England and Wales for the coming year the outlook was bleak. There was some criticism of the pupils' spiritual formation, and it was suggested that a boy would gain more from a good home. This was followed by the observation that there was 'an anti-junior seminary feeling in the country [England]', and 'an increasing number of influential people, especially teachers, are opposed to junior seminaries.' How much of this feeling was generated by the 1960s 'child-centred' experimental teaching methods, how much by interpretations of the Vatican II debates by a liberal press, and how much by studied analysis and reflection is difficult to judge. The difficulty of finding and keeping staff was not mentioned in the report, although this had been a recurring problem since the foundation of the school.

The only person in favour of keeping the school open, prior to the meeting, was Father Murphy, but he said that he had been persuaded to change his view by the Priory staff and the English promotions team. They had favoured closure of both schools from the start, especially if adequate alternatives could be put in place. There had been strong objections to the closure of St Columba's from the Scottish promotions team who, in common with other Scottish clergy, continued to favour junior seminaries. This was probably the reason for the proposal at the start of the meeting that St Columba's should not close. However, there were at that time only 22 Scottish pupils, which was an insufficient number to make a school in Scotland viable. The concluding consensus was that both schools should be closed. It was recommended that vocations directors should encourage future aspirants and maintain contact with them while they continued to live in their own homes and attend their own schools or universities.

The policy of accepting boys of school age was abandoned and arrangements were made to sell the Priory and also St Columba's when it was rebuilt. Henceforth, young men were to be recruited when their university or professional studies were completed. No more students were accepted and their number declined as the members of the upper forms moved out. At the end of June 1967 there were 32 students of whom nine were in the Upper Sixth Form and about to leave for philosophy studies at Blacklion. The remaining 23 were given the option of boarding at St John's or going home to complete their secondary studies.

The first name entered on the school roll on the 12th October 1912, was Germain Aymard from Avignon. The 1031st entry, made on the 3rd September 1965, was that of Norman Turnbull from Leven, Fife. There was space for about three thousand more entries, but Norman Turnbull was to remain the last on the list.[64]

St John's College 1967–1970

A terse announcement in the November 1967 *White Fathers* magazine informed readers that

> The Priory, Bishop's Waltham, ended its function as a junior seminary on 7th July [1967]. Nine of the 32 students have started their [philosophy] studies at Blacklion, Co. Cavan, and ten have made arrangements to continue their studies at schools near their homes. They will eventually apply for entry to Blacklion. The remaining thirteen are now boarding at St John's College, Southsea, and are under the care of Fr W Smith (London) who, until recently, was the Superior at Danby Hall in Yorkshire. This will effect no break in the boys' studies since the Priory has been regularly sending them to St John's for the past few years.[226]

The St John's boys were lodged together in Woodford House with Father William Smith as their housemaster. They wore St John's uniform, participated fully in the academic and sports life of the school and were distributed between the Fifth, Lower Sixth and Upper Sixth Forms. The school fees were paid by the parents or by school grants topped up by the White Fathers where necessary. The intention was that, except for the daytime school activities, they would be a self-contained community apart from the other boarders and subject to a modified seminary regime, but this pious hope was never realised.

Breakfast was taken in the house and was preceded by morning prayers and daily Mass. All other meals were taken with the other boarders in the school dining hall. Evening study was in the house, and the traditional grand silence from night prayers until breakfast should have been the norm. However, such was the lack of discipline and the inability of 'old Father Smith' to exercise control that Brother Swithun, the headmaster, had to come over in the mornings to make sure the boys were up, went to Mass and were ready for school in time. He also required them to go over to the main school for the evening study periods. He put in a later appearance several evenings a week to make sure the boys were in the house and not leaving through a window and down the fire escape for an evening out.[227]

The boys considered Father Smith as elderly, lacking energy, and unable to handle teenaged boys. He was in fact 66 years old when he took the job in 1967, but seems to have been prematurely aged by his years in Tanganyika and by bouts of malaria. The *White Fathers* magazine announcement had said the students would be 'under the care' of Father Smith. He was certainly not a Father Superior and he does not seem to have been able to exercise much care. A younger man would have been much better, but presumably it was a case of not what was best but who was available. He was withdrawn in 1968 and retired to Oak Lodge, Totteridge, London, where he did occasional promotional work. His final move was to Holland Villas Road, London, where he died in November 1978.

The boys that returned in September 1968 were distributed amongst the other houses and lived as ordinary boarders. The last of them, Michael Gallagher and Terry Madden, left in 1970 after taking their A-level examinations.

The boys did well academically, but as an experiment in offsite seminary living it could not be considered a success. Nevertheless, three of the thirteen boys were ordained as priests, one as a White Father and two as diocesan priests.

Closure

With the permission of the General Council, the Priory was offered for sale in June 1967.[228] Within a couple of weeks an acceptable offer had been received and on the 29th December 1967 the sale was completed. The school with its 25 acres of land was sold to the Hampshire Police Authority as a police training college.[229] Prior to the sale, Lord Ashburton, Chairman of the Authority declared 'It has a very large area of land. All in all, quite apart from the thought of the Police Authority and its need for a training school for the increased establishment of cadets, I cannot help thinking it is an extremely cheap proposition'.[230] The price was £50,000.[231] This time the Police Authority had got a bargain.

The signatories to the deed of sale on this occasion were Lord Ashburton and A H M Smyth (Clerk of the Police Authority) for the police, and Fathers Andrew Murphy (Provincial Superior), Francis Briody (Provincial Treasurer), Gerard Rathe (Provincial Secretary) and James Smith. Smith was in Entebbe, Uganda, so getting his signature probably contributed to the six-month delay between the time of the offer and completion of the sale. Fathers Murphy, Briody, Rathe and Smith had replaced the original trustees in 1960 when Father Jean Marie Chollet, the only surviving trustee and by then an old man, had conveyed the property to them.[232]

About an acre of land, at the front of the property adjacent to Martin Street and including the cemetery, was retained and sold for £1000 to the Catholic Diocese of Portsmouth as a site for a parish church. The deed conveying this land was completed on the 17th July 1968 with Mr T K A Walsh (Diocesan Trustee) and Monsignor W Raymond Lawrence (Diocesan Secretary) signing on behalf of the Portsmouth Roman Catholic Diocesan Trustees.[233]

The only residents after the 7th July, when the school formally closed, were Fathers Stanley Lea, Michael Coghlan (the parish priest), and Thomas Conway who was preparing to leave for Zambia. Conway left shortly afterwards. Coghlan moved into 'Old Orchard', a house in Winchester Road where he remained until 1970 when a diocesan priest replaced him as parish priest. Lea stayed in the Fathers' House to see to the disposal of the remaining moveable effects. He then locked the front door for the last time and went off to his next assignment.

If there was any sadness, or misgiving, or nostalgia, none of it found its way into print, nor was it ever apparently expressed. For the White Fathers – nomadic missionaries always on the move – this was another case of rolling up the tent and moving on.

The Bottom Line

The inevitable question at the finish must be 'To what extent was the school successful in its primary objective – producing missionary priests?'

The number of pupils who became priests or brothers was 194: White Father priests – 149; White Father brothers – 11 (excluding one later ordained as a White Father and one later ordained as a diocesan priest); other priests (diocesan and other societies) – 34.

The number of pupils who attended the school over a 55-year period was 1031. Of these, 194, or 18.8%, became priests or brothers; and 160, or 15.5%, became professed members of the Society of Missionaries of Africa. If only the 149 White Father priests are counted, which was the primary purpose of the school, the success rate was 14.5%.

One former pupil became an archbishop (Arthur Hughes), three became bishops (James Holmes-Siedle, Owen McCoy and Michael Fitzgerald), and one became a Benedictine Abbot (Peter [Cuthbert] Johnson).

More important than the numbers, however, is the significant apostolate of this comparatively small band of men. Cathedrals, churches, mission stations, clinics, hospices, universities, schools, seminaries, wells, bridges, translations, dictionaries and grammars of native languages can all be counted, but the number of souls brought to the love of God is incalculable. Many of the African leaders in politics, education, the civil service and the church were baptised and educated by these men. Many of their sportsmen learnt how to play cricket and football under their tuition. Lepers, AIDS sufferers, prisoners and war victims have been tended by them, and they have provided street children in the urban areas with homes and employment skills. Many of them died young, but it is surprising how many have lived to an old age amongst the poor, the sick and the unwanted. The humanitarian aspect of their work can be readily appreciated, but the vocation of a priest is a vocation of consecration to God and the affairs of God. As St Paul reminds us: 'His calling comes from God, as Aaron's did, and nobody can take upon himself such a privilege.' [Hebrews 5, 4.] He is another Christ whose purpose is to bring souls to their loving Father in Heaven, and that is what these White Fathers – these Priorians – have done in abundance.

Epilogue

In 1967 the Hampshire Police Authority was seeking a suitable property for a cadet training school, and the *Hampshire Chronicle* reported that 'Enquiries by the Chief Constable (Mr Douglas Osmond) resulted in information of the impending sale of The Priory being obtained'. Lord Ashburton, Chairman of the Authority, considered the building was easily adaptable and perfectly sound, and a sub-committee of the Authority appointed to consider proposals for acquiring the premises reported that 'The property was excellently situated for the purpose in the centre of the Police area'. A number of additions and adaptations were required to accommodate the proposed 100 cadets, and the costs for this work, in addition to the sale price of £50,000, was estimated at £100,000; this was the figure given to the Home Office.[230] However, considerable extensions and modifications to the buildings and converting the Long Field into additional playing fields, cost more than was anticipated. When the Police Training School opened its doors to public view for the first time in February 1972, the *Hampshire Chronicle* reported that 'The school, which is residential, has cost the county's ratepayers nearly £200,000'.[234]

Ep.1. Police Training School.

On the 18th October 1980 the Hampshire Police Authority approved the proposal to move the school to the former Royal Victoria Hospital at Netley, where it would form part of the new Hampshire Constabulary Support and Training Headquarters[235], but the move was not finally completed until 1988. In July of that year the school was offered for sale and bids were invited.

The buildings lay empty for several years with no interest shown by purchasers except property developers whose proposals did not satisfy the Hampshire County Council who owned the site. After a poll of local electors by the Bishop's Waltham Parish Council in 1991, the parish approached the County Council with an offer of £175,000 to buy the 21 acres of playing fields for use as a recreation area. The parish had by this time secured grants totalling £23,500 towards the cost of bringing the fields, which had been neglected since the police departed, into good working order.[236] At about the same time an offer was accepted from a house building company for the school buildings and part of the elementary school site on Victoria Road, which together totalled 4½ acres. At the end of March 1993 all negotiations were completed. The housing site was sold to Wainhomes (Southern) Ltd who demolished the buildings in mid-1993 and replaced them with an estate of 42 houses. The extensive playing fields were sold to the parish for £119,477, which was considerably less than they had been prepared to pay.[237] The fields were enhanced to provide a recreation area with unusually fine amenities for soccer, rugby, cricket, bowls, children's play, and walking, and this very attractive open space was appropriately named Priory Park.

A

Priory Pupils 1912–1967

Name	Home Town or Diocese	Years
ABBOT Leo Ambrose	Shipley, Yorks.	1936-1938
ADAMS Robert Frederick	London	1919
ADKINS Michael Anthony	Beverley	1956-1958
ADRIAN Francis		1942-43
AHERNE Bernard	London	1956-1957
AIRLEY David	Dundee	1955-1959
AKERS Albert	Portsmouth	1929-1934
ALBARET Casimir	Lozère	1914-1915
ALLAN Joseph Anthony	Paisley	1957
ALLSOP John	Liverpool	1923-1928
ANNELINE G	Nantes	1913
ARCHER Harold	Salford	1919
ARCHER Izidore	Cantal	1912-1915
ARCHER Paul	Birmingham	1961
ARIAS Paul	Bombourcy	1912-1915
ASHBY Paul	South Shields	1954-1958
AUSTIN Alfred Frederick	Frome / Malton, Yorks	1932-1936
AYMARD Germain	Avignon	1912-1915
BAGGOTT Anthony	Birmingham	1959-1962
BAGNELL Michael John Francis	Cardiff	1937
BAGSHAW Kerry Charles	Buxton, Derbys.	1957-1960
BAKER John	London	1945-1948
BAKER William Anthony	Cardiff	1957-1961
BAPTIST Hugh	Leeds	1950-1954
BARLOW John Edward	Govan	1932-1934
BARRETT Desmond Thomas	Co. Clare	1937-1939
BARRIE John	Consett, Durham	1963
BARRINGER George Stanislaus	Plymouth	1922-1927
BARRY James	Renfrew	1934-1936
BARRY Peter Joseph	Middlesbrough	1943-1944
BATTY Vincent Anthony	Stockton on Tees	1934-1935
BEATTIE Hugh	Glasgow	1946-1947
BECKWITH Harold	Portsmouth	1925-1930
BELDON John	Darlington	1924-1927
BELL William Christopher	Dublin	1936
BENTON Christopher	Liverpool	1957-1959
BEX Anthony	Aldershot	1923-1925
BICKERS Geoffrey Maurice	Chandler's Ford	1955-1957

Name	Home Town or Diocese	Years
BIEWER Derek	Middlesbrough	1949-1951
BILLING Terence Joseph	Bury St Edmunds	1936-1937
BILLINGSLEY Maurice	Birmingham	1962-1967
BINGHAM Charles	Bathgate	1955-1959
BINGHAM James Harkness	Bathgate	1957-1960
BION Louis	Lozère	1913-1915
BLAKEMAN William Joseph	Cardiff	1932-1935
BLANDFORD Simon	Southwark	1963-1967
BLEASDALE Edward	Chorley, Lancs	1954-1957
BLUE Patrick Vincent	Rothesay, Bute/Glasgow	1933-1936
BLUNDELL Thomas Joseph	Leeds	1928-1933
BLUNDELL William Aloysius	Leeds	1923-1927
BOLAN Michael	Birmingham	1947-1952
BONIDAN Antonen	Lozère	1912-1914
BONNAFE Albert	Avignon	1913-1917
BOUDON Joseph	Lozère	1912-1915
BOURNIER Adrien	Cantat	1913-1915
BOWEN Leonard Daniel*	Shrewsbury	1931
BOWMAN John	Glasgow	1946-1952
BOYD Gerard	Glasgow	1945
BOYD John	Halifax	1936
BOYD Patrick	Glasgow	1938-1940
BOYD Thomas McGregor	Glasgow	1961-1962
BOYLAN Martin	Hamilton	1946-1951
BOYLE Desmond	Galashiels	1952-1957
BOYLE John	Kelty, Ffife	1959-1961
BRACKEN Robert*	Salford	1922
BRADLEY Thomas	Newry	1949-1951
BRADLEY William	Hamilton	1928-1932
BRADLEY William	Glasgow	1963-1964
BRAMHAM Kenneth	Shipley, Yorks.	1936-1938
BRANKIN John	Birmingham	1963-1965
BRANKIN Joseph	Birmingham	1946-1947
BRASSINGTON Francis	London	1945
BRAZIL William James	Limerick	1937
BREE James	Edinburgh	1922-1927
BREEN Philip	Liverpool	1947
BRENCHER William Ernest	Southwark	1921-1924
BRIGGS Frederick John	Co. Durham	1919
BRIGHOUSE John	Liverpool	1965-1967
BRIODY Francis Patrick	Glasgow	1932-1935
BRITT Joseph	Preston	1933
BROADBRIDGE Ronald Ernest	Toronto	1932-1935
BRODIE Peter	Dundee	1952-1954
BROSNAN Vincent	Coventry	1965-1967

Name	Home Town or Diocese	Years
BROWN Bernard	Portsmouth	1923-1924
BROWN Christopher	Southwark	1964
BROWN Denis	Westminster	1931-1933
BROWN Cyril Basil	Ardrossan	1949-1953
BROWNE Peter	Liverpool	1947-1951
BROWNE Richard John	Co. Wicklow	1936-1940
BROWNE Robert	Hamilton	1946-1950
BRUMECOMBE Norman Louis	Bradford	1937-1939
BRUNDLE Robert Ernest	Portsmouth	1918
BRUNET Hypolyte	Lozère	1912-1914
BUCKLEY Martyn	Sunderland	1962-1964
BUCKLEY Thomas*	Co. Cork	1933-1934
BUDD William*	Salford	1922
BUDDEN Francis Joseph Mary	Southwark	1924-1925
BURBAN Joseph	Morbihan	1913-1915
BURLEIGH Charles Edward	Westminster	1956-1960
BURNS Patrick	Glasgow	1955-1960
BURRIDGE Archibald	Portsmouth	1922-1927
BURTON Arthur Bernard	Birmingham	1920-1921
BURTON Frederick Gerard	Wednesbury	1930-1932
BUTKUS Stanislaus	Leeds	1921-1924
BUTLER Brian	Carlisle	1950-1956
BYRAM Thomas Richard	Leeds / South Osset, Yorks	1935-1940
BYRNE John Philip	Liverpool	1932-1933
BYRNE John Joseph	Westminster	1928-1933
BYRNE Kevin	London	1924
BYRNE Michael	Preston	1962-1966
BYRNE Patrick Joseph	Ilford, Essex	1959-1962
BYRNE Terence Niall	Potters Bar	1956-1958
CAIRNS Clive Anthony	Preston	1961-1962
CAIRNS John Julien	Lancaster	1962
CALCUTT Richard	Southwark	1952-1956
CALLAGHAN Alexander	Glasgow	1946-1947
CALLAGHAN Peter F	Liverpool	1961
CALLAGHAN Vincent	Glasgow	1949-1955
CAMPBELL Christopher David	Glasgow	1960-1963
CAMPBELL Hugh	Edinburgh	1949-1953
CANNON Gerard	Glasgow	1955-1957
CANNON Michael	Glasgow	1965-1966
CAPITANO Arthur Dominic	Leeds	1954-1955
CAPPER William	Leeds	1950-1954
CARABINE Christopher	Birmingham	1961
CARMODY Thomas John	Castle Island, Kerry	1935-1939
CARNEY Oswald	Leeds	1929-1933
CAROLAN John Anthony	Co .Cavan	1957-1959

Name	Home Town or Diocese	Years
CARROLL Edmund Arthur	Westminster	1963-1967
CARROLL Walter	Bradford	1932-1933
CARROLL William Henry	Liverpool	1922-1924
CARVILL Brendan John	Buxton, Derbys.	1957-1959
CASSIDY James Edward	Glasgow	1924-1927
CASSIDY John	Paisley	1934-1935
CASSIDY Joseph Cuthbert	Glasgow	1925-1928
CASSIDY Patrick	Lancaster	1954-1957
CATTERALL Richard William	Wakefield	1930-1931
CAUSEY George Charles John	Westminster	1924-1929
CHALBOT Ernest	Nancy	1912-1915
CHAMBERS Arthur James Edgar	Canterbury	1936-1938
CHAMBERS Martin		1928-1931
CHANDLER Howard	Reading	1918
CHANEY E	Wokingham	1922-1924
CHERREY Edwin John	Hex & Newcastle	1957-1959
CHERRY Anthony	Liverpool	1943-1944
CHEVALIER Louis Albert	Maine et Loire	1915-1917
CHILVER		1920-1921
CIARNS Michael	Glasgow	1963-1967
CLANCY Dermot Joseph	London	1959-1962
CLANCY Leo	London	1954-1958
CLINCH Thomas	Bury	1922-1926
CLYDE Robert	Glasgow	1946-1951
COFFEY Michael Joseph	Bridgetown, Wexford	1935-1936
COGHLAN Michael William	Westminster/Brighton	1928-30, 1935-37
COLDHAM Peter Wilson	Southwark	1942-1944
COLGAN Liam Padraic	Westminster	1960-1962
COLLETT Bernard Cyril Francis	Leigh-on-Sea, Essex	1931-1937
COLLINS Martin Stephen	Edinburgh	1938-1940
COLLYER Peter	Westminster	1947-1948
COLMAN J J G		1920
CONCAGH Hugh	Galway	1954-1958
CONNELL James	Glasgow	1956-1957
CONNOLLY James	Liverpool	1947-1951
CONNOLLY James	Glasgow	1946-1952
CONNOLLY John Anthony	Leeds	1934-1935
CONNOR James	Bradford	1934-1938
CONNOR Paul	Brentwood	1939
CONROY John Dainton	Wigan	1944-1948
CONVY Joseph	Middlesboro	1949-1952
CONWAY John Thomas	Glasgow	1965
CONWAY John	Edinburgh	1942-1943
COOPER Christopher Robert	Southwark	1959-1962
COOPER John Ralph Peter	London	1936

Name	**Home Town or Diocese**	**Years**
COOPER Michael George	Dorking	1926-1929
COPPING Francis George	Brentwood/ Walthamstow	1934-1939
CORCORAN John	Glasgow	1954-1957
CORIO Philip	Mortlake, Surrey	1918-1920
CORK John Naseby	Liverpool	1920-1921
CORMACK George Vincent	Glasgow	1925-1928
CORRIGAN John	Shrewsbury	1965-1967
COSTELLO Patrick	Coatbridge	1919-1920
COTTLE Ernest	Bristol	1922-1927
COURTES Joseph	Lozère	1914-1915
COWE Andrew Inglis	Edinburgh	1957-1959
COWELL Robert	Liverpool	1950-1953
COX Robert Edward	Liverpool	1922-1925
COYLE Andrew Gerard	Dumbarton	1958-1962
COYLE Peter	Glasgow	1963-1966
COYLE Thomas	Widnes	1927-1929
COYNE Gerard	Liverpool	1926-1930
CREANEY Edward	Coatbridge	1953-1956
CREANEY Patrick	Motherwell	1955-1959
CREECHAN Michael	Glasgow	1950-1953
CRONIN Hugh Brendan	Co. Kerry	1936-1939
CRONIN John	Co. Kerry	1938-1939
CROOK John	Lancaster	1922-1927
CROUGHAN Leslie	Liverpool	1947-1952
CRUISE Joseph Francis	Glasgow	1935-1938
CULLEN Francis	Belfast	1934-1935
CUMMINS Gerald Francis	Rutherglen	1959-1962
CUNNINGHAM James William	Hex & Newcastle	1965-1966
CUSHLOW Edmund	Washington, Durh	1962-1963
CUSICK Hugh	Motherwell	1921-1925
CUSICK John	Glasgow	1919-1922
CUTHILL Christopher James	Rotherham	1959-1961
DALTON Paul Gerard	Middlesboro	1965-1967
DALY John Joseph	Kiskeam, Cork	1935-1936
DANGERFIELD Frederick Peter	Portsmouth	1937-1940
DANIELS Albert Edward	Southampton	1935-1938
D'ARCY Bernard Patrick	Carlisle / Southall, Middx	1931-1938
DAVEY Harold Arthur		1932-1933
DAVIES Gerard	Birmingham	1965-1966
DAVIS Francis Rubery	Walsall	1944-1948
DAY Thomas Frederick*	Manchester	1922
DE KERKHOVE Cecil Anthony	Vervius, Belgium	1918-1921
DE LACY Michael Patrick Joseph	Clifton	1958-1959
DE LUSIGNAN Raphael Hugh	London	1951-1953
DE LUSIGNAN Theodore	London	1919-1921

Name	Home Town or Diocese	Years
DE SOUZA Peter	Dumfries	1965-1966
DEEGAN Bernard Ignatius*	Liverpool	1932-1933
DEENEY John Jude	Glasgow	1959-1962
DEENEY John	Glasgow	1932-1934
DELANEY Joseph	Co. Cork	1950-1951
DELÉPHINE Joseph Alexander	London	1929-1931
DELTOUR Marcel	Lozère	1913-1917
DEMPSEY Robert	Birmingham	1962-1966
DENIEUL Prosper	Rennes	1913-1915
DENIS Joseph	St Hilaire	1913-1915
DEQUEMU		1914
DESMOND William	Cork	1928
DEVINE William	Dundee	1933-1934
DIAMOND Francis Alphonso	Manchester	1921-1922
DICKSON Francis William	Edinburgh	1932-1937
DILLON Francis	Edinburgh	1950-1953
DILLON Peter	Edinburgh	1949-1954
DIVER Peter	Carndonagh	1950-1953
DIX Paul	Southwark	1945-1950
DOCHERTY John	Glasgow	1965-1967
DOHERTY John	Derry	1953-1955
DONAGHER Edward	Glasgow	1945-1947
DONNELLY John	Northampton	1946-1950
DONNELLY Patrick	Glasgow	1932-1934
DONOGHUE Andrew Gerard	Edinburgh	1944-1948
DONOGHUE John	Mullingar	1956-1959
DONOGHUE Raymond	Edinburgh	1950-1954
DONOVAN Francis	Rickmansworth	1961-1962
DONOVAN Michael Damian	Rickmansworth	1957-1960
DOOLEY Thomas	Edinburgh	1937-1938
DOOLEY Thomas	Ilford, Essex	1958-1961
DOYLE William	Manchester	1945-1947
DREW Richard		1954
DRIVER Peter	Co. Donegal	1949-1952
DRURY Daniel*	Liverpool	1933
DUBOIS Jean Baptiste	Lozère	1913-1917
DUBOIS Pierre	Epernay	1912-1915
DUFFY Bernard Anthony	Halifax	1936-1937
DUFFY Gerald	Glasgow	1956
DUFFY Thomas	Motherwell	1938-1931
DUGGAN Stephen Vincent	Glasgow	1957-1958
DUNNE Michael	Tralee, Kerry	1934-1935
DUNNION George Joseph	Glasgow	1960-1963
DURKIN John	Edinburgh	1949-1954
DUSSUD Jean	Rhône	1914-1917

Name	Home Town or Diocese	Years
EARLY John	Luton	1946
EARNEY John	Portsmouth	1927
EASTON Alexander	Coatbridge	1944-1949
EBBLEWHITE John William	Hurley Tamworth	1963-1964
EDMUNDS Francis		1916
EGAN John	Leeds	1922-1927
EILERTSON Eilert	Dundee	1965-1967
EKINS James	Glasgow	1950-1951
EVANS Albert Norman	Dublin	1933-1934
FAHY Fiacra	Galway	1950-1955
FAIRHOLME George	Edinburgh	1950-1953
FAIRNEY Francis	Dundee	1954-1955
FARR John	Glasgow	1925-1927
FARRELL Paul	Liverpool	1947-1952
FARRELL Robert	Paisley	1933-1938
FEENEY John	Glasgow	1932-1934
FEENEY Michael Howard	Birmingham	1959-1960
FENTON Maurice Frederick	Hounslow/Brighouse, Yorks	1934
FERRICAIS Gabriel	Gard	1914-1917
FERRY John	Glasgow	1929-1932
FIGUEREDO Francis Gerard	Liverpool	1935
FINN Peter	Liverpool	1947-1952
FINNIGAN Angus	Inverness-shire	1948-1950
FITZGERALD Edmund	Gosport	1923-1928
FITZGERALD Henry Bernard	Liverpool	1949-1950
FITZGERALD Michael Louis	Walsall	1950-1954
FITZMAURICE Patrick Desmond	Newry	1947-1952
FITZMAURICE Louis Raphael	Newry	1946-1949
FITZPATRICK Christopher		1952-1955
FITZPATRICK Finbarre	Bradford	1955-1959
FITZPATRICK James	Rosscarberry, Cork	1935-1941
FITZPATRICK Terence	Bradford	1934-1938
FITZPATRICK Timothy Joseph	Rosscarberry, Cork	1933-1938
FITZSIMMONS James	Glasgow	1943
FLANAGAN Louis	Blackpool	1945-1946
FLANAGAN Peter Joseph	Liverpool	1930-1932
FLANNERY Francis Kevin	Leeds	1935-1940
FLETCHER Paul	Halifax	1962-1965
FOGARTY Francis Arthur	Salford / Manchester	1934-1936
FOLEY Brian	Edinburgh	1954-1956
FOLEY Joseph	Cumberland	1954-1958
FOLEY Michael Bernard	Brentwood	1960
FORD Peter	Salford	1922-1927
FORREST Harold Edgar*	Gloucester	1923-1924
FOWLIE Hector Roderick	Manchester	1959-1960

Name	Home Town or Diocese	Years
FOX Leonard	Liverpool	1932-1933
FRANCIS Edward Lawrence	Westminster	1924-1926
FRANKLIN Arthur Joseph	London	1927-1932
FRASER Keith Alexander	Southwark	1938-1940
FREDRICKSON Peter Anthony	Cardiff	1958-1960
FREILJames Joseph	Glasgow	1961
FROGET Francis	Fougères	1912-1915
FRY George Frederick John	Hounslow/Chiswick, London	1934-1939
GAFFNEY Francis Bernard	Leeds	1923-1924
GALLACHER Anthony Albert	Edinburgh	1962-1963
GALLACHER Michael		
GALLAGHER Clement	Motherwell	1952-1953
GALLAGHER Francis	Newcastle on Tyne	1942-1943
GALLAGHER Michael	Birmingham	1965-1967
GALLEN Michael	Derry	1954-1955
GALLIMORE Ernest Vivian*	Glasgow	1934-1935
GALVIN Jeremiah Christopher	Co. Cork	1959-1962
GALZIN Joseph	Avignon	1912-1915
GARDNER Albert	Edinburgh	1950-1954
GARDYNE James David McDonald	Aberdeen	1933-1934
GASKIN Edward	Ilford, Essex	1923-1925
GATELY John		1953-1954
GAUZY Louis	Lozère	1912-1914
GEDDES Martin	Edinburgh	1950-1953
GERAGHTY Brian	Hex & Newcastle	1947-1952
GERAGHTY Laurence	Hex & Newcastle	1947-1952
GERRY Geddes Alexander	Glasgow	1938-1939
GIBB Andrew	Leeds	1936-1940
GIBBONS Austin	Liverpool	1947-1948
GIBBONS Patrick	Greenock	1955-1959
GIBBONS Thomas	Coventry	1965-1967
GIELTY James Patrick Joseph	Stirling	1943-1947
GILHOOLEY Maurice	Middlesboro	1924-1926
GILHOOLEY Michael	Edinburgh	1942-1943
GILHOOLY Thomas	Edinburgh	1949-1950
GILL Leo*	Leeds	1919
GILMORE Peter	Glasgow	1949-1950
GLEESON Michael Francis	Co. Clare	1937
GLOVER Paul Brendan	Liverpool	1963-1967
GODBOLD Henry	London/Portsmouth	1917-1920
GOLDINGAY Ernest Thomas Jack	Billericay	1932-1934
GOODSTADT Michael	Manchester	1954-1957
GORDON Gerard	Paisley	1961-1963
GORMAN Gerard	Glasgow	1928-1930
GORMLEY Owen	Edinburgh	1961-1966

Name	**Home Town or Diocese**	**Years**
GORNOUVEL François	Ile et Vilaine	1912-1914
GOUBERT Carlos	Bogota, Colombia	1922-1923
GOULD Albert Edward	Portsmouth	1933-1936
GRACE John	Bradford	1934
GRADY Patrick	Glasgow/Motherwell	1934-1936
GREEN Kenneth	Glasgow	1965-1966
GREEN Reginald Alfred	Sheffield	1932
GREENE Michael	Birmingham	1962-1965
GREGSON Kevin Douglas	Aberdeen	1960-1964
GRIFFIN John Joseph	Waterford	1933-1934
GRIFFIN Michael Joseph	Leeds	1959-1963
GRIFFIN Robin	Middlesboro	1954-1958
GRIMES Thomas	Edinburgh	1938-1939
GRIMLEY Desmond	Glasgow	1947-1949
GRINSTEAD Joseph Henry	London	1919-1922
GRITTON Patrick George	Glasgow	1963-1966
GUEINNEC Hervé	Finisterre	1912-1915
GUERET Raymond	Rennes	1912-1914
GUILFOYLE Anthony	Birmingham	1950-1951
GUISARD Arnaud	Nantes	1915
GUNDOLFF Georges	Epernay	1912-1913
GUNNING Terence Joseph	Gurranabraher, Cork	1935
GUNTER Edmund Gottfried	Galashiels	1934-1935
GUTMAN Jean Marie	Paris	1920-1924
HADDAWAY Peter Graham	Harrow, Middx	1938-1940
HAIGH Joseph	Salford	1926-1927
HALL Bernard Thomas	Portsmouth	1922-1926
HALLIGAN William	Co. Westmeath	1936-1937
HALLORAN John Michael	Rotherham	1959-1960
HAMES Anthony Reardon	Ilford, Essex	1929-1933
HAMILTON Gerard	Liverpool	1950-1951
HANCOCK Benjamin Patrick	Leeds	1924-1930
HANCOCK Sidney Louis	Winchester	1921-1922
HANDFORD Frederick John*	Birmingham	1931
HANNON Robert Desmond	Dublin	1924
HARDING George Henry	Portsmouth	1933-1935
HARRISON Alfred	Manchester	1957-1959
HARRISON Philip	West Hartlepool	1949-1956
HARRITY Patrick	Glasgow	1949-1954
HARRITY William	Glasgow	1949-1953
HART William Andrew	Clydebank	1957-1961
HARTE John Michael	Grantham	1937
HARTE Patrick	Leyland, Lancs.	1947-1949
HARVEY Edward	Edinburgh	1955-1959
HASKEW Henry Peter	Stourbridge, Worc	1933-1934

Name	Home Town or Diocese	Years
HASKEW Kenelm	Birmingham	1922-1926
HASKEW Paul	Birmingham	1920-1925
HAWLEY Gerard Hubert Desmond	Dublin	1936-1938
HAYES Harold	Liverpool	1921-1924
HAYWARD Peter Philip	Birmingham	1936-1938
HEALY Francis	Leeds	1922-1924
HEALY John Joseph*	Newcastle	1918-1919
HEGARTY Anthony Stephen	Southwark	1944-1946
HENNEBRY John	Coventry	1963-1964
HENNESSY Thomas	Liverpool	1950-1954
HENRY André	Alger	1912-1915
HERRIDGE Christopher George	Portsmouth	1919-1921
HERRITY Herbert	Glasgow	1946-1947
HESKIN Edward	Chorley	1954
HICKEY Martin	Co. Cork	1950-1952
HICKS Charles Herbert	Dagenham, Essex	1932-1936
HIGGINS Francis	Edinburgh	1942-1944
HIGGINS Hugh	Leeds	1925-1929
HIGGINS John Patrick	Cairo	1934-1935
HILES Edward	Leeds	1936-1938
HILLAS Thomas	Hexham & Newcastle	1963-1967
HODNETT Leo	Liverpool	1944-1948
HODSON John	Liverpool	1950-1954
HOLCROFT Philip	St Anns, Lancs	1956-1959
HOLDAWAY John	Billingham, Durham	1965-1967
HOLLAND William Gerard	Innishannon	1939
HOLLIER Peter William	Westminster	1937-1938
HOLMES Arthur Stephen	Aldershot	1919-1921
HOLMES Patrick	Liverpool	1947-1952
HOPKINS Patrick Joseph	Liverpool	1932-1937
HOSKINS Peter	Cardiff	1952-1955
HOULIHAN Patrick Michael	Southwark	1938-1939
HOWARTH John	Liverpool	1920-1925
HOWELL Alfred Ernest	Menevia	1919. Ph 1920-21
HOWELL John Alfred		1928-1930
HOXLEY Graham James	Southsea	1955-1958
HUDSON Bernard	Middlesboro	1927
HUGHES Arthur Walter	London	1918-20. Ph 20-21
HUGHES Edward	Edinburgh	1945-1948
HUGHES James Peter	Bathgate	1933-1936
HUGHES John/Sean Francis	Liverpool	1960-1965
HUGHES Joseph Vincent	Lancaster	1916-17.Ph17-19
HULSE Michael	Birmingham	1946-1947
HUME Herbert Edward	Westminster	1926-1928
HYNES John	Warrington	1952-1955

Name	Home Town or Diocese	Years
HYNES Kevin	Middlesbrough	1952-1955
HYNES Michael Jarlath	Co. Cork	1950-1952
IMRAY Stewart R	Portsmouth	1924-1925
INNES Gerard	Glasgow	1950-1953
INNOCENT Anthony Thomas	Sheffield	1936
IRVINE Francis William	Derry	1923-1927
IRVINE John	Glasgow	1922-1927
IWEGBUNE Hyacint	Nigeria	1961
JACKSON Cecil Vivian	Westminster	1922-1925
JACKSON Peter	Chorley	1952-1955
JACKSON Peter	Salford	1956-1958
JACKSON William	Nottingham	1946-1947
JASON George	Cape Town, South Africa	1962-1967
JENKINS F		
JOHNSON Arthur Herbert*	Birmingham	1923
JOHNSON Cyril*	Leeds	1924-1925
JOHNSON Peter	Hex & Newcastle	1961-1964
JOHNSTONE Christopher	Southwark	1956-1959
JOHNSTONE Donald	Edinburgh	1954-1956
JOHNSTONE James	Motherwell	1950-1954
JONES John Joseph	Co. Cork	1936-1939
JONES Lawrence James William	Liverpool	1932-1933
JORY Felix	Gard	1913-1917
JOYCE Christopher Thomas	Westminster	1949
JOYCE John	Bamberbridge	1963-1966
KANE Francis*	Glasgow	1929
KANE John	Glasgow	1929-1931
KANE Thomas	Coatbridge	1933-1936
KAVANAGH Joseph	Glasgow	1950-1956
KEANE Stephen W	Brentwood	1927
KEANE Thomas Francis	Brentwood	1921-1922
KEARNEY Lionel	London	1953
KEARNEY William	Westminster	1946-1951
KEEGAN Gerald James	Waterford	1920-1921
KEEGAN Sean Christopher	Dublin	1939
KEENAN Donald		1964-1965
KEENAN Gerard	Birmingham	1946-1947
KEENAN Paul Anthony	Co. Cavan	1962-1964
KELLER Michael Andrew	Bristol	1958-1960
KELLY Gerard Francis	Salford	1927-1930
KELLY James Desmond	Perth	1963-1964
KELLY John Gerald	Motherwell	1951-1954
KELLY Michael	Leeds	1955-1957
KELLY Thomas	Glasgow	1955-1958
KEMPSTON John Edmund Douglas	Westminster/New Southgate	1933-1936

Name	Home Town or Diocese	Years
KENDELLEN Nicholas	Dublin	1956-1959
KENNEDY Bernard	Bradford	1934-1940
KENNEDY Francis	Glasgow	1921-1922
KENNEDY James	Brentwood	1928-1933
KENNEDY Lawrence	Southwark	1926-1931
KENNY James	Winchester	1920-1921
KERVAREC		1912
KILPATRICK Bernard Albert*	Motherwell	1933
KING Anthony Albert	London	1919-1921
KINGSELLER Cornelius	London	1922-1923
KINGSELLER George*	London	1922
KINGSELLER James	London	1925-1930
KINGSTON Thomas John	Co. Cork	1936-1940
KINLEN Richard	Hex & Newcastle	1962-1967
KIRWAN Marcus	Liverpool	1922-1923
KNELL William Adrian	Bermuda	1933-1935
LAGAN Brendan	Gateshead	1956-1957
LANCE Adrian	Westminster	1945-1950
LANE Thomas	Leyland, Lancs.	1947-1949
LARKINS John Paul	Bellshill	1955-1959
LAURENS Justin	Gard	1913-1917
LAVELLE John	Salford	1922-1926
LAW Daniel	Dumbarton	1934-1935
LAW Kenneth	Leeds / Halifax	1935-1938
LAWLESS John	London	1919-1921
LAWLOR William	Co. Carlow	1962-1963
LAYLAND John Francis	Sutton Coldfield	1965
LE ROUX François	Southwark	1947
LEA Stanley	Grantham	1921-1926
LEE Gerard James William	Leeds	1930-1931
LEE James	Glasgow	1952-1955
LEEK Bernard Thomas*	Birmingham	1923
LEMOINE Jules	Ile et Vilaine	1913-1915
LEONARD John Joseph	Motherwell	1960-1961
LEONARD John Joseph	Dundalk, Louth	1929-1931
LEONARD Martin	Glasgow	1956-1957
LETTINGTON David George	Kirkee, / Agra, India	1936
LEVEY Joseph William Gerard	Eastleigh	1934-1935
LEWIS Eugene	Co. Clare	1946-1951
LEWIS George William	Uxbridge, Middx	1935
LILLEY John Bosco	Birmingham	1947-1951
LOCKEY Raymond	Armadale	1961-1962
LOMAS James	Liverpool	1954-1956
LOTH Joseph	Southampton	1939-1940
LOUGHRAN	Peter	1955

Name	Home Town or Diocese	Years
LOWERY Peter	Glasgow	1954-1955
LYDEN John	Southwark	1952-1958
LYNCH Anthony Joseph William	Bradford	1936-1939
LYNCH Brian		1950-1953
LYNCH John	Newmills, Fife	1952-1955
LYNOTT John*	Liverpool	1922
LYONS Jeremiah	Cork City	1935-1937
MACBRIDE Eugene	Glasgow	1950-1954
MACDONALD Patrick	South Uist	1954-1956
MACHIN Peter	Sheffield	1951-1956
MACKLE Francis	Motherwell	1945-1947
MACKLE Thomas	Motherwell	1949-1952
MacLEOD Donald	Glasgow	1964-1966
MACMILLAN Denis Charles	Birmingham	1929
MACNEIL Ian		1953
MADDEN John	Leeds	1961-1965
MADDEN Terence	Kinloss / Selby	1965-1967
MADIGAN Richard Joseph	London	1924-1925
MAGEE Edward Matthew	Portsmouth	1927-1932
MAGEE Gabriel	Magherafelt	1947-1952
MAGGIORE Paul	Sunderland	1961-1964
MAGUIRE Anthony	Portsmouth	1944-1945
MAGUIRE Hugh Patrick	Edinburgh	1959-1963
MAGUIRE John	Salford	1927-1931
MAHUT Georges	Constantine	1913-1914
MAIR Alan Joseph	Newcastle on Tyne	1959-1961
MALLET Privat		1912-1913
MALLON Francis Joseph	Glasgow	1942-1943
MALONE William Bernard	London	1923-1924
MALONEY Gerald Michael Denis	Westminster	1939-1940
MALONEY John	Leeds	1935
MALONEY Michael		1949-1953
MANSFIELD Charles Philip	Southwark	1933-1936
MARCEL Joseph	Paris	1912
MARCHANT Leonard	London	1919-1922
MARR John	Dundee	1919-1923
MARTIN Ernest	Bradford	1934-1939
MARTIN Henry George	Bradford	1936-1939
MARTIN John	Edinburgh	1954-1956
MARTIN John	South Shields	1958-1960
MARTIN Patrick	Coatbridge	1952-1954
MASON Philip	Morpeth	1961-1966
MATTOCK John	Coventry	1962
MAXFIELD James Peter	Sunderland	1964-1967
MAXFIELD Thomas Patrick	Sunderland	1962-1965

Name	Home Town or Diocese	Years
MAY Terence David	Preston	1960-1963
McALPINE Gerald	Salford	1965-1966
McANALLAN Sean Malachy	Armagh	1965-1967
McANAW Peter Joseph	Clydebank	1920-1925
McATEER Gerald	Glasgow	1948-1953
McBRIDE Eugene	Glasgow	1950-1954
McBRIDE Michael	Wishaw	1954-1957
McBRYAN Arthur Cuthbert	Glasgow	1923-1926
McCABE Charles	Aberdeen	1938-1939
McCAFFREY Anthony	Stafford	1954-1958
McCALL Joseph Vincent	Dublin	1936-1939
McCALLION Edward	Wishaw	1927-1928
McCANA Liam Seamus	Dublin	1957-1960
McCARTHY Francis Michael	Co. Cavan	1961
McCARTHY Peter Aloysius	Limerick	1937-1938
McCARTHY Patrick Joseph	Co. Cork	1935
McCLUSKIE Peter	Irvine	1965-1967
McCOMBIE Peter	Gateshead	1946-1951
McCOMISKEY Daniel	West Calder	1932-1935
McCOMISKEY Peter	Edinburgh	1950-1954
McCORMACK Eric	Motherwell	1953-1957
McCORMACK Robert	Paisley	1930-1933
McCORMICK John Joseph	Toronto, Canada	1937-1940
McCOY Owen	Liverpool	1921-1926
McCULLOCH John	Hamilton	1932-1935
McCUNNIN Patrick	Dublin	1926-1928
McDERMOTT James	Sutton Coldfield	1956-1959
McDERMOTT Joseph	Motherwell	1952-1957
McDERMOTT Liam	Blackburn/West Lothian	1959-1960
McDEVITT Hugh Patrick	Motherwell	1957-1958
McDONALD John Joseph	Glasgow	1957-1961
McDONNELL Michael	Liverpool	1950-1956
McERLEAN Patrick	Dumbarton	1936-1937
McEVOY James	Newcastle on Tyne	1944-1948
McEWAN Patrick*	Stirling	1932
McFADDEN Lawrence	Preston	1961-1966
McGARRAGHY Paul	Blackburn	1954
McGARRY Alexander	Glasgow	1946-1951
McGHEE Owen	Clydebank	1922-1927
McGILL Daniel	Glasgow	1921-1922
McGOVERN Sean Michael	Co. Cavan	1958-1962
McGRAIL Thomas	Edinburgh	1932-1933
McGRATH Michael	Glasgow	1949-1953
McGRORY James	Glasgow	1929-1931
McGUINNESS Ciaran	Longford	1962-1965

Name	Home Town or Diocese	Years
McGUINNESS Francis Joseph	Westminster	1938-1939
McGUIRE Brian Manus	Edinburgh	1954-1957
McGUIRE Christopher	Edinburgh	1954-1957
McHALE Gerard Thomas	Pontefract	1934-1935
McHALE Patrick	Edinburgh	1962-1966
McHUGH Dennis Anthony	Aberdeen	1956-1959
McILVENNEY Thomas	Dumbarton	1933-1934
McINTYRE John	Liverpool	1942-1944
McINTYRE Joseph Patrick	Newcastle	1960-1965
McKAY George	Edinburgh	1964
McKEITH Thomas	Glasgow	1963-1964
McKENNA Richard Clement	Coventry	1957-1958
McKENNA Thomas	Glasgow	1949-1950
MACKENZIE John	Perth / Rothsay, Bute	1916-1917
McKENZIE Peter	Glasgow	1959-1962
McKEON Brendan	Dublin	1956-1957
McKEOWN Michael	Shrewsbury	1956-1958
McKINLAY James	Stirlingshire	1962-1964
McKINLAY Patrick	Larbert, Stirling	1965-1967
McLAREN Charles	Dundee	1955-1959
McLAUGHLAN Joseph	Coatbridge	1938-1939
McLAUGHLIN James	Clydebank	1963-1965
McLAVERTY John Maxwell	Portsmouth	1960-1961
McLEAN Hugh*		1929
McLEOD Alexander	Dunoon	1957-1958
McMANUS Joseph	Blantyre	1949-1954
McMURRAY Peter	Sutton Coldfield	1954-1958
McNALLY James	Glasgow	1932-1934
McNAMARA Donald Patrick	Shrewsbury	1937-1939
McNAMARA Peter Desmond	Welling, Kent	1937-1939
McNAMARA Michael	Birmingham	1963-1966
McPHARLANE Cormac	Dublin	1952-1953
McQUADE James	Paisley	1956-1958
McREYNOLDS John Joseph	Portadown	1963-1964
McSHERRY John	Paisley	1933-1936
McSHERRY Maurice	Armagh	1948-1953
McVEY Hugh	Stirling	1962-1967
MEARNS Michael	Chiswick, London	1955-1959
MEEHAN Patrick Joseph	Portsmouth	1926-1929
MELLING Joseph Bernard	Preston	1959-1962
MENZIES Patrick	Glasgow	1946-1951
MEYER Pierre	Alger	1912-1915
MIDDLEMASS Cyril Leo Stephen	Whitley Bay	1958
MILLER John Oliver	Portsmouth/Salisbury	1919-1924
MILLER Vincent	Portsmouth/Salisbury	1927-1932

Name	Home Town or Diocese	Years
MILLS John	Menevia	1963
MILNER Charles John	London	1920-1923
MONAGHAN Gerard James William	Glasgow/Airdrie	1933
MONAGHAN Hugh	Glasgow / Airdrie	1933-1936
MONAGHAN Patrick Francis	Glasgow / Airdrie	1933-1936
MONTEITH James	Glasgow	1928-1930
MOODY Paul Francis	Armagh	1938-1939
MOONEY Andrew Joseph	Glasgow	1957-1958
MORAN Adrian	Birmingham	1961-1966
MORAN Damien Joseph	Birmingham	1963-1966
MORAN Gerard	Leeds	1925-1928
MORAN John Patrick	Edinburgh	1930-1931
MORAN Thomas	Wigan	1927-1932
MORRIS Edward William	Salford	1927-1930
MORRISSEY John	York	1947-1951
MORTON John	Sutton Coldfield	1950-1953
MULLANE Denis	Cowie, Stirling	1959-1960
MULLANE Michael	Cowie, Stirling	1959-1960
MULLER Nicholas	Portsmouth	1954-1957
MULLIGAN John	Shrewsbury	1950-1954
MULLOY Daniel	Rutherglen	1961-1962
MULQUEEN Leo Alfred Vincent	Southwark	1931-1934
MULRANEY Edward	Motherwell	1950-1952
MURNANE Patrick	Cork/Dagenham, Essex	1935-1936
MURPHY Andrew	Dumbarton	1935-1936
MURPHY Andrew	Luton	1962-1967
MURPHY Francis	Liverpool	1958-1959
MURPHY James Henderson	Grangemouth	1943-1945
MURPHY John Joseph	Brentwood	1927-1928
MURPHY John Joseph	Co. Cork	1936-1937
MURPHY John	Leeds/Pontefract, Yorks	1935-1940
MURPHY Joseph Patrick	Leeds	1929-1934
MURPHY Peter	Leeds	1925-1929
MURPHY Sean	Coventry	1962-1967
MURPHY Thomas	Hamilton	1932-1936
MURRAY Charles Robert	Glasgow	1937
MURRAY James Patrick	Paisley	1960-1963
MURRAY John	Glasgow	1961-1964
MYTTON Anthony John	Walsall	1944-1950
NAPPER Gerald Cyril	Barnet, Herts.	1938-1939
NELSON James Francis*	Macclesfield	1933
NERTNEY Michael Joseph	London	1957-1959
NETTON Ian Richard	Warrington	1962-1964
NEVILLE James Henry*	Westminster	1925
NEWMAN Arthur	Northampton	1922-1927

Name	Home Town or Diocese	Years
NEWTON Philip	Birmingham	1933-1938
NICHOLAS John	Glasgow	1965-1966
NIMMO-SCOTT William	Southampton	1955-1957
NIXON Peter	Dumbarton	1924-1928
NOLAN Michael Joseph	Co. Tipperary	1957-1960
NORTH Richard Edward John	Plymouth	1933-1934
NOONAN Joseph Patrick	Ballydesmond, Cork	1935-1938
O'BRIEN Dennis	Westminster	1947-1950
O'BRIEN Francis	Glasgow	1956-1959
O'BRIEN Joseph Matthew	Westminster	1938-1939
O'BRIEN Peter	Co. Clare	1946-1952
O'BYRNE Gerard	Dublin	1954-1957
O'CONNOR Bernard	Leeds	1925-1932
O'CONNOR Daniel Brendan	Co. Cork	1936
O'CONNOR Daniel	Co. Cork	1939-1940
O'CONNOR Dermot	Barnsley	1936-1937
O'CONNOR John Edward	Ludd, Palestine/Farnborough	1935-1940
O'CONNOR Kevin	Glasgow	1959-1962
O'CONNOR Liam	Newcastle	1959-1960
O'CONNOR Ronald	Glasgow	1965-1967
O'DOHERTY Christopher Joseph	Limerick	1937-1939
O'DONNELL Hugh	Coventry	1952-1954
O'DONNELL Thomas	Preston	1933-1938
O'DONOHUE John Francis	Manchester	1942-1943
O'GORMAN Anthony	Edgware, Middx	1954-1956
O'HAGAN Daniel	Glasgow	1956-1959
O'HAGAN James Kerr	Glasgow	1939
O'HARA James	Glasgow	1946-1951
O'HARA Patrick	Glasgow	1947-1952
O'HARE Edward	Manchester	1922-1927
O'HARE Patrick Joseph	Motherwell	1942-1947
OLDERSHAW Peter Francis	Southport	1932
O'LEARY Jeremiah Joseph	Ballydesmond, Cork	1933-1939
O'LEARY Patrick Joseph	Kingwilliamstown, Cork	1933-1939
OLHER John	Co. Cork	1934-1935
OLIVIE Gabriel	Avignon	1914-1917
O'NEILL James	Glasgow	1939
O'NEILL Patrick	Northampton	1946-1951
O'ROURKE Dennis	Grangemouth	1957
ORR Francis Bulger	Sunderland	1919
OSBORNE Cyril Bernard	Aldershot	1919-1920
O'SHEA William	Cardiff/Neath, Wales	1936-1939
OSOWSKI Thomas Joseph	Whitehaven	1963-1964
O'SULLIVAN Cornelius	Ballydesmond	1932-1933
O'SULLIVAN David	Plymouth	1963-1965

Name	Home Town or Diocese	Years
O'SULLIVAN Denis Cornelius Joseph	Co. Cork	1934-1937
O'SULLIVAN Denis	Millstreet, Cork	1935-1936
O'SULLIVAN Joseph Patrick	Dublin	1939
O'SULLIVAN Michael	Tralee, Kerry	1933-1934
O'SULLIVAN Patrick	Co. Cork	1947-1953
O'SULLIVAN Patrick	Ashford, Kent	1951-1955
OTAKI Allan Fadaski	Middlesbrough	1937-1939
O'TOOLE James	Liverpool	1952-1955
OVERTON Peter		1950-1953
PARKER John	Leeds	1963-1965
PARKINSON James Bertram	Portsmouth	1922-1924
PARSONS Michael	Twickenham	1956-1957
PARSONS Richard	Southwark	1964-1966
PENDLEBURY David Vincent	St. Helens	1957-1958
PENISTONE George Roland	Salford	1937-1938
PÉRAIS Louis	Morbihan	1914-1917
PERRY Walter	Warrington	1950-1954
PETT Terence	Stanmore, Middx	1946
PETTIT Terence Anthony	Bromley, Kent	1954-1958
PHILLIPS John	Warrington	1950-1955
PIGNIDE Leon	Lozère	1912-1915
PILKINGTON Sidney Jack Ch David	Southampton	1934-1938
PINEAU Henri	Maine et Loire	1913-1915
PINKNEY Alban Lawrence	Westminster	1944-1945
PITT Gerard William	Birmingham	1932-1938
PLANK Vincent Edward	Portsmouth	1922-1923
POLLARD Cedric Anthony	Brentford	1963-1967
POLLARD Joseph	Salford	1922-1924
PONS Emmanuel	Lozère	1912-1915
POTTON Maurice	Glasgow	1945-1948
POWER Thomas	Glasgow	1957-1960
PRENDERVILLE Maurice	Portsmouth	1928
PREST John Percy	Aberdeen	1932-1935
PRESTON William Michael	Edinburgh	1952-1953
PRICE Thomas Reginald	Derby	1919
PRICE Thomas	Newry	1951-1954
PRIEUR Eugene	Lozère	1914-1917
PRIOR Nicholas	Southwark	1964-1966
PUMPHREY John Thomas	Portsmouth	1922-1926
PUTMAN John	Portsmouth	1928-1933
QUINN Anthony Francis	Ilford, Essex	1959
QUINN Anthony	Enniskillen	1961-1963
QUINN Brendan	Newry	1954
QUINN James J	Co. Tipperary	1956-1960
QUINN John	Liverpool	1950

Name	Home Town or Diocese	Years
QUIRKE Thomas Michael	Birmingham	1965-1966
RADCLYFFE John Arnold Ayscough	Auckland	1936-1938
RAFFERTY Gerard Stephen	London	1921-1923
RATHE Harold Gerard	Middlesbrough	1935
RATHE Thomas	Shrewsbury	1938-1939
REGAN Hugh	Edinburgh	1948-1950
REGGIO John	Southampton	1918
REILLY Joseph Henry	Portsmouth	1927-1931
REILLY Patrick	Coatbridge	1927-1930
RESSOUCHES Georges	Avignon	1912-1915
RICE Patrick	Clydebank	1954-1957
RILEY John	Southwark	1942-1945
RING Thomas Joseph	Ballydesmond, Cork	1933-1938
RITSON David	Jarrow	1961-1964
ROBERTSON John Ronan	Bathgate	1957-1960
ROBERTSON Peter	Birmingham	1961-1964
ROBERTSON Thomas Dominic	Bathgate	1958-1961
ROBIN Edouard	Alger	1913-1914
ROBINSON Charles	Leyland	1949-1951
ROBINSON Gerard	Liverpool	1952
ROBINSON John Metcalfe	Preston	1925-1930
ROBINSON John Lawrence	Liverpool	1923-1928
ROBINSON John Joseph	Motherwell	1932-1933
ROBINSON William	Motherwell	1945-1948
ROCKS John George Smith	Paisley	1937-1939
ROCOPLO Gabriel	Avignon	1913-1915
RODDEN John	Durham	1950-1951
ROGAN John	Southwark	1944-1945
ROGAN Peter	Westminster	1963-1966
ROGERS William Michael	Liverpool	1931-1932
ROGERSON Samuel*	Leeds	1918-1919
ROMAN Stanislaus George	Bradford	1935-1937
RONIÈRE Jean-Baptiste	Lozère	1913-1917
ROONEY Patrick	Glasgow	1922-1927
ROUGEOT Gaspard	Saone	1912-1915
ROUVIÉRE Felix	Lozère	1913-1917
ROWSE Anthony	Hex & Newcastle	1949
RUMBOLD Leonard	Portsmouth	1923-1925
RUSSELL Patrick Francis	Dorking	1957-1960
RUSSELL Thomas	Kelty, Fife	1959-1962
RUTLEDGE Gordon Francis	Stanmore, Middx	1955-1958
RYAN Anthony Joseph	Westminster	1960-1963
RYAN Francis	Glasgow	1950
RYAN Michael	Portsmouth	1923-1927
RYAN Michael	Widnes	1946-1950
RYAN Michael	Wigan	1952-1956

Name	Home Town or Diocese	Years
RYAN Thomas Patrick	Glasgow	1944
RYAN Vincent Joseph Manuel	Co. Cork	1937-1938
RYAN William Patrick	Waterford	1936-1937
RYCE Joseph	Hamilton	1935-1937
SADDLER Francis	Edinburgh	1949-1951
SALAVILLE Rigis	Lozère	1912-1915
SALMON Joseph Gerard	Liverpool	1939
SAVAGE Charles	Glasgow	1962-1966
SCOTT Joseph	Wallsend on Tyne	1949-1951
SCOTT Terence Ford	Hex & Newcastle	1944-1948
SCOTT Ian	Selkirk	1961-1966
SCRIVEN Gerard Francis	London	1927-1928
SEATON Francis	Hex & Newcastle	1950
SEDGWICK Edward	Westminster	1923-1925
SEED William	Lancaster	1959-1960
SELBY Robert Robertson	Edinburgh	1943-1945
SEXTON Gerard Francis	Dublin	1957-1959
SHANN Anthony	Coventry	1955-1959
SHANN Joseph Alfred	Leeds	1924-1925
SHANN Richard Terence	Coventry	1960-1961
SHANAHAN Patrick Joseph	Mill Hill, London	1955-1959
SHANNON Brendan	Newtownbutler	1952-1955
SHARKEY Patrick*	Co. Sligo	1923
SHAW Robert	Birmingham	1961-1965
SHELTON Angus James Patrick	Birmingham	1939-1940
SHERIDAN Thomas	Glasgow	1921-1922
SHERRY Daniel	Edinburgh	1939-1940
SHERWIN George	London	1922-1923
SHERWOOD Thomas*	Guisborough	1930
SHEVLIN Stephen John	Armagh	1957-1960
SHIELDS Brendan	Birmingham	1965-1966
SHIELDS Dennis	Edinburgh	1950-1952
SHIELDS John	Glasgow	1936-1937
SHIRLEY Christopher	Birmingham	1962-1963
SHORROCK Peter Joseph	Salford	1965-1967
SHORT Gerard	Birmingham	1956-1959
SIBLEY John Huxley Francis	Brentwood/Hove, Sussex	1933-1938
SIDGREAVES John	Manchester	1961
SIEDLE James	Cardiff/London	1927-1928
SIMS Maurice Edgar	London	1919-1921
SINIGAS Georges	Bordeaux	1914-1917
SLEVIN John	Hex & Newcastle	1945-1950
SLOAN Richard	Liverpool	1965-1967
SMALL John	Motherwell	1949-1953
SMIT Jonathan Michael	Lechlade, Glos	1963-1967
SMITH Desmond Patrick	Middlesbrough	1955-1959

Name	Home Town or Diocese	Years
SMITH Donald Archie	South Uist/Glasgow	1933-1936
SMITH George Harold	Menevia	1922-1927
SMITH George	Hamilton	1954-1957
SMITH James	Menevia/Liverpool	1920-1924
SMITH John McKinnon	Glasgow	1938
SMITH John	Middlesbrough	1949-1952
SMITH Leo	Dublin	1950-1952
SMITH Matthias Francis	Edinburgh	1959-1961
SMITH Peter	Middlesbrough	1956-1960
SMITH Reginald	Nottingham	1920
SMITH William	London	1923-1924
SMYTH Anthony David	Hex & Newcastle	1962-1967
SMYTH Dennis	Glasgow	1962
SOUTHALL Patrick	Coventry	1956-1958
SPENCER John	Liverpool	1919-1921
SPITTLE Sidney Lawrence	ThorntonHeath	1931-1935
STACK Gerald James	Leix, Ireland	1935-1940
STACK Robert Brendan James	Nottingham	1959-1960
STANLEY John Frederick Sidney	Cloyne/Newport, Wales	1923-1928
STAPLETON Christopher	Southwark	1922-1925
STAPYLTON Walter	Leeds	1934-1936
STARKEY Brian Dennis	Altrincham	1965
STEWART Edward	Westminster	1923
STOKER Joseph Francis	Leeds	1919-1923
STOKER Thomas	Leeds	1932-1933
STOKES Bernard Brian Kieran	Dublin	1957-1958
STRAIN John	Blackpool	1962-1964
SULLIVAN Daniel*	Brentwood	1924-1925
SULLIVAN William	Motherwell	1950-1952
SURDIVAL Sean	Dublin	1953-1956
SUTCLIFFE John	Southall, Middx	1932-1933
SUTHERLAND Walter	Edinburgh	1938-1939
SWAINE James	Dublin	1927-1931
SWEENEY Charles Geoffrey	Bradford	1932-1936
SWEENEY Raymond Joseph	Reading	1963-1966
SYMONDS Edward Charles	Leeds	1922-1923
TAIT John	Heston, Middx	1956-1958
TAIT Paul	Heston, Middx	1956-1959
TALBOT George William	Birkenhead	1919-1921
TANNIOU		1912
TAPPENDEN Guy	Southsea	1920-1925
TAYLOR Edward	Liverpool	1925-1930
TAYLOR Gerard David	Sunderland	1934-1939
TAYLOR Robert	Liverpool	1952-1954
TEAGUE John James	Glasgow	1939-1940
THOMAS Henry Huish	Westminster	1936

Name	Home Town or Diocese	Years
THOMPSON Laurence Alan	Stockton on Tees	1943
THORNTON Robert Peter	Glasgow	1936-1937
TICKLE Edward	Leeds	1929-1931
TIERNEY Joseph	Glasgow	1950-1955
TIERNEY Patrick	Glasgow	1950-1956
TIMSON Stephen Jude	Wallasey	1965-1966
TITAIRE Reni Marcel	Rouen, France	1936-1937
TOBIN Henry	Glasgow	1929-1930
TOBIN James	Glasgow	1929-1934
TOBIN Michael	Portsmouth	1963-1965
TOBIN Richard	Airdrie	1956
TOBIN Richard*	Glasgow	1930
TOBY Eric	Salford	1921-1926
TOBYMaurice	Salford	1921-1926
TOGHER John William	Hamilton	1933-1936
TOLMIE Alexander	Glasgow	1939-1940
TOLMIE James	Bellshill, Scotland	1933-1936
TONNER William	Glasgow	1965
TONNER William	Stirling	1950-1955
TOOP Francis	London	1963-1967
TORTOLANO Francis	Bannockburn	1950-1953
TOYE William	Glasgow	1929-1931
TRIVERS Charles	Motherwell	1950-1953
TRYERS Francis Xavier Patrick	Liverpool	1934-1937
TRYERS Thomas Augustine	Liverpool	1933-1934
TUCKEY David Paul	Southwark	1944-1949
TURK George	Glasgow	1933-1938
TURNBULL Norman	Leven, Fife	1965-1967
TURNER George Henry	Preston	1931-1932
TWOMEY Patrick	Berehaven, Cork	1932-1937
TYE John Thomas	Westminster	1925-1930
UNSWORTH William	Leigh, Lancs	1919
VALE-HUMPHREYS Peter	Birmingham	1959-1962
VALLELY James Francis	Glasgow	1919-1923
VAN HOORN George	Louvain	1918-1919
VAN WELL Hans Gerhard	Reading	1962-1964
VELLAS Emile	Gard	1913-1917
VERRALL Samuel Joseph	Dublin	1934-1935
VIDEAU Adrian	Sierra Leone	1921-1923
VISOCCHI Anthony Mariano	Edinburgh	1952-1956
VOSE William	Darlington	1946-1949
WAGSTAFF Francis William*	Banbury	1930
WALKER David	Winsford, Chesh	1961-1964
WALKER Ronald Joseph	Bishops Waltham	1916
WALLACE James	Northampton	1946-1951
WALLBANK Christopher	Leamington Spa	1961-1967

Name	Home Town or Diocese	Years
WALSH Daniel Joseph	Cork	1919-1922
WALSH Joseph Edward	Leeds	1922-1925
WALSH James Patrick	Leeds	1928-1933
WALSH Richard Mortimer	Kerry	1925-1930
WALSH Thomas Aidan	Leeds	1965-1967
WALTERS Peter Percival	Clifton/Bristol	1934-1939
WARING Francis	Liverpool	1928-1930
WAROM Anthony	Birmingham	1950-1953
WATTERS Seamus Edward	Co. Cavan	1959-1962
WEBB Christopher	Grantham	1946-1947
WEBB Patrick	Grantham	1949-1950
WELHAM Robert John	Southwark	1926-1927
WENGEWORTH Godfrey	Glasgow	1942-1943
WEST John	Heston, Middx	1954-1956
WEST Paul	Heston, Middx	1955-1957
WETZ Peter	Wimbledon	1953-1954
WHARTON Christopher John	Birmingham	1960-1961
WHISTON Gerald	Edinburgh	1938-1940
WHITE Christopher Gordon	Southsea, Hants	1935-1939
WHITE Ernest		1951-1954
WHITE Frederick Cecil	Southwark	1922-1926
WHITE Joseph	Inverness	1932-1934
WHYATT Thomas John	Salford	1962-1967
WILLIAMS James Joseph	Enniscorthy, Wexford	1935-1936
WILLIAMS Martin	Portsmouth	1930-1933
WILLIAMS Peter	Middlesbrough	1949-1952
WILLOX Vincent	Glasgow	1938
WINDSCHEFFEL Bernard Kenneth	Devonport	1921-1925
WINDSCHEFFEL Clement John	Plymouth	1925-1926
WINTER James	Glasgow	1949
WISEMAN Francis Carl	Sheffield	1943-1945
WISEMAN Joseph Kevin	Wakefield/Sheffield	1936-1938
WISEMAN Vincent Paul	Sheffield	1944-1948
WOOD John	Birmingham	1919-1923
WOODHOUSE Thomas James	Bradford	1935-1938
WOODS John Frederick	Dublin	1937-1939
WOODWARD Charles Leo*	Sunderland/Southampton	1919
WOOLER Frederick John	Brentwood	1939-1940
WOOLF John Louis	Leeds	1943-1944
WYLIE Peter	Liverpool	1947
WYNNE Gerald	Edinburgh	1950-1954
YEOMANSON Francis	Brighton	1950
YOUDALE James	Cumberland	1951-1956
YOUNG Robert Godfrey	Scarborough	1958-1959

* Postulant brothers

B

Priory Staff 1912–1967

Name		Years
Bro AELRED	(Peter Biewer)	1956-59
Bro AIDAN	(John Ryan)	1926-27
Bro ALBAN	(Arthur H Johnson) (Oblate)	1924-26
Bro ALEXANDRE	(Christian van Herpen)	1921-25
Bro ALYPE	(Jean-Louis Bruynius)	1915-22
Mr ANDERSON W	(Resident lay teacher)	1919-21
Bro ANDREW	(Andrew Cathie)	1956-58
Bro AUBERT	(Pierre van der Wijst) †	1913-50
BALL	Francis	1952-53
BOLDUC	Joseph	1925-31
BOUCAUSAUD	Claude	1922-26
BOUNIOL	Joseph	1912-14, 1919-37
Bro BOYD	Patrick (Theology-student teacher)	1946-47
BRADLEY	John	1938-40
BRASSAC	Adolphe	1913-14
BRENCHER	Ernest (Th-student teacher'30-'31)	1930-31,1932-33
BRENNAN	William	1948
BRULS	Louis (Priest-student teacher)	1946-47
BRUTEL	Emile	1915
BURRIDGE	William	1936-39, 1957-60 (PP)
BURTON	Gerard	1955-57 (PP)
Bro CAMILLE	(François Viel)	1912-13
CANTWELL	Richard	1958-60
Bro CASIMIR	(Kazimerz Warszylewicz)	1957-60
CASSIDY	John	1953-54
CAZIN	Clotaire (Priest-student teacher)	1947-48
CHOLLET	Jean Marie	1912-14
COGHLAN	Michael	1944-45, 55-56, 65-70 (PP)
COLLINS	Stephen	1950-54
Bro COLUMBKILLE (John Mennie) See Bro MENNIE John		
CONLON	John	1962-64
CONWAY	Thomas	1954-55, 1967
CÔTÉ	Henri °	1925-34
COUCHE	John (Resident lay teacher)	1918-19?
COUTU	Rémi	1912-15
Bro CUTHBERT	(Lionel O'Neill)	1942-43
Bro CYPRIEN	(Eugene Cassidy)	1939

Name		Years
Bro DANIEL	(Désiré Vanderwegen)	1954-55
D'ARCY	Bernard P	1945-49
Bro DAVID	(James Kennedy)	1948, 1954-56
DELAEY	Alban	1914
DERY	Joseph	1922-24
DICKSON	Francis	1948-56
DONNELLY	Patrick	1951-53
DROST	Balthazar	1914-15
DUCOURANT	Albert	1914-19
DUFFY	Bernard #	1948-53, 1961-63
EGAN	John	1955
Bro EGBERT	(Cornelis Verheugd)	1912-15
EISELE	Adolf	1949-50
ENGLISH	Pierce	1959-60 †
Bro EVARISTE	(George Kingseller)	1925-26, 1933-34
FADY	Joseph +1	1951
FALGUIÉRES	Eloi	1912-14, 1919-21
FITZGERALD	Patrick	1954-61
Bro FLORIAN	(Charles Andrews)	1931-35
FOLLIOT	Albert	1914-20
FORBES	John +2	1914-16
FORTIN	Robert	1949-50
FOWLES	John	1953-59, 1962-66
GAFFNEY	Bernard #	1931-36
GAGNON	Charles	1921-25
Bro GARDNER	Albert (Agricultural student)	1964-65
GARVEY	Brian	1962-66
GERAGHTY	Lawrence	1962
Mr GILBERT	(Non-resident lay teacher)	1918-20/29(?)
Prof GUILBERT	(Non-resident lay teacher)	1929
GUNTER	Edmund	1934-35
HAIGH	Joseph	1934-37, 1961-66
HALLIGAN	William	1952-54, 1956-57, 1966
HARTMANN	Bernhard	1939-40
Mrs HEATH	Doreen (Non-resident lay teacher)	1959-62
Mr HEATH	John (Non-resident lay teacher)	1946-63
HOULIHAN	Patrick	1947-48
HOWELL	Alfred Ernest #	1926-28
HUGHES	Arthur ++ †	1927-30
Bro JEAN	(Jean Fréring)	1912-13
Bro JOHN OGILVIE	(James Sweeney)	1950-52, 1959-60
JONES	John Joseph ##	1946-47
Bro JOSEPH FRANCIS (Eugene Leonard) See LEONARD Eugene		
KAPPEL	Pierre	1914-15
KEANE	Thomas	1929-37

Name		Years
Bro KELLEY	David	1960-62
Bro KELLY	Michael (Architectural student)	1966-67
KINGSELLER	Cornelius	1930-44
LABRECQUE	Edouard	1921-22
LASSOUMERY	Francisque	1915
LEA	Stanley	1934-35, 44-47, 66-67
LEFEBVRE	Emile	1913-14
LEFILS	Paul	1925-27
Bro LEO	(Charles Woodward)	1922-23
Bro LEONARD	Eugene	1957-58
Bro LUCIEN	(Louis Murrer)	1913-19
LYNCH	John	1964-65
LYNCH	William	1957-60
MADELEINE	Auguste	1915-16
MARCHANT	Leonard	1929-36
Bro MARCIEN	(Antoine Barrette)	1926-31
MARTIN	Patrick	1965-66
Bro MAX	(Valentin Kirtscher)	1912-13
Bro MENNIE	John	1958-59, 1960-61
Bro MODESTE	(Petrus Broekman)†	1914-31, 1936-56
MOLONEY	Michael	1961-64
MONAGHAN	Hugh	1951-58
MOODY	Paul Francis	1953-54, 1955-58
MORAN	Thomas	1939, 1945-51
MORETON	Henry	1960-65 (PP)
MONTAU	Louis	1913-14
MURPHY	Andrew #	1943-48
MURPHY	Donald	1938-40
MURPHY	J P (Diocesan priest)	1924-38
MURPHY	Joseph	1943-48
NADON	Adhemar-Darcy	1919-20
Bro NICAISE	(Hendricus Bouwmans)	1914-15
NICOLE	Romuald	1926-29
NOLAN	Francis	1965
O'DONNELL	Thomas	1948-52
O'DONOHUE	John	1958-62
OP DEN KAMP	Piet	1914-15
O'SULLIVAN	Cornelius	1947-54
Bro PATRICK	(John Leonard)	1934-56
Bro PAUL-ANTHONY (Joseph Sullivan)		1946-48
PRENTICE	Arthur	1920-21 (Philo), 1921-24
RATHE	Thomas	1956-59
REGAN	Hugh	1960
RICHARD	Donat	1927-34
RIJKERS	Jean-Marie	1936-40

Name		Years
ROBERT	Joseph	1915-25
ROBINSON	John	1943, 1944-47
ROY	Armand	1924-27
RUDD	John (Theology-student teacher) ⋆	1947-48
RYAN	Michael	1934-40, 1942-44
Mr SAVAGE	Michael (Resident lay teacher) ⋆⋆	1964-65
Mr SIMS	Alfred (Non-resident lay teacher)	1912-13
SMITH	James	1938-43
SMITH	William (Priest in Charge at Southsea)	1967-68
STANLEY	Sidney	1935-39, 1942-44
Mr STEWART	(Resident lay teacher)	1923-24
SWEENEY	Charles Geoffrey	1944-45, 1955-56
TAYLOR	Edward	1936-38
Bro TERENCE	(J Coghlan)	1943, 1953-54
TÉTRAULT	Philippe	1950
Bro THOMAS MORE	(Alphonsus Toland)	1948-54, 1962
THOMPSON	Lawrence Alan	1954-61
TOLMIE	James	1944-53
TRAVERS	Pierre Marie †	1912-14, 1915-27
TRYERS	Thomas	1951-53
VAN DEN HOEVEN	Leo	1940-43
VAN HISSENHOVEN	René	1920-22
VAN UDEN	Corneille ‡	Jan 1916 - Sept 1916
WALSH	Francis +3	1930-31
WALSH	Patrick	1959-60
WALTERS	Peter	1949-50
Miss WILEY	(Non-resident lay teacher)	c1962-65
Mr WILLIAMS	Daniel J (Resident lay teacher) ⋆	1960-62

⋆ Later ordained priest for Cardiff diocese, Wales.
⋆⋆ Later ordained priestfor Mbala diocese, Zambia.
Later Provincial Superior of Britain & Ireland.
Later Provincial Superior of Ireland.
++ Later Archbishop of Apro & Papal Internuncio to Egypt.
+1 Later Bishop of Lilongwe, Malawi.
+2 Later Bishop of Vaga & Coadjutor Vic Apostolic of Uganda.
+3 Later Bishop of Aberdeen, Scotland
° LaterProv'l Superior of Canada & Assistant to Sup General.
PP Parish Priest of Bishop's Waltham.
‡ Chaplain to Belgian soldiers.
† Buried in the Priory cemetery.

C

Priory Superiors 1912–1967

Years	Name
1912-14	Pierre Marie Travers
1914-15	John Forbes
1915-26	Pierre Marie Travers
1926-38	Joseph Bouniol
1938-44	James Smith
1944-47	Stanley Lea
1947-51	Thomas Moran
1951-53	Patrick Donnelly
1953-54	John Cassidy
1955	John Egan
1955-58	P Francis Moody
1958-61	Patrick Fitzgerald
1961-63	Bernard Duffy
1964-66	John Fowles
1966-67	Stanley Lea

D

Priory School Captains 1922–1967

Years	Name
1912-22	(Unknown)
1922-23	Leonard Marchant
1923-24	James Smith
1924-25	Paul Haskew
1925-26	Stanley Lea
1927-28	John Robinson
1928-29	Richard Walsh
1929-30	Richard Walsh
1930-31	Martin Chambers
1931-32	Vincent Miller
1932-33	Anthony Hames
1933-34	Joseph Murphy
1934-35	William Blakeman
1935-36	Donald Smith
1936-37	Michael Coghlan
1937-38	George Penistone
1938-39	Gerard Taylor
1939-40	Bernard Kennedy
1940-41	None
1941-42	None
1942-43	John Conway
1943-44	Peter Coldham
1944-45	James Murphy

Years	Name
1945-46	Anthony Hegarty
1946-47	James Gielty
1947-48	Francis Mackle
1948-49	Louis Fitzmaurice
1949-50	Michael Ryan
1950-51	John Morrissey
1951-52	Peter Finn
1952-53	Francis Dillon
1953-54	Walter Perry
1954-55	John Hynes
1955-56	Richard Calcutt
1956-57	Brian McGuire
1957-58	Hugh Concagh
1958-59	Patrick Shanahan
1959-60	John Quinn
1960-61	John McDonald
1961-62	Sean McGovern
1962-63	Michael Griffin
1963-64	Sean Hughes
1964-65	Sean Hughes
1965-66	Ian Scott
1966-67	Andrew Murphy

E

St John's Pupils 1967–1970

Name	Town or Diocese	Years
BRIGHOUSE John	Liverpool	1967-68
EILERTSEN Eilert	Dundee	1967-69
GALLAGHER Michael	Donegal	1967-70
GIBBONS Thomas	Coventry	1967-68
GLOVER Paul Brendan	Liverpool	1967-68
HOLDAWAY John	Billingham, Durham	1967-68
MADDEN Terence	Kinloss	1967-70
MURPHY Sean	Coventry	1967-68
POLLARD Cedric Anthony	Brentford	1967-68
SLOAN Richard	Liverpool	1967-68
SMIT Jonathan Michael	Lechlade, Glos	1967-68
TOOP Francis	London	1967-68
TURNBULL Norman	Leven, Fife	1967-69

Priest in Charge: William Smith 1967-68

F

Domestic Staff 1918–1967

Name	Years
APPS, Mrs Rose	1940-42
BELSTONE, Mrs	1934-40
BREWER, Mrs	1947-48
BROWN, Mrs	1959-60s
BUTLER, Mrs	1940-41
CLEMENT, Mr	1918-19
COOPER, Mrs	1919-33
CREIGHTON, Mrs	1959-60s
FENNER, Mrs	1954-55
FLOOK, Mrs	1959-60s
HAMMOND, Miss	1960s
HARFORD, Mrs	1936-40
IACOBUCCI, Mrs Gilda	1962-67
MERCIER, Mrs	1933-36
POND, Mr Len	1950s & 60s
RODGERS, Mrs Norah	1943-61
SCOTT, Mrs	1962-67
SMITH, Mrs Lilian	1955-56, 58-61
TILBURY, Mr	1941
TILBURY, Mrs	1939-41
TILLNEY, Mrs	1954
WARD, Miss Ivy	1958-60s
WHEELER, Mr	1930s, 45-49

G

Priory Cemetery Graves

P M Travers WF
First Superior of this Missionary School
Died 17 April 1927, aged 52 years

Peter Murphy, Seminarist
Died 6 April 1929

Peter Joseph Flanagan, Seminarist
Died 24 October 1932

Cornelius Willem Marie de Waal WF Deacon
Died 1 November 1935

Archbishop Arthur Walter Hughes WF
Titular Archbishop of Apro
Apostolic Internuncio to Egypt
Died 12 July 1949, aged 46 years

Brother Aubert WF
Died 28 June 1950

Brother Modeste WF
Died 22 February 1956

Andreas Johannes Verdonk WF
Died 22 July 1958

Pierce John English WF
Died 1 April 1960

Henry Moreton WF
Died 26 January 1965

John Burdett-Clark
At rest 25th Jan 2001
Aged 79 years

The little school cemetery is now within the grounds of the Catholic parish church in Martin Street. Before 1968, the entrance to the cemetery was where the large crucifix now stands, entry being from the Boys' Drive. The crucifix was moved to the opposite end of the plot to provide access from the present church grounds.

H

Internment Camp 1940–1944

The philosophy students of 1939 were unable to continue using the college at Autreppe in Belgium because of the imminent war. Nor could they use Rossington Hall in Yorkshire, which had been recently purchased to replace Autreppe, because it had been requisitioned by the army. A disastrous decision was then made to send them to Kerlois, the French college of philosophy. This was at Hennebont on the southwest coast of Brittany which, French contacts assured them, would not be invaded. The 22 students and their two professors (Father Jan Deltijk, the intended Rector of Rossington Hall from Autreppe, and Father Jack Maguire, fresh from the Angelicum University in Rome) were told to report in the meantime to the Priory. They started their studies there on the 6th November, but the accommodation was unsatisfactory.

They set out for France a month later in separate groups for safety's sake. On the 8th December the second year students left with Father Maguire, and the others followed on the 26th December with Father Deltijk. They crossed the Channel by the ferry from Southampton to Le Havre and continued by train to Hennebont. Throughout the journey a blackout was maintained as a safeguard against aerial bombing. They arrived safely at Kerlois ('House of St Louis' in Breton) and were together again in time to celebrate New Year's Day 1940. Their French superiors were still convinced that the Germans would not reach Hennebont, but in July 1940, the invading army occupied the area and the English-speaking group was marched off to a local prison. They were moved on to prisoner-of-war camps before being finally incarcerated in an all male internment camp at St Denis, near Paris.

Three of the group who had Irish passports, William Brennan, John Jones and Joseph McCall, were not arrested. The Irish Consul was willing to issue Irish passports to people who could establish a personal connection with Ireland, and under this scheme Bernard D'Arcy and Patrick Houlihan, who had British passports, obtained Irish papers and were released. The Priory records show that D'Arcy was from Carlisle and Houlihan from Southwark, although both became members of the Irish Province when it was established in 1971. Father Jan Deltijk, a Dutchman, was not arrested and returned with the Irish students to Kerlois. Kerlois was soon afterwards requisitioned by the German army and the neutral nationalities went to a White Fathers' house in the then unoccupied south of France. Joseph McCall attempted to return home and obtained visas for passage through Spain and Portugal. However, the German authorities would not grant him a visa to leave France, so he got a post as resident English Master in a Marist Fathers' school at La Seyne-sur-Mer, near Toulon, in October 1942. In November 1942 he witnessed the invasion of Toulon, which until then was unoccupied territory, and the scuttling of the French fleet in the harbour.

Father Jack Maguire was the superior in the camp and solely responsible for the students although he was not much older than they were, being only 28. His black beard, large physique and military bearing, however, gave him an authoritative air.

Father Tom Moran, aged 27, was among those detained at Hennebont. He had been teaching English at the Tournus Apostolic School from March 1940, but had to leave in May when the school was forced to close because of the war. He went to what appeared a safe haven at Hennebont, but within two months he was arrested with the others.

In difficult circumstances the little group continued their community and seminary life in the camp. Their religious devotions and studies were maintained and, as much as possible, they wore their white habits. For studies they were divided into two groups: those that had completed the philosophy course in July were taught theology by Tom Moran, using a single textbook. The others, who by now had completed their first year, were taught second-year philosophy by Jack Maguire using books sent from Kerlois. Father Tom Dooley recalled that through the good offices of Colonel Schmidt, the Camp Commandant, more books were obtained from Germany.

Fortunately, at this time, scholastic philosophy and theology books were in Latin so a student was not limited to books in his native language.

H.1. Fathers Moran and Maguire in internment camp.

The daily diet in the camp was cabbage soup with occasional slices of sausage, one loaf of bread between four men, and ersatz coffee made from roasted barley. Many of the other internees, being domiciled in France, had friends or relations in the Paris area who brought them food. These prisoners gave their soup ration to the White Fathers, who were known as the 'cabbage soup boys' or 'crazy English boys', for they existed on cabbage soup and bread, wore white habits at their lessons and played football several times a week on the parade ground. Later their condition was alleviated a little by Red Cross food parcels, but this was too late for one of the boys, Billy O'Shea, who died in the camp in 1941. As Father Dooley later remarked: 'The food parcels were literally lifesavers ... More than a few of us would not have made it without them'.

Shortly after New Year 1942 a Mademoiselle Demeur contacted Kevin Wiseman (one of the students) with an offer to help him and some friends to escape. He was advised by Jack Maguire to be prudent, whereupon he decided to stay put. Unfortunately, in an act of misplaced trust, the address of the safe house, which he had been given, was passed to a fellow internee. This was a soldier, Jock Phelps, who had been left behind after the evacuation of British troops from Dunkirk in May and June 1940. He had discarded his uniform, obtained civilian clothes, and was now interned as a civilian. He and some companions made their escape. In a short time and with hardly believable crassness they entered a bar looking for alcohol. Their stupidity resulted in dire consequences for themselves and others. The Gestapo followed them to the house of Mademoiselle Demeur, who fortunately was not at home, and were arrested. They were never seen again, but under questioning they implicated Kevin Wiseman. He was taken to the Gestapo bureau in the Hotel Crillon in Paris for interrogation on the 18th February 1942, just a week after his 21st birthday. There he was told that the woman was to be shot. The interrogators were convinced he was a British soldier, doubtless having discovered that the escaping Jock Phelps was an army man. Wiseman persisted in claiming to be a civilian and was thereupon condemned to be shot as a spy. Before being led away, he was told that the woman had escaped. He was taken to Fresnes prison and placed in solitary confinement. Eight days later, on the 26th February, the president of the tribunal that tried him came with an interpreter to tell him that he would be shot at 3pm that day. He was given pencil and paper and wrote letters to his parents and to Father Maguire.

H.2. Kevin Wiseman in the camp before death sentence.

Later the same day he was told that he would not be executed. What had happened was that the prison chaplain, a German priest who brought the sacraments to the prisoners and accompanied condemned men to the place of execution, received the list of those to be shot that day. He immediately contacted the general who governed Paris and told him it would be adverse propaganda if a churchman were to be executed when the occupying force was trying to avoid hostilities with the Church. Wiseman's relief was short-lived, for on the 2nd March the Gestapo officer returned to tell him that the sentence would be carried out but, because of the

H.3. Sketch of Kevin Wiseman after release from condemned cell.

complications that had been introduced by the countermanding order, authorisation was being sought from Berlin. He was given pencil and paper again, and this time he wrote to the Provincial Superior of the White Fathers in Paris as as well as to Father Maguire. The Provincial Superior, Father Joseph Boudon – a former Priory boy, lost no time in calling on the German prison chaplain, the Swiss authorities (which represented British interests) and the Archbishop of Paris. Their intervention, and possibly the stronger political clout in Berlin of the Paris military governor in his contest with the Gestapo, resulted in a pardon being granted on the 17th May. Five days later, on the 22nd May 1942, he was taken back, a very skinny bearded young man, to the camp and to his lessons.

H.4. Capt Reiner, Colonel Schmidt (Commandant), and Lieut Leisinger. St Denis Camp, June 1941.

The internees were liberated on the 25th August 1944. Unfortunately, their nearly five years in France counted as only two years of study; they were required to continue with a novitiate year and four years of theology before ordination.

Tom Moran, who had contracted tuberculosis in the camp, was later appointed Superior of the Priory. Jack Maguire became rector of the College of Philosophy at Broome Hall, Surrey, then British Provincial Superior, and afterwards rector of St Augustine's College of Philosophy at Blacklion, County Cavan.

The internees were:

Father Jack Maguire	Joe O'Brien ⋆
Father Tom Moran	Tom O'Donnell ⋆
Vincent Batty	Billy O'Shea
Francis Copping	George Penistone
Tom Dooley⋆	Gerry Pitt
George Fry	Tom Rathe ⋆
Gerry Geddes⋆	Gerry Taylor ⋆
Garry Gewey	Peter Walters ⋆
Frank Moody ⋆	Kevin Wiseman⋆
Gerry Napper	

Not interned: Father Jan Deltijk, William Brennan⋆, John Jones⋆, Joseph McCall, Bernard D'Arcy⋆, and Patrick Houlihan⋆.

All those interned were former Priory boys except for Brennan and Gewey. Of the 22 students, Billy O'Shea died in the camp, George Fry died shortly after liberation, and 13 (indicated by ⋆) were ordained as White Fathers.

(Information in this appendix has been derived from *Destined for a Mission* by Kevin Wiseman, KAAS Publishing Corporation, Houston, USA, 1999; letter from Kevin Wiseman to the author, 13 July 1999; unpublished typescript of Thomas Dooley, 1984; 'Missionary Studies in a World at War' by Patrick Boyd, in *White Fathers – White Sisters*, No. 335, August-September 1997; and 'The Battle of Toulon 1942' by Joseph McCall, in *The Pelican*, Summer 1957.)

I

Saint Laurent d'Olt Apostolic School

The school at St Laurent d'Olt was originally established not for aspirants to the priesthood, but for poor Arab boys to prepare them for careers in the professions. About 1870 Archbishop Lavigerie set up in Algeria an 'Arab Junior Seminary' (a college for teenaged boys) for the more able of the orphans under his care. Later, other able boys were admitted with the permission of their fathers. In 1874 Lavigerie transferred the seminary to France after rumours that the government was going to take the orphans and place them in their own establishments. In the uncertain situation, he thought it wise to get the boys out of Algeria, and turned to his friend Bishop Bourret in Rodez for help. Eventually a château big enough to house the pupils was found in the village of Saint Laurent d'Olt in the south of France and 70 pupils were installed there in November 1874.

Problems that were later to become familiar at the Priory arose immediately. 'The Society of Missionaries however still had very few members, and there were so many other urgent tasks to be done that there were frequent changes in the staff of St Laurent d'Olt. New faces kept appearing in the classroom, and they were not always faces well equipped for the task'. There was also the problem of money, 'so they [the priests] went begging round the parishes.'

Lavigerie insisted on the boys being educated as 'Christians and apostles, not as Frenchmen or Europeans', and on 'the necessity of respect for African traditions'. He drew up a list of the subjects they were to be taught, and ordered that 'the study of Arabic will have a preponderant place in their classes'. 'Some of the pupils did well ... Some became legal interpreters, some entered the Cavalry School of Saumur, some joined the Navy. Thirteen went on to study medicine, and five of them ... reached the doctorate.'

In 1877 French boys wishing to enter the Society of Missionaries of Africa were admitted. The number of Arab pupils steadily declined for many reasons including the austere form of life and homesickness. The perceived government threat had not materialised, and by 1882 all the Arab boys, except for a few that wished to study for the priesthood, had returned to the more congenial atmosphere of their homeland. From 1882 the school admitted only boys wishing to become missionary priests and was no longer an Arab school.

It was now called an Apostolic School and it continued as such until 1948 when staff and pupils were transferred to Bonnelles, Seine-et-Oise, near Paris.[238] The building then served as a rest home for sick and aged missionaries until finally closing in 1953.[239] In 1955 it was sold for local government use, and it currently belongs to *La Fédération Générale des Association Départementales des Pupilles de l'Enseignement Public*.[240]

(Most of the information and the quotations in this appendix have been drawn from *Cardinal Lavigerie – Churchman, Prophet and Missionary* by François Renault, translated by John O'Donohue, The Athlone Press, 1994.)

J

Political Background to the White Fathers' 1912 Decision

In France at the turn of the 19th–20th century, Republican policies and Radical sentiments were militantly anti-clerical. Probably the issue that most invigorated the politics of the Third Republic between 1870 and 1914 was the role of the Catholic Church. Jules Ferry, as a government minister and then as President in the 1880s, took strong steps to reduce the Church's influence in education, concerning himself actively with the laicisation of schools and the expulsion of teaching orders. However, many schools continued to be staffed by religious brothers and sisters who had no legal status, but were allowed to remain in the country and operate outside the law because of the shortage of lay teachers.

The Dreyfus affair provided a trigger for further action against the Church. The newspaper *La Croix*, published by the Assumptionist order, expressed anti-Dreyfus and anti-Semitic opinions. This was sufficient for denouncements of clerical involvement although the bishops and clergy had remained aloof, not wishing to get involved in a political and judicial contest. When the pro-Dreyfus faction triumphed, the Church was once more a target of retribution. The Assumptionists were declared an illegal association and dissolved in 1900 under Article 291 of the Penal Code.

To pursue the other religious orders (the teaching orders and the Assumptionists having been disposed of), the Law of Associations requiring all religious orders to seek government authorisation was enacted in 1901. This law, which expressly gave recognition to all associations *except* religious orders, prevented an unauthorised association from owning property or receiving gifts. In 1902 Waldeck-Rousseau was succeeded as prime minister by Emile Combes 'the personification of anti-clericalism'. He was animated by a profound hatred of the Church and saw to it that nearly all religious congregations were denied authorisation and were dissolved.

Having dealt with the religious orders, the government then turned its attention to the diocesan clergy; a confrontation with the French bishops and the Pope unsurprisingly ensued. A separation of Church and State bill was called for, but Combes hesitated fearing he would lose control over an independent Church. He failed to satisfy the more militant anti-clericals and was replaced by a new premier, Rouvier, in 1905, and the separation bill became law. This was a unilateral repudiation of the 1801 treaty negotiated by Napoleon I and Pius VII. However, it was not simply a separation, the Church was now required by law to restructure itself into *associations cultuelle* (worship associations) which were to be registered with the State. A further stipulation was that inventories of all Church property were to be made; this resulted in massive confiscations of Church property. The government was prepared to hand back churches to *associations cultuelles*, but the Church resisted the restructuring. Ugly incidents in some parts of the country between the State's agents and the local people caused the downfall of Rouvier, and the taking of inventories was suspended.

The hard line anti-clericalism persisted until 1914, but there was a very unsettled state of affairs. Since the disestablishment of the Church and the removal of most religious congregations, the republican unifying power of anti-clericalism was much weaker leaving no consensus on how to govern. There were 11 governments between July 1909 and August 1914. Those religious congregations, including the White Fathers, still with establishments in France were naturally concerned for there was no knowing which political group's policies would be implemented and there was no assurance of security. In this period, the White Fathers and others took the sensible precaution of preparing for exile.

On the 3rd August 1914 Germany declared war on France. This necessitated a policy of national unity and the setting aside, for the time being, of conflicting domestic issues. In order to foster continued national unity after the war, the Republicans of the

Alliance Démocratique promoted a policy of 'religious appeasement'. The law was not enforced against unauthorised congregations, the dioceses were accepted as *associations cultuelles*, and diplomatic links with the Vatican were restored in 1921. In this post-war atmosphere of toleration it was not necessary for the French students to continue at the Priory.

Bibliography

McManners J, *Church and State in France 1870–1914*, London, 1972.
McMillan J F, *Twentieth Century France*, London, 1992.
Randell K, *France: The Third Republic 1870–1914*, London, 1986, 1992.
Tombs R, *France 1814–1914*, London, 1996.

K

Cardinal Lavigerie

K.1. Cardinal Lavigerie.

It is no exaggeration to say that Charles Martial Allemand Lavigerie, the founder of the White Fathers, was one of the outstanding ecclesiastical figures of the 19th century. He was a big man with a commanding presence, a patriarchal beard and a short temper. A strong, vigorous and imperious figure, 'he had all the qualities of a great commander and unrivalled powers of organisation' ... 'he had the wisdom, the foresight, the tact, the unfailing courtesy, the invincible resolution of a great statesman.'[Leahy] 'As biographer I want to say in advance that no other personage has ever intimidated me to the same extent. I approach him almost with fear ... Inflexible self-will is the dominant trait in the character of this man ... Lavigerie belonged to that class of men who keep a clear outlook and dominate events.'[de Arteche]

He was Archbishop of Algiers (with the suffragan sees of Oran and Constantine) and simultaneously Archbishop of Carthage, Primate of Africa, Apostolic Delegate to the Sahara and the Sudan, Apostolic Delegate to St Anne's Seminary in Jerusalem, Vicar Apostolic of four immense territories in Equatorial Africa, Founder of the White Fathers' and White Sisters' Societies, and a Cardinal – the first African bishop to receive that privilege. He was also a leader of the international anti-slavery movement. He toured Europe, including Britain, appealing for an end to slavery, and on the 31st July 1888 he was the principal speaker at the British Anti-Slavery Association Conference in London

He was a distinguished scholar, having doctorates in Literature, Theology, Civil Law and Canon Law. He had been a professor at the Sorbonne, which he found stifling; Director of *L'Oeuvre des Ecoles d'Orient* (Society for the Promotion of Education in the Near East), which he organised and put on a sound footing; Advisor to the Congregation for Oriental Rites where he pressed for decentralization from the Latin rite; and Auditor for France in the Court of the Rota in Rome, which involved diplomatic duties and judging civil court cases that he felt were not the province of a priest. He was appointed Bishop of Nancy in 1863 at the early age of 37, and Archbishop of Algiers in 1866 at the age of 42. He participated in the First Vatican Council; founded the Melkite[74] seminary of Saint Anne in Jerusalem; built the Basilica of Saint Louis in Carthage and the Basilica of Our Lady of Africa in Algiers; established churches, colleges and schools; and set up and ran homes for multitudes of orphaned Arab children.

He had no hesitation in going straight into the presence of Emperor, King, Pope, President or Governor to insist on what he believed to be right. He went to see King Leopold II to express disapproval of the 1876 Brussels Conference which divided Africa amongst European nations for commercial exploitation; he faced down the French government which opposed Christian missionary work in Algeria; he extracted from the President of the Council a promise not to enforce in French North Africa the decrees dissolving religious societies; and he rejected Emperor Napoleon III's blandishments including the offer of the prestigious Archdiocese of Lyons (the 'Primatial See of the Gauls') to get him away from Africa where he was a constant irritant to the French government. He was not one to avoid head-on confrontation: when, for example, the Mayor of Algiers forbade religious processions, he organized a procession with 20,000 in attendance and had the military fire their guns to salute the Blessed Sacrament; then he got the Minister of the Interior to rescind the Mayor's order. At the defeat of France in the Franco-Prussian War, Algiers descended into anarchy; the army disbanded and mob-rule prevailed. Lavigerie was the only figure able to impose authority and quell the mutinous crowds.

Throughout his adult life, he was acquainted with violent death. The Archbishop of Paris, Denis Affre, who ordained him sub-deacon, was shot dead six months later as he tried to mediate at the barricades between rebels and the authorities in June 1848; Archbishop Sibour who ordained him priest was murdered at the altar; and Lavigerie's predecessor in the see of Nancy, Bishop Georges Darboy, who became Archbishop of Paris, was cold-bloodedly executed during the anti-clerical violence of 1871. He even fell into the hands of the Commune himself while visiting Paris, but was released.

As Director of *L'Oeuvre des Ecoles d'Orient*, Abbé Lavigerie spent time in Lebanon and Syria dealing with the political and humanitarian problems resulting from the massacre of tens of thousands of Christians by the Druses in 1860 and with the accompanying refugee problems. For this work he was awarded the Cross of the Legion of Honour by Emperor Napoleon III and the Order of the Medjidieh by the Sultan of Turkey. In 1867, the year he arrived in Algiers as Archbishop, there was cholera, a plague of locusts, drought, heavy hail and snow and inevitable famine. The cholera epidemic alone killed 60,000 people, and 500 of the children he rescued and many of the nuns who cared for them died of typhus. Then, in 1876, a group of three White Fathers he sent into the Sahara were murdered by Tuaregs; another three were murdered in 1881 while trying to reach Timbuktu; in the same year three others shed their blood in Central Africa; and, by the time of his death, 14 of his priests and five brothers had perished in Central Africa and many lay people had been martyred in Uganda.

K.2. Abbé Lavigerie in Lebanon.

Although born of middle class parents, Lavigerie had the temper of an autocrat. Obedience to the Church helped to curb his arrogance, aggressiveness, impetuosity and obstinacy. But these tendencies were the very characteristics of a strong leader and without them and against such great obstacles he would never have accomplished what he did. He was also capable of great sensitivity, self-abasement and obedience to his spiritual superiors, and particularly in his 'Toast of Algiers' speech he acted completely contrary to his own strong inclinations.[241] He had a gift for diplomacy when it was required, but his diplomacy was not that of compromise, it was astute manoeuvring to achieve his desired ends.

Grand conceptions, bold enterprises, calamities and rejections, the poor and oppressed, weighty responsibilities, long and frequent journeys, and begging for money constantly occupied him. But none of these concerns prevented him from being above all a man of prayer with a fervent devotion to Our Lord, Our Lady and St Joseph. Personal sanctity, he maintained, was the first duty of an apostle. His day started at 4am and for three hours he remained at prayer, meditating and saying Mass. He spent hours in the evening in spiritual reading. He recited the divine office every day, went to confession every week, and visited the Blessed Sacrament daily.

He lived an energetic, demanding and stressful life in turbulent times. His punishing schedule eventually caught up with him: prematurely aged by his exhausting work, he breathed his last in November 1892 at the age of 67. He died an acclaimed international figure and his death was reported in the European press. At his death, the French Republic, despite its anti-clericalism, decreed that the highest honours of State should be paid to the dead Cardinal, both on account of his distinguished position and of the services which he rendered to France. The funeral route was lined by troops, flags were at half-mast, the procession advanced to the sound of muffled drums and the guns of Algiers thundered a salute.

Bibliography

Attwater D, *The White Fathers in Africa*, Burns Oates & Washbourne Ltd, London, 1937;
Bouniol J, *The White Fathers and their Missions*, Sands & Co, London, 1929;
de Arteche J, trans. Mitchell M, *The Cardinal of Africa*, Sands & Co (Publishers) Ltd, London, 1964;
Leahy E, *Light in Darkest Africa*, Catholic Truth Society of Ireland, Dublin, 1922;
Renault F, trans. O'Donohue, J, *Cardinal Lavigerie – Churchman, Prophet and Missionary*, Athlone Press, London, 1994.

L

The Society of Missionaries of Africa (White Fathers)

The White Fathers have been described as 'men who are fascinated with Christ and with Africa'.[72] They come from every continent and from different backgrounds and occupations, but all are dedicated to working for the people of Africa out of love for Jesus Christ.

The Society of Missionaries of Africa is an institute of priests and non-ordained brothers living in community and dedicated to proclaiming the Gospel to the peoples of the African world.[242] The priests and brothers are celibate, their ownership of private property is restricted, and they live in a community of at least three. Their first obligation is to the spiritual life – complete dedication to God, and this dedication is expressed in their apostolic life. Great importance is attached to meditation and daily prayer, and throughout their lives the missionaries are required to spend long periods in retreat.

They are committed to the service of others and to solidarity with the people among whom they live. Their Constitutions declare that 'Sharing the sufferings of others and making their aspirations our own, demands of us a particular care for the poor, a commitment to justice and peace, a concern that people's lives be fuller and richer, more truly human'.[243] They are specifically called to side with the powerless, live in solidarity with those surrounded by misery and suffering, help the poor retain their dignity and self-respect, care for the sick, be at the side of all those who experience oppression, and to join forces with those who struggle for justice, for human rights and for peaceful democratic change.[244] They are required to study the native languages, not resort to an interpreter when evangelising, and never impose any European model or custom. Absorbed in the daily life of their people, White Fathers can be found working in shanty towns, urban prisons, bush dispensaries, desert outposts, AIDS hospices, and guerrilla war zones. As the African clergy take over the parishes and dioceses, more White Fathers can be found assisting the native African priests and bishops, teaching in higher educational establishments, and working for justice and peace particularly through the media. Over many years they have published dictionaries, grammars, anthropological treatises and research work in the natural sciences; they have composed and arranged African music; made outstanding archaeological discoveries; provided social and economic analyses; and been responsible for the education of many of the present day African leaders in politics, medicine, education, the civil service, and the Church.

The Society was founded in 1868 by Charles Lavigerie, Archbishop of Algiers. In 1871 a Mother House (Headquarters) was established at Maison Carrée, near Algiers, but moved to Rome in 1952 where it is known as the Generalate (Curia Generalizia). The supreme legislative authority of the Society is the General Chapter, which meets every six years and at that time elects the Superior General and his council of four members. The Superior General is represented by a provincial superior in each province.

The dress adopted by the Society was that of the Algerian Arab: a white tunic (*gandoura*), a white cloak (*burnous*), small red hat (*chechia*), and a black and white rosary in place of the Mohammedan's *tesbiha* – a string of beads used for reciting the names of God. Because of their dress, the missionaries became commonly known as White Fathers. Lavigerie insisted that his missionaries must dress as Arabs, speak Arabic fluently, and live, think and eat like those to whom they were sent. Later, when the members penetrated Central Africa, Lavigerie instructed his missionaries that 'African children must be brought up as Negroes. It is an unforgivable mistake to try and turn them into Frenchmen. I forbid you to dress them *à la française*; they are not to sleep *à la française*; they are not to eat *à la française*. I forbid you to teach them to read and write French. They must learn to read and write in the language of their own country …'[245] By the end of the 1960s the white habit, although not discarded, was out of favour except in Arab countries and on formal occasions. Clothing more suited to the environment in which a missionary is working is now worn. By 1990 the Society had dropped the name White Father in favour of the strictly correct Missionary of Africa, the members now writing 'M.Afr' after their names rather than 'WF'. Good reasons have been given for these changes, but one cannot but regret the virtual disappearance of the white habit, which was immediately recognisable, an attention winner, and a strong and singular statement. The easily recognised and remembered name and such a strong brand image would be the envy of many an organisation.

Aspirants to priesthood within the Society must have finished their general education to university entrance level or higher. They are sent to a college of scholastic philosophy for two years, then to a novitiate (or spiritual year as it is now called). After the novitiate all students spend two years in an African country other than their own (most of the students are now Africans), learning the language, engaging in mission work, and discovering their suitability for life in the Society. They then attend a theology degree course for three or four years, usually abroad with international student bodies. The theological colleges are affiliated to universities which grant the degrees. The training thus takes about nine years, which is a long time for the candidate but also a huge investment on the part of the Society. The training may well continue with further university studies after ordination. The student commits himself to the Society, and the Society to him, when he takes an oath one year before ordination to the priesthood. Until this time the candidate is free to leave, and the Society is free to ask him to do so.

The brothers' training is identical to that of the clerics in formation for the spiritual and community life. It is much more diversified, however, in the professional field. Their training can last four or more years, and may involve further study to acquire professional qualifications. According to their skills, they may go on to work as builders, technicians, surveyors, architects, civil engineers, agriculturists, administrators, bursars, or teachers.

The White Fathers are called to share in the life and mission of Jesus by their own exemplary life and by proclaiming that we are all children of the same loving Father. '*His Word has touched and transformed us. We have received His Spirit to continue His Mission, not a Spirit of timidity but a Spirit of power and strength*.'[244]

Notes

Abbreviations
AG: Archivio Generale, Curia Generalizia, Missionari d'Africa, Rome.
HRO: Hampshire Record Office, Winchester.
PCDA: Portsmouth Catholic Diocesan Archives, Portsmouth.
PD: Priory Diary, UK Provincial Office, Missionaries of Africa, London.

1 *Cardinal Lavigerie – Churchman, Prophet and Missionary*, Renault F, tr O'DonohueJ, AthlonePress,London, 1994.

2 Howell A E, 'The Priory 1912–1922' in *The Pelican*, Jubilee Number, 1962. Although moving the school is discussed in the minutes of the 1912 General Chapter, there is no mention of government threats. It may be assumed that those attending, nearly all of them French and on French territory, did not wish to go on record as criticising the State and thus incur the further wrath of an inimical government.

3 *Hampshire Chronicle and General Advertiser*, December 6, 1913.

4 The General Chapter is the supreme legislative authority of the Society with delegates from many areas. It meets every six years and at that time elects the Superior General and his four assistants who together constitute a General Council for the ensuing six years. The Superior General is represented by a Provincial Superior in each province.

5 AG. Report: 14° Chapitre, 1912, 10° Séance, p 273.

6 Father Voillard, a future Superior General, was fluent in Arabic, but this was the first time he had been exposed to English. Father Travers recounted the following anecdote of their train journey to Bishop's Waltham which required a change of trains at Eastleigh. When Travers prepared to get out, his companion refused to move.
'Il faut descendre ici, mon Père, et changer de train', said Travers.
'Mais non!' declared Voillard, 'Ce n'est pas Eastleigh.'
'Mais, si!' insisted Travers.
'Mais, non, je vous dis. Regardez: c'est Va-ee-oot!' he said pointing to the Way Out sign.
However, Father Travers managed to get him off the train before it departed. – Howell A E, 'The Priory 1912–1922' in *The Pelican,* Jubilee Number, 1962.

7 Henri Gaudibert, who was born in London and later lived for a short while in Nottingham, was the first White Father from Britain. He entered the Society in 1884 and was ordained in 1889. His first appointment was as secretary to Cardinal Lavigerie. A year later he was a member of the ninth caravan of missionaries to Central Africa. At the departure of this caravan on 29 June 1890, Cardinal Lavigerie emphasised that the Society was an international society and purposely included priests from Belgium, England,

France and Germany. Gaudibert ended his days as Professor of English at Maison Carrée, Algeria, where he died, aged 66, in 1929. – AG. *Bionotes* and *Curriculum Vitae of Henri Gaudibert*. Arthur Prentice, born in London and a convert Anglican, entered the White Fathers' college of philosophy in France in 1896 and was ordained priest in North Africa in 1903. He remembered, as a young man, seeing Henry Morton Stanley on his way to the London Guildhall to receive the freedom of the City, and maybe it was this that first set him thinking about Africa.

8 Arthur Helps (1813–1875) was knighted (KCB) in 1872. Educated at Eton and Trinity College, Cambridge, he was a gifted writer who had many publications to his name including histories, essays and novels. He was private secretary to several government ministers. From 1860 till his death in 1875 he was Clerk to the Queen's Privy Council. – *Concise Dictionary of National Biography*, 1995. He edited Prince Albert's *Speeches and Addresses* (1862) and Queen Victoria's *Journal of Our Life in the Highlands* (1868). – *Chambers Biographical Dictionary*, 1974. He was largely responsible for the construction of the Botley to Bishop's Waltham railway, the building of the Bishop's Waltham gasworks, and the establishment of the Bishop's Waltham Clay Company. He owned and lived in Vernon House, but also rented the Palace House, which included the palace ruins and massive 13th century stone barn with a fine oak-beamed roof in which he entertained his royal guests in 1865. – Sargeant F H, *The Story of Bishop's Waltham Ancient and Modern*, published by the author 1961.

9 *Illustrated London News*, August 13th, 1864.

10 *The Hampshire Chronicle, Southampton and Isle of Wight Courier*, November 11th, 1865.

11 Sergeant F H, *The Story of Bishop's Waltham Ancient and Modern*, published by the author 1961.

12 *Illustrated London News*, November 15th, 1865.

13 *The Hampshire Chronicle, Southampton and Isle of Wight Courier*, August 6th, 1864. A lengthy and detailed description of the ceremony, banquet and speeches is given in this edition.

14 The statue was the gift of the three-times mayor of Southampton, Alderman (later Sir) Frederick Perkins (1826–1902). 'The statue is of terracotta, made by Mr Blashfield, at Stamford, from a model by Mr Theed, the sculptor, resembling, in its attitude and arrangement, the colossal bronze statue which the Queen inaugurated the other day at Coburg, another copy of which, in marble, has been sent to Sydney, New South Wales. The Prince is represented in the robes of the Garter, holding a Field Marshal's baton in the left hand, while the right hand points to a scroll on a pedestal, upon which is indented the façade of the Crystal Palace of 1851. The pedestal has upon it a medallion portrait of her Majesty, and a wreath of flowers is entwined round the pedestal. The colour of the terracotta is of warm buff, like Caen stone; and the outlines of the features and the details are beautifully wrought. The figure, inclusive of the plinth on which it stands, is 7ft 2in

high. It has been burnt in one piece, is without flaw, and is as hard as black marble. The materials used in the formation of the statue are clays – from the estate of Mr Arthur Helps at Bishop-Waltham and from the Marquis of Exeter's pit at Wakerly – mixed with felspar and Lynn sand'. – *Illustrated London News*, November 15th 1865.

[15] Known as the 'New Town Elementary School', it was built in 1865 and enlarged in 1894 and 1895 to accommodate 300 children. – *Kelly's Directory of Hampshire 1907*. The new school site was the gift of Arthur Helps. The school formally opened on June 4, 1866 with the Rev Maunsell, a Congregational Minister, in charge. – *Bishop's Waltham Society Newsletter*, September 1993. It was opened under the auspices of the British and Foreign School Society – a Noncomformist organisation, and passed to the School Board in 1870. The original parish school was a Church of England elementary school near St Peter's churchyard.

[16] Robert B Critchlow seems to have few recorded buildings to his name, though he does appear as the architect of Rownham's Church, Hampshire (1885) and of the Annexe to St Joseph's School, Bugle Street, Southampton (1870) in Lloyd's and Pevsner's *The Buildings of England: Hampshire and the Isle of Wight*, Penguin Books, Harmondsworth, 1967. His offices were at 5 Portland Street, Southampton. – *Craven's Directory of Hampshire 1857*.

[17] In the 1871 census 'The Royal Albert Hospital' was counted as two dwellings. The first was occupied by Andrew Deacon, a butcher, aged 58, born in Fareham, and his daughter Emma E. Deacon, a dressmaker, aged 24, born in Gosport. The second was occupied by Joseph Phillips, a brickmaker, aged 39, born in Aldershot, and his wife Sarah, aged 34 and born in Bishop's Waltham.

[18] Vernon Hill House was built by Admiral Vernon, who captured Porto Bello in 1739. Arthur Helps entertained many distinguished people here, including the Prince of Wales. – *Southampton Geographical Society Report 1901*.

[19] 1871 Census. James Butler Fellowes, aged 51, 'Late Captain of 77th Foot', born in Burghlere, Hampshire. His wife was Georgina Eustatia Player Fellowes, aged 45, born in the Isle of Wight. They had three daughters and three sons between the ages of two and 24, and two servants living in the house.

[20] 1881 Census. Lieutenant General Frederick R[obert] Elrington, aged 61, born Burghlere, Hants, his wife Emilie J Elrington, aged 42, born at Hampton, Surrey; eight children, a governess and seven servants. The *Southampton Geographical Society Report 1901* describes General Elrington as 'one of the heroes of the Crimean War'.

[21] Sale Particulars relating to Vernon Hill Estate auction Tuesday 19th October 1875, HRO 30M87/9. A map attached to the sale particulars identifies the various parts of the estate by lot numbers, but the infirmary is shown as an anonymous building without a lot number. A plan of the infirmary shows a wing, which later would be replaced by the bar of the H shaped school buildings, protruding from the middle of the back of the building; and the

carriage drive leads from the front door in a straight line directly to the lane (later Martin Street). The future Priory playing fields and farm area appear as Lot 118, which came into the possession of the West family. The estate being auctioned includes virtually all the country surrounding Bishop's Waltham – 1280 acres.

[22] *Victoria History of Hampshire and the Isle of Wight*, Vol III, p.277 (1914).

[23] The statue of Prince Albert, which had cost £300, was given freely to the Southampton Borough Council. The statue had been designed for a niche; it was not suitable for a free-standing pedestal, the back being 'quite unfinished'. The Council had it placed on the east side of the Gaol Tower, later renamed God's House Tower, not in a niche but on a pedestal with its hollow back against the tower wall. Once in place the statue was neglected and it steadily deteriorated. In 1907 it was removed on the dubious grounds that its shabby condition might offend Prince Albert's grandson, Kaiser Wilhelm II, who visited the docks in that year but went nowhere near the tower. It was deposited in a Corporation yard, and although there were calls for it to be returned, it never was. Early in the First World War, some Royal Engineers constructing a nearby railway line, chanced upon the neglected statue. Upon learning that it was a representation of the grandfather of the hated Kaiser – albeit Queen Victoria's beloved Consort – they broke it up in a burst of misdirected patriotic zeal. – Leonard A G K, 'The Saga of the Prince Consort's Statue' in *The Journal of the Southampton Local History Forum*, No. 4, Spring 1993.

[24] Sale particulars published by Mr Richard Austin, auctioneer, Bishop's Waltham, 1877. – Bishop's Waltham Museum. Lots that were tenanted are noted as such.

[25] *Hampshire Chronicle*, September 25th, 1884.

[26] 1891 Census of Bishop's Waltham. The Hurley family were Richard H Hurley aged 48, born in London; his wife Elizabeth aged 40, born in Ely; their children Edith Mary (12), Jessie Muriel (9), Frank (8), Ellen M (7), Arthur (5), Fred (4); visiting governess Laura Bays Poole (21) from Northington; and servants Alice Littlefield (27) from Bishopstoke, Emma R Crouch (22) from London, and Margaret Adams (24) from Sussex. All the children were born in Bishop's Waltham. They had previously been living at the Abbey Mill, Bishop's Waltham – *White's History Gazetteer and Directory of Hampshire 1878.* In *The Register of Persons Entitled to Vote 1875*, Richard Hurley is referred to as 'occupier of the mill, near the pond'.

[27] *Kelly's Directory of Hampshire 1898 and 1899, Warren's Directory of Winchester 1900, 1901,1902, and 1903.*

[28] It was built of the finest terracotta brick from the brick works at Bishop's Waltham. The Bishop's Waltham works were originally set up by Arthur Helps, but were taken over by MH Blanchard, who moved his operation from Lambeth in 1880. – Leonard A G K, 'The Saga of the Prince Consort's Statue' in *The Journal of the Southampton Local History Forum*, No. 4, Spring 1993. Another well-known brick and tile works in the town was Churchers

at Winters Hill and Coppice Hill. – *Southampton Geographical Society Report 1901* and *Kelly's Directory of Hampshire 1911*.

[29] *Kelly's Directory of Hampshire 1903 & 1911, Warren's Directory of Winchester 1903, 1908 & 1911*. Mrs Robson appears in place of her husband in *Warren's Directory of Winchester 1912*.

[30] *The Priory Sale, May 1908* by Messrs Edwin Fear and Walker of 49 Jewry Street, Winchester. Sale document in the possession of Mr and Mrs Terry Butler, Bishop's Waltham.

[31] AG. Conseil Général, Séance du 10 Juin 1912.

[32] Thomas Grant Hickey, DD PhD, 'short, stocky and a bundle of energy', was the parish priest of Eastleigh from 1903 to 1916. He was born in Guernsey and educated at Oscott and the Venerable English College, Rome, where he was ordained. He was appointed an honorary canon of Portsmouth Cathedral in 1936 and a chapter canon in 1941. In 1941 he was appointed Vicar General of the Channel Islands where he was a parish priest but, because the islands were occupied by the German army, the appointment was made through the Irish Ambassador to the Vichy government. He died in Guernsey in 1952 aged 74. – Isherwood F, *Priests Who Have Worked in What is Now the Portsmouth Diocese from Reformation Times up to 1989*, Diocesan Information Office, Portsmouth, 1990.

[33] Letter: Rev R B Ellwood, SMM, to the author, 11 October 1999. Father Pierre Raimbault was the first superior of the Montfort College at Romsey, which opened in 1910. The establishment of the Montfort College had a history similar to that of the Priory. 'In 1901, the Apostolic School at Pontchâteau [in France] was forced to go into exile because the government had decreed that religious communities were no longer to be recognised by the law, and in particular that they were not to be allowed to continue teaching the young. The Apostolic School moved to Santbergen in Belgium on 25 September. This was looked upon as an interim move, and when the Belgian government appeared to be contemplating actions similar to the French government, it was decided by the Superior General and his advisors to look further afield . . . It seemed that the Apostolic School must move again, so in 1908 land was obtained at Whitenap, just outside Romsey . . . By February 1910, it [the Whitenap building] was partly habitable, and so the first occupants began to cross from Belgium.' It became a college for British seminarians in 1927 and closed in June 1977, being sold to a commercial company as offices and training centre. (Commonly known as the Society of Montfort Missionaries, The Company of Mary was founded in 1715 by St Louis Marie Grignion de Montfort.)

[34] PD. Vol 1, p 6.

[35] PCDA. The Priory Conveyance Deed, 22 November 1912. The vendor trustees were Elizabeth Sarah Robson of Westcliffe-on-Sea, James Mark Dietrichsen of Loughton, Essex, and the Reverend Paul Petit (Honorary Canon of Canterbury Cathedral) of St George's Square, London.

[36] AG. Conseil Général, Séance du 29 Août 1912.

[37] AG. Undated handwritten draft of letter from Bishop Livinhac to Bishop Cotter. '1912 debut Mai' has been added later in different handwriting, but it is unlikely that it could have been written in early May, because Voillard had not yet returned from England.

[38] AG. Conseil Général, Séance du 9–11 Juin 1913.

[39] *Missionary Districts 1865–1958*, Diocese of Portsmouth Information Office, 1985. England had ceased being a designated mission territory in 1908, but some subdivisions of the Portsmouth diocese were still referred to as missionary districts and the priests as missionaries.

[40] PD. Vol 1, p 10. An undated copy of the letter was transcribed into the school diary. It has not been possible to check Bishop Cotter's papers because the Portsmouth diocesan archives were mostly destroyed by bombing in the 1939–45 war.

[41] PD. Vol 1, p 1.

[42] Pierre Marie Travers was born at Livre, France, in 1874. He was the eldest of eight children, and two of his sisters became missionaries in Africa as White Sisters. He was not quite 26 at his ordination in 1900, and his first appointment was to teach philosophy at Binson, France, where he remained for four years. In 1904 he was sent to a mission post at Mpanda in Nyasaland, and in 1906 was appointed financial administrator of the Vicariate of Nyassa. In November 1910 he was nominated Vicar General of the southern part of the vicariate. The Vicariate of Nyassa at that time was under the jurisdiction of a renowned Vicar Apostolic – Bishop Joseph Dupont, whose life is a thrilling adventure story. He became King of the Brigands of Ituna in 1898, wrote on the flora and fauna of Nyassa, and discovered in Lake Tanganyika a new kind of shellfish, which was named 'Dupontia' in his honour. His story is told in *Eveque-Roi des Brigands* by Père Pineau, and in *Bishop-King of the Brigands*, a translation by A E Howell. Both publications are now sadly out of print.

[43] PD. Vol 1, p 14 records 14 pupils travelling on 10 October 1912 from St Laurent d'Olt to Paris where they spent the night at the White Fathers house. On 11 October they set off for England arriving on Saturday 12 October when 27 pupils were enrolled.

[44] PD. 11 October 1912.

[45] PD. Vol 1, p 18.

[46] The striking habit of the White Fathers is the common dress of the North African Arab: *gandoura* (long white tunic), *burnous* (white cloak with a hood), black and white rosary beads around the neck similar to the Moslem *tesbiha* with 99 beads used for reciting the names of God, and, in the early days, a *chechia* (small red hat) was also worn. This was but one indication of Lavigerie's directive that 'you are to share the exterior life of the natives amongst whom you work, as regards language, food and clothing'.

[47] PD. 4 April 1913.

[48] 'Our Fifty Years' in *White Fathers* magazine, No. 122, February 1962.

[49] All these religious communities came from France to England seeking sanctuary. The Brothers of the Christian Schools (de la Salle) came originally to Dover then founded their school at Southsea in 1908. The Brothers of Christian Instruction did not at first intend opening a school, but did so in 1922 when most of the French community at Bitterne went to Jersey. The community of the Abbey of Solesmes moved to the Isle of Wight in 1901. After some years in the south of the island they moved to Quarr in 1907 where they set about building the great Abbey of Our Lady. Most of the French monks returned to France in 1922, and the Abbey continued as an English foundation. – Anon, *Quarr Abbey Past and Present*, Quarr Abbey Publications, c1970, and e-mail from Lord Abbot Cuthbert Johnson to the author, 5 January 2001. The Trappist monks returned to France in 1916 without establishing an English foundation. The Montfort Fathers' junior seminary established at Romsey in 1910 for French students became an English-speaking school in 1927. – Letter: Rev R B Ellwood, SMM, to the author, 11 October 1999.

[50] PD. 8 May 1913.

[51] Dr J J Griffiths Whittindale lived at Lime House, Bishop's Waltham. – *Kelly's Directory of Hampshire 1911*.

[52] Father R P Elrington seems to have been the eldest son. He was not living at home when the 1881 census took place, although six sisters and two brothers (aged ten and eight) were. Presumably he went away to school at the age of twelve or thereabouts. Nor was he living at home in April 1891 when the two younger brothers, described as [university?] students, were. Interestingly, the census of 1881 records General Elrington as having been born in the Tower of London.

[53] AG. Conseil Général, Séance du 17 Septembre 1913.

[54] PD. 8 March 1913 and *County of Hants Register of Electors, 1918*. The Sims family lived in the School House in Albert Road. Alfred Sims later became headmaster of the elementary school.

[55] This was the original St Peter's Chapel, built in 1792 and the first Catholic church to be consecrated since 1588. It was built by Rev John Milner, and is now known as the Milner Hall. The large and beautiful church of St Peter that replaced the chapel was opened in 1926.

[56] PD. 5 March 1913.

[57] PD. 13 September 1912.

[58] PD. 6 March 1913.

[59] PD. 25 May 1913.

[60] PD. 27 May 1913.

[61] Conversations: Brother Patrick, M.Afr, with the author, 30–31 May 1998.

[62] PD. 22 April 13.

[63] PD. 12 August 1913.

[64] The Priory school registers. – Society of Missionaries of Africa, UK Provincial Office, London.

[65] E-mail: Fr Richard Kinlen, M.Afr, to the author, 19 February 2001, referring to a typed note in the UK Provincial Office of the Missionaries of Africa. The offices of Jurd and Sanders were at 23 Portland Street, Southampton (the same street as the original architect, Robert B Critchlow).

[66] Henry Ingalton Sanders was the surviving partner at this time. – *Kelly's Directory of Hampshire 1911*.

[67] AG. Letter: Father Travers to Mother House, 20 June 1913.

[68] PD. 6 April 1913.

[69] E-mail: Fr Fernand Gruber, M.Afr, to the author, 16 September 2000.

[70] Father John Forbes joined the Society in 1886 at the age of 22. He returned to Canada in 1900 to establish a house in Quebec for seminarians who had completed their classical and philosophical studies and who wished to join the White Fathers. He was superior from 1901 to 1914 when he departed for Africa via England. He arrived in England accompanied by his brother, Guillaume, a missionary to the Iroquois people and Bishop of Joliette, who was attending the Eucharistic Congress in London before going on to Rome. Forbes was effectively the founder of the Society's flourishing North American province. He became Coadjutor Vicar Apostolic to Monsignor Streicher in Uganda, and died in 1926 aged 62.

[71] The Melkites are Catholic Arabs of the Byzantine rite in Syria, Lebanon, Israel, Jordan and Egypt. Their liturgy is conducted in Greek and Arabic. The White Fathers, who teach at the seminary of St Anne in Jerusalem, do not allow the students to enter their Society or to join the Latin rite, for to do so would deprive their own people of their services.

[72] *The White Fathers in North America 1901–2001*, published by *Mission Magazine*, Montreal, Canada, 2001.

[73] PD. 21 October 1914.

[74] PD. 5 February 1915.

[75] PD. 2 September 1914.

[76] PD. 10 February 1917.

[77] The College of St Maurice at Valais in Switzerland had been established as an Apostolic School in 1913 for boys from Savoy, 'Suisse Romane', and Northern Italy; they were taught by the Canons Regular of St Augustine. Another Apostolic School was founded at Rietberg in Westphalia, Germany, in 1914. The establishment of junior schools in Europe was in contrast to Canada where young men were recruited from the senior diocesan seminaries or universities and sent to North Africa for study and training.

[78] AG. Conseil Général, Séance du 26 Janvier 1914.

[79] PD. 15 September 1917.

[80] PD. 11 February 1919.

[81] Many years later, on 14 June 1944, the Fathers learnt that a pottery bowl owned by 'our respected neighbour' Mr Austin was made at the Bishop's Waltham brickworks to commemorate the foundation of the Royal Albert Infirmary.

[82] AG. Letter: Father Joseph Bouniol to the Superior General, 3 June 1919.

[83] Pau is in the far southwest of France in the Basses Pyrénées and is not far from Lourdes. The White Fathers had a sanatorium there originally intended for sick missionaries who returned from Africa, but many who were taken ill in Europe were also sent there.

[84] AG. Conseil Général, Séance du 9 Juin 1919.

[85] AG. Conseil Général, Séance du 11 Août 1919.

[86] *Register of Electors 1918, Bishop's Waltham Division II*. Mr Gustave Reginald John Couche was the only person at the Priory entitled to vote in government elections.

[87] *Register of Electors 1918, Bishop's Waltham Division II.*

[88] AG. Conseil Général, Séance du 11 & 12 Mai 1914.

[89] Smith J A, 'Forty Years Ago' in *The Pelican*, Jubilee Number, Summer 1962.

[90] PD. 19 November 1920.

[91] Father Robert, never having been in good health, was diagnosed with pneumonia in June 1925 and left permanently, first for Maison Carrée, then for the Society's sanatorium at Pau where he died a year later, having served ten years at the Priory. He was 36. – *Le Petit Messager des Missions*, Sept–Oct 1926, Diocèse de Nantes.

[92] Holmes-Siedle J, 'Memories of a Year at The Priory' in *The Pelican*, Jubilee Number, 1962.

[93] Kerlois at Hennebont in Brittany accommodated British philosophy students until 1924, when St Mary's, Autreppe, Belgium, was opened as a college of philosophy for English-speaking students.

[94] PD. 19 March 1924.

[95] John Patrick Murphy was assistant priest at Gosport from 1919 to 1928, then parish priest from 1928 to 1946. He was also an honorary canon of Portsmouth Cathedral. He was educated at the Venerable English College, Rome, where he was ordained in 1917, but continued his studies in Rome until 1919, presumably to obtain a higher degree. He died in 1962 at Reading aged 71. – Isherwood F, *Priests Who Have Worked in What is Now the Portsmouth Diocese from Reformation Times up to 1989*, Diocesan Information Office, Portsmouth 1990.

[96] 'Chosen Men' in *White Fathers* magazine, No. 122, February 1962.

[97] *The Tablet*, April 18, 1925.

[98] PD. 16 April 1927.

[99] Maguire J, 'The Happiest Days . . .' in *The Pelican*, Jubilee Number, 1962.

[100] Anonymous, *The Pelican*, Summer 1955.

[101] PD. 14 September 1927.

[102] Brother Patrick, M.Afr, *Reminiscences of The Priory*, published privately, 1998.

[103] *Hampshire Chronicle*, October 27, 1934.

[104] Armand Roy travelled to New York [PD. 30 November 1927] and then went to Canada in July 1928. He and Fathers Filion and Baurman set up the first United States house in Cleveland, Ohio, in 1929, and in 1935 he went to Zambia where he spent most of his priestly life. – AG. *Bionotes: Roy Armand.*

[105] PD. 6 April 1929.
[106] PD. 24 October 1932.
[107] Marchant L, *The White Fathers in Scotland 1934–1984*, unpublished typescript, c1984. Society of Missionaries of Africa, Rutherglen, Scotland.
[108] Marchant L, *Bishop Francis Walsh, White Father, 1901 – 1974*. An unpublished biography, c1975, Society of Missionaries of Africa, Rutherglen, Scotland.
[109] PD. 7 September 1934.
[110] '...plans should be made for the digging of slit trenches by local inhabitants in their gardens, ... slit trenches give almost equal protection against bombing and more protection against shellfire as compared with standard shelters although of course, they do not provide a weatherproof cover.' – HRO W/C21/3/1/(3): Civil Preparations at Anti-Tank Islands. City Engineer's File, detailing emergency planning during the war 1939–45. Quoted by Marter P and McConnell R in 'Preparation for War: World War II Civil Defence in the City of Winchester', *Proceedings of The Hampshire Field Club and Archaeological Society, Vol 54, 1999.*
[111] AG. *Bionotes: Bernhard Hartmann*.
[112] Duffy B, 'The Priory 1936–40' in *The Pelican*, Jubilee Number 1962.
[113] Letter: Father Patrick Boyd, M.Afr, to the author, 8 March 1999.
[114] Boyd P, 'Missionary Studies in a World at War', *White Fathers – White Sisters*, No. 335, August-September 1997.
[115] Wiseman K, *Destined for a Mission*, KAAS Publishing Corporation, Houston, USA, 1999.
[116] O'Donohue J, 'The Priory at War' in *The Pelican*, Jubilee Number, 1962.
[117] PD. 18 September 1942.
[118] Letter: Peter Barry to Eugene MacBride, 17 December 1998.
[119] PD. 26 May 1944.
[120] Letter: Fr James P O'Kielty to the author, 26 March 2000.
[121] PD. 18 June 1944.
[122] PD. 12 July 1944.
[123] Conversation: Brother Vincent Martin, M.Afr, with the author, 24 October 1999.
[124] Letter: Father J P O'Kielty, M.Afr, to the author, 5 February 2000.
[125] *Priory Annual Report June 1950 – June 1951*, UK Provincial Office, Missionaries of Africa, London.
[126] The single line railway between Bishop's Waltham and Botley Junction was constructed in 1862. The line and the Bishop's Waltham station were opened on 1 June 1863. The line ran from a single platform terminus, along the river via Durley Halt, to Botley. It closed to passengers on 2 January 1933 but continued to be used for freight until it closed finally on 30 April 1962. The line was 3 miles and 56 chains long. [1 mile = 80 chains.] – Body G, *Railways of the Southern Region*, Patrick Stephens Limited, Cambridge, 1984. From Botley passengers could take a train northwards to Waterloo Station in London or southwards to Portsmouth or, with a change at Eastleigh, to Southampton.

[127] Outfit List, August 1948. In the possession of Mr Charles Robinson, Leyland, Lancashire.
[128] Stevens D, 'The White Fathers', *Hampshire – The County Magazine*, Vol 1, No 11, September 1961.
[129] MacBride E, *Father Patrick Donnelly, WF. An Appreciation*, unpublished typescript, 1997.
[130] *Provincial Visitation Report, May 1951*, UK Provincial Office, Missionaries of Africa, London.
[131] Author's recollection.
[132] E-mail: E MacBride to the author, 16 May 2001.
[133] PD. 12 December 1952.
[134] E-mail: Bishop Michael Fitzgerald to the author, 13 June 2000.
[135] Sandom J, 'Father Patrick Donnelly WF – RIP. An Appreciation' in *White Fathers – White Sisters*, No. 338, February–March 1998.
[136] E-mail: Eugene MacBride to the author, 26 May 2000.
[137] Conversation: Mrs Norah Rodgers with the author, 4 May 2001.
[138] *The Hampshire Telegraph and Post*, 25 January 1959.
[139] *The Pelican*, 1959.
[140] *The Pelican*, 1958.
[141] *The Pelican*, 1957.
[142] Letter and attachment: Fr Patrick Boyd to the author, 8 March 1999.
[143] PD. 22 July 1916.
[144] E-mail: Fr Patrick Fitzgerald to the author, 27 May 2001.
[145] Conversations: Abbot Cuthbert Johnson of Quarr Abbey with the author, 6–7 February 2001.
[146] Shaw R, 'Christian Unity Week' in *The Pelican*, 1964; and McGuinness C, 'The Changing Liturgy' in *The Pelican*, 1965.
[147] PCDA. The Priory Conveyance Deed, 29 December 1967, Second Schedule.
[148] Telegram from FMC Fareham, 24 February 1959. UK Provincial Office, Missionaries of Africa, London.
[149] *The Pelican*, 1960.
[150] Daniel J Williams, BA, BD, was ordained as a Baptist minister in 1952 after studying for six years at the South Wales Baptist College, Cardiff. His first and only church as a minister was in East Monmouthshire. He resigned his pastorate in 1958 and went to teach at Portsmouth where he was received into the Catholic Church. – DJW, 'Glancing Back' in *The Pelican*, 1960.
[151] Mills R, 'Bishop's Waltham comes to St John's' in *The Pelican*, 1966.
[152] *The Pelican*, 1964.
[153] Letter: Sean McGovern to the author, 14 January 1999; and *St John's Gazette*, Midsummer 1965 (Robert Dempsey).
[154] MacBride E, Personal Diary, 1951.
[155] AG. Conseil Général, Séance du 12 Août 1918.
[156] Fenwick K (ed), *Southey's Life of Nelson*, The Folio Society, London, 1956.
[157] Hubback JH & EC, *Jane Austen's Sailor Brothers*, Ian Hodgkins & Co, Stroud, 1986.

[158] Alethea Hayter A (ed), *The Backbone*, Pentland Press, Edinburgh, 1993.
[159] Sherley-Price L (tr), *A History of the English Church and People*, Bede, Penguin Books, London, 1955
[160] Sale DM, *The Hymn Writers of Hampshire*, Winton Publications Ltd., Winchester, 1975.
[161] Attwater D, *The White Fathers in Africa*, Burns Oates & Washbourne Ltd, London, 1937.
[162] de Arteche J, tr Mitchell M, *The Cardinal of Africa*, Sands & Co (Publishers), London 1964.
[163] *The Pelican*, 1965.
[164] Tyerman C, *A History of Harrow School 1324–1991*, Oxford, 2000.
[165] *Priory Annual Report, June 1948–June 1949*.
[166] *County of Hants Register of Electors, 1935–36*.
[167] Letter: Fr James Wallace to the author, 8 August 2000.
[168] Fitzgerald P, 'The Crucible' in *The Pelican*, 1961.
[169] Mahon B, 'The Lark. A Review of the Christmas Play' in *The Pelican*, 1966.
[170] Letter: Father Stephen Collins, M.Afr, to Eugene MacBride, February 1999.
[171] Letter: Father J P O'Kielty, M.Afr, to the author, 5 March 2000.
[172] *The Pelican*, 1960 & 1963.
[173] AG. Conseil Général, Séance du 6 Septembre 1912.
[174] AG. *Bionotes. Cornelis Verheugd*. Brother Egbert (Cornelis Verheugd) left the Society in September 1917 and was later ordained as a priest for the diocese of Algiers.
[175] Brother Patrick, *The Pelican*, Christmas 1950.
[176] Letter: Father Patrick Fitzgerald, M.Afr, to the author, 27 February 1999.
[177] Letter: Brother Patrick to the author, 5 February 2001. I am indebted to Brother Patrick for much of the information about the domestic staff.
[178] Conversations: Mrs Norah Rodgers with the author, 4 & 5 May 2001; *London Gazette*, November 6, 1898; *Kentish Gazette*, March 1942. Private Thomas Byrne was a cavalryman in the 21st Lancers at the battle of Khartoum in 1898. Despite having lost his lance, being severely wounded in the right shoulder, and wielding his sword with his left hand, he fought off many Dervishes and rescued a stranded officer. Winston Churchill, who was in the same charge and witnessed his courage, said it was the bravest act he had ever seen. Thomas Byrne lived with his daughter at Brooklands Farm for a short while and then returned to his home in Canterbury where he died in 1945. Arthur Rodgers was one of the first soldiers to be billeted at the Priory when he returned from Dunkirk. His wife came from Sheffield to be near him and lodged at Brooklands Farm where she worked as a Land Girl until she moved to the Priory bungalow in 1946.
[179] Anon., 'Back Room Girls' in *The Pelican*, 1960.
[180] PD. 8 February 1955.
[181] Geraghty L, 'Modern Times 1947–1962' in *The Pelican*, Jubilee Number, 1962.

[182] Conversation: P Desmond Fitzmaurice with the author, 18 May 1998.
[183] Letter: Father James P O'Kielty, M.Afr, to the author, 4 March 1999.
[184] Conversation: Peter Barry with the author, 9 March 2001.
[185] Corporal punishment continued in many schools for the next 25 years or more. In 1976 the Hampshire Education Committee issued school punishment regulations, which included 'Pupils over the age of eight may be caned on the palm of the hand, or slippered or caned on the clothed buttocks'. – *Hampshire Chronicle*, July 30, 1976.
[186] E-mail: Sean Murphy to the author, 14 November 2000.
[187] PD. 29 March 1965.
[188] Conversation: Fr Richard Kinlen, M.Afr, with the author, 7 June 2000.
[189] Conversation: Sean McGovern with the author, 24 February 1999.
[190] PD. 12 January 1920.
[191] PD. 3 December 1923.
[192] PD. 2 May 1924.
[193] PD. 7 May 1925.
[194] PD. 18 January 1928.
[195] PD. 19 June 1933.
[196] PD. 30 July 1935.
[197] PD. 26 November 1919.
[198] PD. 15 September 1926.
[199] PD. 5 March 1954.
[200] PD. 16 September 1965.
[201] PD. 4 March 1924.
[202] PD. 2 November 1928.
[203] Conversation: Brother Patrick with the author, 19 February 2001.
[204] DJW, 'Glancing Back' in *The Pelican*, 1960.
[205] Conversation: Fr James Wallace with the author, 28 June 2000.
[206] PCDA. Land Sale Agreement, 23 December 1913, between the Reverend Norman Salusbury, James Charles Warner and Alfred Charles West of the one part, and the Reverend Pierre Marie Travers, the Reverend Jean Marie Collet, the Reverend Joseph Bouniol and the Reverend Eloi Falquières of the other part.
[207] PCDA. Land Sale Agreement, 29 March 1923, between Alfred Charles West of the one part, and the Reverend PM Travers, the Reverend JM Collet, the Reverend J Bouniol and the Reverend E Falquières of the other part.
[208] Letter: Brother Patrick to the author, 5 February 2001.
[209] Conversation: Father James Wallace with the author, 10 July 2000.
[210] Galley Down Wood, a 41-acre plantation of beechwood between Dundridge Lane and the B3035 road, was notified as a Site of Special Scientific Interest in 1988. The site has a rich and very well developed specialised beechwood flora, including the largest known populations in Hampshire of two particular species. – *Bishop's Waltham Society Newsletter*, April 1988.
[211] The 1957 General Chapter allowed the brothers to drop their 'name in religion' and use their family name; newly professed brothers were to keep

their family name. Some of the older brothers continued to be known from habitual usage by their religious name.

[212] Conversation: Sean McGovern with the author, 14 January 1999.

[213] Hughes S, 'Bill Matthews' in *The Pelican*, 1965, and conversation of Brother Patrick with the author, 20 February 2001. Bill Matthews died in 1965.

[214] *The Pelican*, Summer 1955.

[215] Melling B, 'The Dancing Seminarists' in *The Pelican*, Jubilee Number, 1962.

[216] Letter: David Ritson to the author, 3 February 2001.

[217] PD. 8 March 1963.

[218] Conversation: Sean McGovern with the author, 16 February 2001; and loose, one-page letter of thanks from a gentleman of the road, undated and with illegible signature, found in school diary.

[219] Editorial in *The Pelican*, 1966.

[220] Letter: Father Patrick Fitzgerald, M.Afr, to the author, 28 August 1999.

[221] Letter: Father Patrick Boyd, M.Afr, to the author, 24 February 1999.

[222] Letter: Father Christopher Wallbank, M.Afr, to the author, 19 February 1999.

[223] AG. *Meeting Regarding Junior Seminaries in the Province* – Report of British Provincial Council Meeting, July 1965. Those attending were Fathers Andrew Murphy (Provincial Superior), John Maguire (former Provincial Superior), Patrick Donnelly, Patrick Fitzgerald, John Fowles, Michael Moloney (former and current Priory staff), Ben Henze (Vocations Director), and Brother John Ryan (formerly known as Brother Aidan).

[224] Decree on Training for the Priesthood, *Optatam Totius*, 3, CTS, London, 1966.

[227] E-mails to the author from Michael Gallagher, 4 Nov 2000; Sean Murphy, 14 Nov 2000; Fr Terry Madden, M.Afr, 31 Oct 2000; Fr Paul Glover 20 Nov 2000.

[228] AG. Conseil Général, Séance du 12 Juin 1967.

[229] *Hampshire Chronicle*, November 25, 1967. The agents were Messrs Frank Stubbs and Son of Bishop's Waltham in conjunction with Messrs Gerald Eve and Co. of London acting on behalf of the Trustees of the Society of Missionaries of Africa.

[230] *Hampshire Chronicle*, October 14, 1967.

[231] PCDA. The Priory Conveyance Deed, 29 December 1967.

[232] PCDA. Deed of Appointment of Trustees, 1 July 1960. The original trustees had been Fathers Travers (died 17 April 1927), Falquières (died 28 September 1924), Bouniol (died 21 December 1950), and Chollet who was living at St Joseph's College, Thibar, Tunisia, in 1960, and died there in May 1962.

[233] PCDA. Deed of Conveyance of Land at Bishop's Waltham, 17 July 1968.

[234] *Hampshire Chronicle*, February 18, 1972.

[235] *Hampshire Chronicle*, January 11, 1981.

[236] *Bishop's Waltham Society Newsletter*, September 1991 and January 1992.

[237] *Bishop's Waltham Society Newsletter*, May 1993 and September 1993.

[238] AG. *Rapport Annuel 1945–1946*, Province de France, Missionaires d'Afrique.

[239] Letter: Father P Ivan Page, Archivist, Missionari d'Africa, Roma, to the author, 16 September 1999.

[240] *Le Château de Saint-Laurent* (a leaflet published by Le Mairie de Saint-Laurent-d'Olt). St Laurent d'Olt is in the Département de l'Aveyron, a few miles north of Millau, and in the diocese of Rodez. The Château de Saint-Laurent is on a peak overlooking the village and was originally a 10th century fortress. The White Fathers rented the château from 1874 to 1878 when they bought it from the Valette des Hermaux family who had owned it since 1766.

[241] 'The Toast of Algiers' was a speech that rocked the French establishment and turned the Catholic Church in France against Lavigerie. He had been asked by Pope Leo XIII to publicly accept the Republican government of France as the legitimate rulers, despite their having overthrown the monarchy and being committed to the eradication of Church influence. The bishops in France could not be relied upon to do it. Knowing full well the unfortunate consequences for himself, and dreading them, Lavigerie went ahead. He took advantage of a visit by the French Fleet to Algiers to make a statement that would be widely publicised. He arranged a banquet to welcome the visitors, and in his speech toasting the French navy he publicly acknowledged the *de facto* government. The navy was anti-republican, and the admiral and his entourage walked out, the French bishops and Catholic intellectuals turned against him, and the newspapers had a field day.

[242] *Constitutions and Laws*, Section 1, Society of Missionaries of Africa, Rome, 1988.

[243] *Constitutions and Laws*, Section 7, Society of Missionaries of Africa, Rome, 1988.

[244] 'A Statement on Mission for Today', *Documents of the General Chapter1992*. Society of Missionaries of Africa, Rome, 1992.

[245] Attwater D, *The White Fathers in Africa*, Burns Oates & Washbourne Ltd, London, 1937.

Index

Italic page numbers indicate illustrations.
'n' indicates a note.